Living in Chri

Church
History

Apostolic Times to Today

Gloria Shahin
with Joanna Dailey

saint mary's press

The Subcommittee on the Catechism, United States Conference of Catholic Bishops, has found that this catechetical high school text, copyright 2013, is in conformity with the *Catechism of the Catholic Church* and that it fulfills the requirements of Course Elective B: "History of the Catholic Church" of the *Doctrinal Elements of a Curriculum Framework for the Development of Catechetical Materials for Young People of High School Age.*

Nihil Obstat: Rev. William M. Becker, STD
                          Censor Librorum
                          May 7, 2013
Imprimatur: † Most Rev. John M. Quinn, DD
                          Bishop of Winona
                          May 7, 2013

The nihil obstat and imprimatur are official declarations that a book or pamphlet is free of doctrinal or moral error. No implication is contained therein that those who have granted the nihil obstat or imprimatur agree with the contents, opinions, or statements expressed, nor do they assume any legal responsibility associated with publication.

The publishing team included Gloria Shahin, editorial director, and Maura Thompson Hagarty, development editor. Prepress and manufacturing coordinated by the production departments of Saint Mary's Press.

The publisher also wishes to thank the following individuals who advised the publishing team or reviewed the work in progress:
Adrian Mison Fulay, MTS
Rev. Mark Francis O'Malley, HistEcclD

Printed in the United States of America

1154 (PO6706)

ISBN 978-1-59982-148-1, Print

Contents

Section 2: The Church in the Middle Ages

Section 3: An Age of Renewal and Growth

Section 4: The Church in the Modern Era

Section 5: The Church in the Post-Modern Era (Twentieth to Twenty-First Centuries)

Introduction

The *Catechism of the Catholic Church* tells us, "The Church is in history, but at the same time she transcends it. It is only 'with the eyes of faith' that one can see her in her visible reality and at the same time in her spiritual reality as bearer of divine life"[1] (770).

Studying Church history requires studying both a visible and a spiritual reality. The Church is more than what we can see; she is a spiritual reality. Through the constant action and presence of the Holy Spirit, the visible aspects of the Church communicate with us and put us in touch with her divine aspects.

Studying the history of the Church reveals many reasons to rejoice in her holiness. The Church has made wonderful and significant contributions to human life. And from her earliest history, the Church has faced many challenges. But the Holy Spirit has never abandoned the Church and guides her to continue to be what she was intended to be from the beginning of God's plan: a sacrament, a holy sign of his presence, and a means to union with him.

Even though the Church has a divine origin and a divine mission, that mission is carried out in the midst of human events; therefore, to study the history of the Church, it is also necessary to study the events of the Church's life intertwined with events in the life of the world. The Church, like Jesus Christ himself, is incarnated in the world.

As you learn about the Church's history, recall that the nature of the Church transcends the actions of specific individuals who have shaped her human character, and that despite any human failings, the Church that you are a part of is willed by the Holy Trinity—planned by the Father, instituted by Christ, and sanctified by the Holy Spirit.

Blessings,
Gloria Shahin

The Church in the Early Christian Centuries

Part 1

The Origin of the Church

This first section of this student book on Church history begins even before human history to discern the plan that God had formed before time. That plan was gradually revealed through salvation history. Through God's plan revealed in Sacred Scripture, we find the formation of the Church.

In the Old Covenant, which God made with Abraham, God formed his people. Through Abraham, he began a pact with the human race. The prophets renewed the promises of God and called his people to faithfulness. The prophets announced the coming of the Messiah, Jesus Christ.

When the Word of God became flesh in the Incarnation, the Father's promise of a New Covenant was fulfilled. In the New Covenant offered to us in Jesus Christ, the Church takes shape as Jesus shares the Good News and gathers followers who will spread this news to others.

After the Paschal Mystery is complete, the Holy Spirit descends upon the Apostles. Following this Pentecost event, the Apostles responded to the call of the Holy Spirit in their lives and Christ's call to them to bring the Good News to all people. (See Matthew 28:19–20.)

The articles in this part address the following topics:

- Article 1: From the Father's Heart (page 10)

- Article 2: Sent by the Holy Spirit (page 14)

- Article 3: After Pentecost (page 17)

Article 1 From the Father's Heart

covenant
A personal, solemn promise of faithful love that involves mutual commitments and creates a sacred relationship.

When Jerusalem had been destroyed (in 587 BC) and the People of Israel—God's Chosen People—who were exiled in Babylon, were made to serve a foreign power who did not know God, the Word of the Lord came to the Prophet Jeremiah. What would God say to his people who were at such a low point in their history? This is what is recorded in the Book of Jeremiah:

> For I know well the plans I have in mind for you—oracle of the LORD—plans for your welfare and not for woe, so as to give you a future of hope. When you call me, and come to pray to me, I will listen to you. When you look for me, you will find me. Yes, when you seek me with all your heart, I will let you find me—oracle of the LORD—and I will change your lot. (29:11–14)

In these words God the Father renewed the plan that had been in his heart before time began, a plan that included the creation of the universe, the creation of human beings to share his own divine life, and the sending of his Son to gather all people into one family of God.

Scripture relates that God showed Abram the night sky, which must have been ablaze with stars in the total darkness of the ancient desert. Such a sight has moved many to reflect on the depth of God's mysterious power.

© wong yu liang/Shutterstock.com

The Old Covenant

Original Sin had disrupted the harmony between God and all people, and what could restore it? Only God's forgiving initiative, only a new beginning, sealed with a **covenant**. God had called Abraham into a new land, and promised Abraham that his descendants would be as many as the stars in the sky. God made a covenant with Abraham, and by this covenant he formed his people. In Abraham, God began a pact with the human race.

Yet the story of Israel, Abraham's descendants, is not a story of perfect response to God's initiative of love. It is a story full of sorrow and failure. Still, God remained faithful to his people. He saved them from slavery in Egypt and led them to the Promised Land; he gave them wise kings to lead them and extended his mercy when they sinned, even forgiving the evil deeds of King David; and he sent his prophets to call them back to him when they faltered. Throughout the Old Testament, we see that God's loving fidelity and mercy endured, and that he always called his people back to himself.

God's saving plan, and the willing response of a man named Moses, turned the slavery of Egypt into the freedom of the Promised Land. But by Jeremiah's time, the glory days of Israel again seemed to be behind them. The great King David had come and gone. The People of God were in exile in a strange land. Yet God had revealed his heart, and hoped for a free and loving response in return: "I will place my law within them, and write it upon their hearts; I will be their God, and they shall be my people" (Jeremiah 31:33).

The Hope

Presented with the hope of a new covenant, written in their hearts, the People of God rallied. Through the **providence of God** and the agency of King Cyrus of Persia (a pagan), they were allowed to return to Israel. They slowly pulled themselves together as a nation.

But without a central Jewish authority to mediate laws, many petty kings and leaders had sprung up. Roman occupiers took over. The religious leaders encouraged the people to keep God's Law but piled on many other petty rules and regulations that seemed to separate people from God and even from one another. The hope for a new covenant, a new pact with God, seemed dim. But God further revealed his plan.

The New Covenant

In God's plan for our **redemption**, the **New Covenant** was the Son's great task. Jesus Christ was the center of this New Covenant. He lived it, preached it, explained it, and called God's people into it—not through the prophets, as of old, but in his very Person, both true God and true man. The Son of God became man to rescue us from the sin and death that were the consequences of the Fall. The fullness of our redemption from sin and death was made possible through the Paschal Mystery—Jesus' work of salvation through his Passion, death, Resurrection, and Ascension.

To carry out the Father's plan, Jesus Christ made a new and eternal pact between God and human beings, the New Covenant, ultimately in his own blood. Thus began the Kingdom of Heaven on earth. This beginning, this community of people Jesus gathered around him, is the Church.

Christ himself is the head of the Church and the light of the Church: "The Church has no other light than Christ's;

providence of God
God's loving care throughout salvation history and in each individual life, bringing what is needed into every situation and even bringing good out of evil.

redemption
From the Latin *redemptio*, meaning "a buying back," referring, in the Old Testament, to Yahweh's deliverance of Israel and, in the New Testament, to Christ's deliverance of all Christians from the forces of sin.

New Covenant
The covenant or law established by God in Jesus Christ to fulfill and perfect the Old Covenant, or Mosaic Law. It is a perfection here on earth of the Divine Law. The law of the New Covenant is called a law of love, grace, and freedom. The New Covenant will never end or diminish, and nothing new will be revealed until Christ comes again in glory.

Mary, Mother of the Church

Mary was named Mother of the Church by Pope Paul VI in 1964. Although this was a new title, it was also an acknowledgment of something the Church, the Body of Christ, has always known: Mary is our Mother. Mary is Mother of the Church because she is the Mother of Christ, the one whom God chose from among all women, all the descendants of Eve, to be the virgin mother of his Son. Mary, ever virgin, was preserved from Original Sin from the moment of her conception and remained free of personal sin during her whole life—a dogma called the Immaculate Conception. Mary, full of grace, said yes to the New Covenant, to the Incarnation—the wonderful union of the divine and human natures in the one Divine Person of the Word, the Son of God.

Mary is also Mother of the Church because she was the first disciple and the Mother of all other disciples. After Jesus' death she continued to nurture the early Church with her prayers. Through her continual obedience, faith, and hope, she cooperated with her Son's work of redemption. Because of the unique grace given to Mary through her Immaculate Conception, as well as her singular role in bringing forth our Savior, she is the first and best fruit of the redemption of Christ. We, the members of the Church, share the life of Christ, especially through Baptism and the Eucharist. Mary is our mother because we are one with her son, Jesus Christ.

© Saint Meinrad Archabbey

according to a favorite image of the Church Fathers, the Church is like the moon, all its light reflected from the sun [Christ]" (*Catechism of the Catholic Church [CCC]*, 748).

Christ began the Church first through his preaching of the Good News of salvation. In his preaching, Jesus taught a new way to live—not negating the Old Covenant or basic Ten Commandments but enhancing them with the pervasive influence of love: Jesus said, "I give you a new commandment: love one another. As I have loved you, you also should love one another" (John 13:34). Jesus taught a love that not only meets expectations but goes beyond them. Jesus also taught his disciples a new way of relating to God, not only as their Creator and Ruler of all but also as their loving Father, saying: "This is how you are to pray: / Our Father in heaven . . ." (Matthew 6:9). This prayer that Jesus taught, the Lord's Prayer, is the prayer of the New Covenant and thus the prayer of the Church.

Christ established the Church primarily by the saving gift of himself, which was fulfilled on the cross and anticipated when he instituted the Eucharist. His words, "This is my body, which will be given for you" (Luke 22:19), express his complete self-giving in sacrificing his life for the sake of humanity.

Apostle
The general term *apostle* means "one who is sent" and can be used in reference to any missionary of the Church during the New Testament period. In reference to the twelve companions chosen by Jesus, also known as "the Twelve," the term refers to those special witnesses of Jesus on whose ministry the early Church was built and whose successors are the bishops.

Structure and Sign

Jesus also gave his Church two more important elements: a structure and signs of his self-giving love, the Sacraments. The Church's structure from the beginning was the **Apostles** united with Peter, the head. The Twelve Apostles represent the Twelve Tribes of Israel and are the symbolic foundation stones of the New Jerusalem, the Church. This structure survives today in the union of all the bishops in the Church with the successor to Peter, the Pope.

Catholic Wisdom

The Holy Spirit Leads People to the Church

These words from *Dogmatic Constitution on the Church (Lumen Gentium)* speak of Christ's work in the Church and for the Church.

> Rising from the dead (see Rom 6:9) he [Christ] sent his life-giving Spirit upon his disciples and through him [the Spirit] set up his body which is the church as the universal sacrament of salvation. Sitting at the right hand of the Father he is continually active in the world in order to lead people to the church and through it to join them more closely to himself. (48)

The signs that Jesus left to his Church, the signs of his self-giving love, are the Sacraments. They come from him, for Christ is the original sacrament, the original sign, of our salvation. From Christ comes the Church. From Christ, through the Church, come the Seven Sacraments: Baptism, the Eucharist, Confirmation, Penance and Reconciliation, the Anointing of the Sick, Holy Orders, and Matrimony. The Seven Sacraments, instituted by Christ, are a visible sign of an invisible reality. Christ's words and actions during his public ministry were part of his work of salvation, and they announced the gift of the Sacraments he would give his Church through the actions of the Holy Spirit. ✝

Article 2 Sent by the Holy Spirit

The origin of all things, including God's plan for the human race, is the Holy Trinity, the central mystery of our Christian faith and our Christian life. God has made his mystery known to us by revealing himself as Father, Son, and Holy Spirit. The Divine Persons are distinct from one another, yet the three are perfectly united. Inseparable from the Father and the Son, and existing, like them, always and forever, the Holy Spirit participated with them in Creation itself, as they together are the "one, indivisible principle of creation" (*CCC*, 316). When the Word of God became flesh in the Incarnation, the Holy Spirit participated fully with the Father and the Son, each in his own proper way, in this divine mission and in the gift of the New Covenant. The Holy Spirit was with Jesus from the moment of his conception in the womb of the Virgin Mary, uniting both his divine and human natures. The Spirit was with him, working with him to complete the Father's plan of establishing the Kingdom by planting the seed of the Church.

Because John baptized for the repentance of sin, he resisted Jesus' request for Baptism at first, but Jesus insisted, demonstrating his obedience to God's plan.

© Blair Howard/iStockphoto.com

A key moment in the ministry of Jesus was his Baptism by his cousin John. In that experience of humility, of identifying most closely with those who repented and were preparing for the coming of the Kingdom, Jesus was assured that both the Father and the Holy Spirit were with him as he began his public work of announcing the Kingdom of God. His Father's voice proclaimed, "You are my beloved

The Solemnity of Pentecost

The fifty days of the Season of Easter end with the Solemnity of Pentecost. On this Solemnity the Church prays a special vigil Mass, which may be celebrated on the Saturday evening prior to Pentecost. At this vigil Mass, we may hear this Collect, or Opening Prayer:

> Almighty ever-living God,
> who willed the Paschal Mystery
> to be encompassed as a sign in fifty
>   days,
> grant that from out of the scat-
>   tered nations
> the confusion of many tongues
> may be gathered by heavenly grace
> into one great confession of your
>   name.
> Through our Lord Jesus Christ, your Son,
> who lives and reigns with you in the unity of the Holy Spirit,
> one God, for ever and ever.

(Roman Missal)

On the day of Pentecost, the Paschal candle, symbol of the Risen Christ, is moved from the sanctuary, in the front of the church, to a place near the baptismal font. Candles of the newly baptized will be lit from it, and, at funeral Masses, it may be placed near the casket in place of the usual candles.

Son; with you I am well pleased" (Mark 1:10). And the Holy Spirit, in the form of a dove, descended from the heavens upon him. The Spirit then drove Jesus out into the desert, where he remained for forty days to prepare himself for his public ministry. (See Mark 1:10–13.)

Then, on the feast of Pentecost, after the Paschal Mystery—Jesus' work of salvation through his Passion and death, Resurrection, and Ascension—had been accomplished, the Holy Spirit descended from on high. Pentecost was a great

charism
A special gift or grace of the Holy Spirit given to an individual Christian or community, commonly for the benefit and building up of the entire Church.

feast day for the Jews. It was a harvest feast, the feast of first-fruits, a feast of rejoicing in the first evidence of abundant life to come. The Apostles, with Mary in their midst, were gathered in an upper room. The Holy Spirit came upon them in flame and wind, to remove all fear, and to send them out to proclaim the message of Christ and begin the spread of the Gospel to all nations.

The Gifts of the Holy Spirit

The Church has never been without the Gifts of the Holy Spirit, for the Holy Spirit was sent to continually make the Church holy. It is the Holy Spirit who builds, enlivens, and sanctifies the Church.

How does the Holy Spirit aid the Church in fulfilling her mission today? In the same way he did with the Apostles: through his gifts or **charisms**. In the First Letter to the Corinthians, Saint Paul outlines those gifts clearly (see chapters 12–14.) These gifts are given to us, to the Church, not only for our own advancement in holiness, although individual holiness is necessary, but also for the good of others. And even though our individual gifts may differ, each one is given for the benefit of the entire Church, as Saint Paul explains:

> Now you are Christ's body, and individually parts of it. Some people God has designated in the church to be, first, apostles;

Pray It!

Your Lord and Savior

"Have you accepted Jesus Christ as your Lord and Savior?" Sometimes evangelists of other Christian communities ask others this question. What answer would you give? A good answer for Catholics is this: "Yes. I accepted Jesus Christ as my Lord and Savior at my Baptism—at least my parents and godparents accepted for me. I accepted Jesus Christ as my Lord and Savior, with the Gift of the Holy Spirit, at my Confirmation. I accept Jesus Christ as my Lord and Savior every time I go to Mass and receive Holy Communion. I accept Jesus Christ as my Lord and Savior every time I try to live the New Covenant of love."

Use this question and your answer as a prayer. Choose a time each day when you can say to Jesus: "Yes, I accept you as my Lord and Savior! Help me to live your covenant of love today." Remember that through the power and Gifts of the Holy Spirit, Jesus is with you always.

second, prophets; third, teachers; then, mighty deeds; then gifts of healing, assistance, administration, and varieties of tongues. Are all apostles? Are all prophets? Are all teachers? Do all work mighty deeds? Do all have gifts of healing? Do all speak in tongues? Do all interpret? Strive eagerly for the greatest spiritual gifts. (1 Corinthians 12:27–31) ✝

Messiah
Hebrew word for "anointed one." The equivalent Greek term is *christos.* Jesus is the Christ and the Messiah because he is the Anointed One.

Article 3 After Pentecost

After Pentecost everything changed for Jesus' followers. The Apostles themselves were no longer hiding in fear. Suddenly they were in public, proclaiming the Good News, announcing that Jesus was the Messiah and Savior that everyone had been seeking for so long. In his speech to the crowds gathered to hear the disciples speak, Peter invited them to repent, be baptized, and live a different way.

Peter proclaims to the crowd that Jesus *is* the **Messiah**, Jesus *is* risen, Jesus *is* with us, and we can still hear his message and follow him. Peter offers the crowds what they have been seeking for so long: a New Covenant with God and with one another, in love, and the opportunity to participate in it. (See Acts 2:14–41.) For the crowds and the Church, it is a new beginning. For the Church it is the beginning of proclaiming the Good News of evangelization. Now, after

The Gifts of the Holy Spirit poured out at Pentecost empowered the followers of Christ to share the Gospel effectively.
© Francis G. Mayer/CORBIS

Successors to the Apostles

The Twelve Apostles had a unique role in the Church. They were the foundation stones, specially chosen by Christ himself, to be the witnesses to his Resurrection, to be his emissaries, his ambassadors, who would carry the Good News of the New Covenant to the ends of the earth.

The Church realized that the promise of Christ, to be with us always, could not have been made simply for the first generation of Christians. The Apostles realized, in designating their successors, that the presence and power of Christ would be just as much with those successors, the bishops. Apostolic preaching and authority is transmitted uninterrupted from the Apostles to the bishops through the laying on of hands when a bishop is ordained in the Sacrament of Holy Orders. This is called **Apostolic Succession**.

The Pope and bishops of the Church today are the successors of the Apostles. It is their responsibility to govern and shepherd Christ's Church, leading Christ's flock to good pasture through the Word of God and the Sacraments. To them, as to his Apostles, Christ gives this awesome responsibility and privilege. He proclaims to the Apostles: "Whoever listens to you listens to me" (Luke 10:16).

Pentecost, the Apostles are beginning to do what Jesus asked of them as he gathered them together on a mountain in Galilee: "Go, therefore, and make disciples of all nations, baptizing them in the name of the Father, and of the Son, and of the holy Spirit, teaching them to observe all that I have commanded you. And behold, I am with you always, until the end of the age" (Matthew 28:19–20).

This is called "the Great Commission," Jesus' great "sending out" of the Apostles before his Ascension. Before Pentecost the Apostles were simply Jesus' followers. After Pentecost they became truly *apostles*, from the Greek word *apostoloi*, which means "emissaries." They were now Jesus' emissaries and could continue his mission and invite the whole world into the New Covenant in his name.

The Apostles could do this because Jesus kept his promise to send the Holy Spirit. He was still with them. He had not left them orphans. Jesus not only gave the Apostles their mission but also helped them to carry it out. Jesus, who suffered, died, and rose from the dead to establish the New Covenant, would be with his emissaries through the Holy Spirit, no matter what.

Apostolic Succession

The uninterrupted passing on of apostolic preaching and authority from the Apostles directly to all bishops. It is accomplished through the laying on of hands when a bishop is ordained in the Sacrament of Holy Orders as instituted by Christ. The office of bishop is permanent, because at ordination a bishop is marked with an indelible, sacred character.

Live It!

You'll Never Walk Alone

The picture of the early community of the Way in the Acts of the Apostles is almost idyllic. The followers of Jesus certainly formed a significant community united in purpose.

Today we might envy that unity. Often, it seems, we gather for Sunday Mass and then scatter our separate ways, not meeting again all week. This is not the model of Christian life presented to us in the Acts of the Apostles.

Some parishes have tried to remedy this situation with small-group communities, prayer groups that meet during the week, or other interest groups that draw people together. Almost every parish has a teen group. Look for something in your parish that interests you and to which you can bring your particular gifts. If one group doesn't fit, try another. Ask the Holy Spirit to help you to find other followers of the Way to support your faith in Jesus.

The People of the Way

Not everyone, of course, was called to be an Apostle or an evangelist. Not everyone of that time was called to preach. So how did the ordinary followers of Jesus live their New Covenant lives after Pentecost? The Acts of the Apostles helps us to see:

> They devoted themselves to the teaching of the apostles and to the communal life, to the breaking of the bread and to the prayers. . . . All who believed were together and had all things in common. . . . Every day they devoted themselves to meeting together in the temple area and to breaking bread in their homes. They ate their meals with exultation and sincerity of heart, praising God and enjoying favor with all the people. And every day the Lord added to their number those who were being saved. (2:42–47)

The early members of the Church were living a Jewish life as before, centered on the Temple, but they were living it in a different way because they were following the way of Jesus, their Lord and Messiah. That is what they came to be called among the Jews: followers of the Way.

Eventually the word *Christian* emerged. When Gentiles began to join the community, they used the Greek word for *Messiah* (which means "anointed one"). That word is *christos*. In the community at Antioch, made up of mostly Gentiles, the followers of the Way, the followers of Christ, were first called Christians. ☨

Part Review

1. Knowing that the Church has both visible and spiritual aspects, what attitude should we take in studying Church history?

2. What plan did God have in his heart before time began?

3. Besides preaching the Good News, what did Christ give his Church?

4. What is the significance of the first Pentecost in the life of the Church?

5. Describe how the early Christian community lived.

6. What is the Great Commission?

7. Why do we call Mary the Mother of the Church?

Part 2

The Mission of the Church

Although the life of the early Christian community, as described in the Acts of the Apostles, may seem perfect to us (see 2:42–47 and 4:32–35), the early Church still had to overcome obstacles in order to grow.

In this part we will learn about two events in the early Church that greatly influenced her growth. The first involves Saint Paul. Paul, formerly known as Saul, was a persecutor of the early Christians. But on one of his raiding journeys, Paul encountered Christ and came to believe in him. Paul was baptized and began the work of evangelization through his writing and missionary journeys that reached to the ends of the Roman Empire.

The second event is the decision of Saint Peter, under the guidance of the Holy Spirit, to allow Gentiles to be baptized. Under Peter's leadership, Jewish Christians came to understand that Christ had come for all people, not just followers of the Old Law.

Finally, in this part we will learn about the development of the New Testament and the role of the Church in discerning and preserving the Word of God for us today, as we live the New Covenant.

The articles in this part address the following topics:

Article 4 The Conversion of Saint Paul

As previously described in the Acts of the Apostles, the life of the early Christian community may seem perfect to us (see Acts of the Apostles 2:42–47, 4:32–35). The account in the Acts of the Apostles 2:42–47 ends with: "They ate their meals with exultation and sincerity of heart, praising God and enjoying favor with all the people" (verses 46–47).

© Ken Welsh / The Bridgeman Art Library

Yet a devout Jew named Saul was suspicious of the Christians. He began persecuting them. In the Acts of the Apostles we read, "Saul . . . was trying to destroy the church; entering house after house and dragging out men and women, he handed them over for imprisonment" (8:3).

But on one of Saul's raiding journeys, something dramatic happened. The Acts of the Apostles describes the event as follows:

> As he was nearing Damascus, a light from the sky suddenly flashed around him. He fell to the ground and heard a voice saying to him, "Saul, Saul, why are you persecuting me?" He said, "Who are you, sir?" The reply came, "I am Jesus, whom you are persecuting. Now get up and go into the city and you will be told what you must do." (9:3–6)

The Lord had meanwhile instructed Ananias, a disciple, to find Saul. Ananias did as the Lord asked and found Saul and laid hands on him. Saul, who had been struck blind in his encounter with Christ, regained his sight. He was filled with the Holy Spirit, and was baptized. Under his Roman name, Paul, he would come to be known as the Apostle to the Gentiles. His letters and his teachings would reach to the ends of the Roman Empire.

Saul's aim may have been to eradicate a misguided Jewish sect, but the Risen Christ identifies *himself* as the one being persecuted. The Church as the Body of Christ later became a theme in the letters he wrote.

grace
The free and undeserved gift of God's loving and active presence in our lives, empowering us to respond to his call and to live as his adopted sons and daughters. Grace restores our loving communion with the Holy Trinity, lost through sin.

The conversion (the "turning around") of Saint Paul was one of the most significant events in the life of the early Church. Through Paul, the Gentiles (the non-Jews of the world) would hear the Good News of salvation through Jesus Christ. But this mission to the Gentiles was not immediately discerned by Paul or by the other leaders of the early Church. Peter, for example, did not at first associate with Gentiles. (At first, he preached exclusively to the Jews, as did Paul. He later welcomed Gentiles into the Church. See the Acts of the Apostles 10:1–49.) It was only when the Jews rejected his message that Paul began preaching to the Gentiles. They began to meet together in their homes, just like the Jewish Christians, and to form Christian communities.

The Jewish Christians were both pleased and confused by this phenomenon. They viewed following Christ as a continuation of the religious tradition they had already been following. To some the Gentile Christians seemed to be going around Jewish Law, not observing its customs but then being baptized as Christians. They believed that because the Law of God was for everyone, new Gentile Christians should be taught to follow Jewish Law, be circumcised, and then be baptized.

The Council of Jerusalem

Paul and his assistant Barnabas met in Jerusalem in AD 49 or 50 with the apostles and the presbyters, or the leaders of the Church, to discuss the important matter of welcoming the Gentiles into the Church. Would the Gentiles be required to first follow Jewish Law? Some in the group, especially former Pharisees, who were great proponents of following the Law, said, "It is necessary to circumcise them and direct them to observe the Mosaic law" (15:5).

After much debate Peter stood up. He asked the assembly to consider what God was doing. Peter noted that the Gentile converts had also received the Holy Spirit, and, if God gave Gentiles the Holy Spirit, he was making no distinction between Jews and Gentiles. Peter went on to say: "Why, then, are you now putting God to the test by placing on the shoulders of the disciples a yoke that neither our ancestors nor we have been able to bear? On the contary, we believe that we are saved through the **grace** of the Lord Jesus, in the same way as they" (Acts of the Apostles 15:10–11). At this the entire assembly fell silent and then listened to Paul and Barnabas tell of the wonderful things God had done among the Gentiles through them.

The Apostle James volunteered an opinion that the Gentiles should not be made to follow Jewish Law but should observe only some basic regulations that the Law of Moses had always commanded; that is, they should avoid pollution from idols, unlawful marriage, the meat of strangled animals, and blood. They wrote a letter to the Gentiles in Antioch saying that "if you keep free of these, you will be doing what is right" (Acts of the Apostles 15:29).

The History behind the Acts of the Apostles

Luke, the writer of both the Gospel of Luke and the Acts of the Apostles, takes care to note that his writings, though not history in the way we think of it, are true to the message of Jesus. At the beginning of his Gospel (written for a certain Theophilus, which means "friend of God"), Luke explains that he has investigated everything accurately, to write it down in an orderly sequence. (See Luke 1:3–4.)

At the beginning of the Acts of the Apostles, Luke again addresses Theophilus and continues at the point where his Gospel left off: at the Ascension of Jesus and Jesus' instructions to his Apostles: "You will be my witnesses in Jerusalem, throughout Judea and Samaria, and to the ends of the earth" (1:8). It is the witnessing of the Apostles that comprises the contents of the Acts of the Apostles.

The Old Covenant and the New Covenant

From this debate we get a glimpse of the tension that existed between followers of the Old Law, the Old Covenant, and the New Law, the New Covenant given to us in Jesus Christ. The Jews had always thought of the Law as God's great gift to them, a gift he had given to no other people. It would seem natural for Jewish Christians who had accepted Jesus as the Messiah to want to share both the Old Law and the New Law with new converts. Both were gifts from God, and God has never renounced or revoked his covenant with the Jews.

But the Church discerned at the Council of Jerusalem that God had another vision, sealed by the gift of the Holy Spirit. This vision was a law not written on tablets of stone or even on scrolls or in books but written in the human heart. This was the vision that the patriarchs and prophets had been pointing toward, and, finally, in the Church's mission to the Gentiles, it was beginning to take shape. ✝

Article 5 The Significance of Saints Peter and Paul

In the iconography of the Church, Saints Peter and Paul are often honored together. In the liturgy they share the same feast day, on June 29. They are often called "the pillars of the Church" because from the beginning they held it up and carried it as pillars hold up a roof and carry the weight of the building. We still look to them today as our fathers and teachers in the faith.

Catholic Wisdom

Wisdom and Love in the Cross of Christ

In the ancient world, crucifixion was reserved for criminals and traitors. Yet Saint Paul emphasizes the cross of Christ, seeing in it the wisdom and love of God. In effect he says, "This is how far God's love will go." It was countercultural to the expectations of his age, and is to ours. Saint Paul says, "Jews demand signs and Greeks look for wisdom, but we proclaim Christ crucified . . . the power of God and the wisdom of God" (1 Corinthians 1:22–24).

The Mission of Saint Paul

We have already learned of the conversion of Saint Paul. We learned that he was baptized by Ananias in Damascus, visited with the Apostles in Jerusalem, but then, threatened with death from Jewish leaders who still could not accept that "one of their own" had accepted Jesus, was forced to flee back to his hometown of Tarsus. There he stayed for ten years, until he was called to help Barnabas in Antioch.

Antioch (in Syria) became the starting point for each of Saint Paul's three missionary journeys to the Gentiles. His first journey took him to the cities nearest to Antioch; his second journey took him farther afield, to cities in present-day Greece; and on his third journey, he revisited many of the places he had evangelized on his second journey. Saint Paul did take a fourth journey, to Rome, but it was not a missionary journey. This journey had another purpose. Paul went to Rome to defend himself, as was his right as a Roman citizen, in a trial before the emperor against a charge for which he had been accused and placed under house arrest, the charge of being a Christian.

After he had evangelized and established a church in a city, Paul kept in touch with the new Christians by writing letters. These letters, which are still read in our liturgies

Scholars have estimated that Saint Paul covered over 15,000 miles on his journeys, on land and by sea.

© Saint Mary's Press

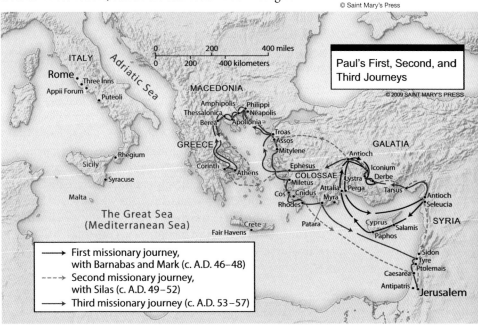

Paul's First, Second, and Third Journeys

© 2009 SAINT MARY'S PRESS

→ First missionary journey,
with Barnabas and Mark (c. A.D. 46–48)
---→ Second missionary journey,
with Silas (c. A.D. 49–52)
→ Third missionary journey (c. A.D. 53–57)

today, instruct the new Christians in the doctrines of the Christian faith and in the practical living-out of that faith in their everyday lives. In Paul's time, letters were often carried by friends and acquaintances traveling to the letter's destination. Paul frequently begins a letter by thanking the person who carried it (usually a member of the community to which the letter was addressed) and by greeting the recipients of the letter.

The Mission of Saint Peter

We have learned about the importance of Saint Peter to the early Church through the earlier discussion of the Council of Jerusalem. At this Council Saint Peter took everyone's view into consideration and thoughtfully considered, with the help of the Holy Spirit, the best course for the Church to take.

Early Christian writings, like the letters of Paul and the Acts of the Apostles and the writings of Tertullian, Clement, and Cyprian, clearly show that Peter is the leader of the Church. From the beginning he moves the Church forward. For example, he advises choosing a replacement for Judas, and his advice is accepted (see Acts of the Apostles 1:15–26). At Pentecost he was the first to give witness to Jesus in a speech to the crowd (see 2:14.) Throughout the Acts of the Apostles, the Twelve Apostles are often referred to as "Peter and the other apostles," in acknowledgment of Peter's leadership role.

One of the most pivotal events of the New Testament concerning Peter is his gradual realization, under the guidance of the Holy Spirit, that the Gentiles should be welcomed into the Church along with the Jews. Chapters 10 and 11 of the Acts of the Apostles describe Peter's dream during prayer and its influence on his acceptance of the Gentile converts, Cornelius the centurion and his family, into the Church. When confronted by Jewish Christians who accused him of eating with the uncircumcised, Peter carefully explained his decision. With care and concern, he led the Church along with him in his decisions, guided by the Holy Spirit.

Just as the office of the Apostles continued with the bishops, the office of Peter continued in the role of the Pope. The Pope and the bishops have taken the place of Peter and the other Apostles as pastors and shepherds of the Church, and the teaching authority of the Apostles has been handed down to them through Apostolic Succession. ✝

Article 6 The Development of the New Testament

At the time Saint Paul was writing letters to the churches he had founded, there was no New Testament. The Scripture known to the early Church was the same Scripture known to the Jews, which is what we know today as the Old

Pray It!

In the Footsteps of Saints Peter and Paul

On the Solemnity of Saints Peter and Paul (June 29), the Mass concludes with a Prayer over the People. This prayer encourages us to imitate the faith and witness of Saints Peter and Paul:

May almighty God bless you,
for he has made you steadfast in Saint Peter's saving confession
and through it has set you on the solid rock of the Church's faith.
R. Amen.

And having instructed you
by the tireless preaching of Saint Paul,
may God teach you constantly by his example
to win brothers and sisters for Christ.
R. Amen.

So that by the keys of Saint Peter and the words of Saint Paul,
and by the support of their intercession,
God may bring us happily to that homeland
that Peter attained on a cross
and Paul by blade of a sword.
R. Amen.

(Roman Missal)

When your faith falters, ask Saints Peter and Paul to strengthen you and encourage you, as they strengthened and encouraged the first Christians.

The Martyrdoms of Saints Peter and Paul

Tradition relates that Saint Peter journeyed to Rome during the last part of his life and was martyred there in AD 64, in the persecutions of Emperor Nero. According to Origen, an early Church writer, Peter was crucified upside down, at his request, because he did not consider himself worthy to be crucified in the same way as his Savior. For this reason an upside-down cross is one of the symbols of Saint Peter the Apostle. The great Basilica of Saint Peter in Rome was built over his tomb.

© Christie's Images/CORBIS

Paul's story ends in a similar fashion. He was in Rome at the time of the persecution of Christians by Emperor Nero and was beheaded in AD 67. The Basilica of Saint Paul-Outside-the-Walls near Rome was built over his burial place, and his tomb can still be visited today.

Testament. This was the Scripture the early Christians read in their assemblies. Following the Jewish custom, they also prayed the Psalms several times a day, a practice that became the basis for the Church's official prayer, the Liturgy of the Hours.

At the time of Saint Paul, the Gospels had not yet been written. As the Apostles and disciples evangelized, they shared their recollections of Jesus and his teachings. Because people in those days did not have ready access to writing tools, they were more practiced in remembering what was told to them than we are today. This would be especially true in important matters, such as the teachings of Jesus. And the Holy Spirit was with them, helping them to remember and to proclaim the Good News. Only at a later time were these recollections and teachings compiled into scrolls and books.

The formation of the New Testament occurred in three broad stages:

1. **The life and teaching of Jesus** Jesus lived and taught among us until his Ascension.

Early missionaries first preached in the synagogue when they arrived in a new location. If the Jewish community did not welcome them, which was often the case, they took their message to the Gentiles in the marketplace.

Live It!

Share the Gospel in Words and Deeds

An old African American spiritual called "Balm in Gilead" contains this verse:

If you can't preach like Peter,
If you can't pray like Paul,
Just tell the love of Jesus,
And say He died for all.

We are all called to evangelize, to share the Gospel with others, in words and in deeds. To share your faith, you don't need to be a great orator; you can share it in ordinary ways. Someone around you may need to hear that God loves and cares for them! But don't just talk the talk; also walk the walk. In other words, follow up your words with actions, even small ones, that bring God's love to others and make life better for those around you.

Sacred Tradition
From the Latin *tradere*, meaning "to hand on." Refers to the process of passing on the Gospel message. It began with the oral communication of the Gospel by the Apostles, was written down in Sacred Scripture, and is interpreted by the Magisterium under the guidance of the Holy Spirit.

Magisterium
The Church's living teaching office, which consists of all bishops, in communion with the Pope, the bishop of Rome.

Deposit of Faith
The heritage of faith contained in Sacred Scripture and Sacred Tradition. It has been passed on from the time of the Apostles. The Magisterium takes from it all that it teaches as revealed truth.

2. **The oral tradition** The Apostles handed on, in their preaching and writing, what Jesus had said and done, in that fuller understanding brought about by the Resurrection of Christ and the guidance of the Holy Spirit.

3. **The written books** The inspired authors selected certain elements from what had been handed on, either in oral or written form, often with synthesis and explanation (that is, in a process of editing), to bring us the truth about Jesus (see *CCC*, 126). These written accounts eventually became what we know today as the New Testament.

Scripture, Tradition, and the Magisterium

How did the Church discern which writings about Jesus were true and authentic? In order to answer this question, we must understand the relationship among Sacred Scripture, **Sacred Tradition**, and the **Magisterium**, or teaching authority, of the Church.

Christ governs the Church through the Pope and the bishops in communion with him—the successors to Peter and the Apostles. The Pope and the bishops in union with him form the Magisterium—the living, teaching office of the Church. The Magisterium is entrusted with transmitting and interpreting Divine Revelation. The Church's handing on of the Gospel message and transmission and interpretation of Divine Revelation are known as Sacred Tradition.

The writings of the New Testament (the Gospels; the Acts of the Apostles; the epistles, or letters; and the Book of Revelation) were authenticated by the Church as the truth revealed by God. Eventually the New Testament was authorized with twenty-seven books and the Old Testament with forty-six. Together this list of books is called the canon of Scripture. The word *canon* comes from the Greek word *kanon*, meaning "measure" or "standard," which evolved into the word *canon*, meaning "rule."

Sacred Scripture together with Sacred Tradition "make up a single sacred deposit of the word of God" (*Dogmatic Constitution on Divine Revelation* [*Dei Verbum*, 1965], 10). Both are necessary. Depending on Scripture alone for the truths of our salvation would deprive us of the living transmission of ancient Church practice and teaching through the ages; and looking to Sacred Tradition without Sacred

Scripture would be an exercise in futility, empty of meaning. We need to live the life God intends for us, and we also need the teaching authority of the Church (the Magisterium), as it draws all that it teaches from the **Deposit of Faith**, the heritage of faith contained in Scripture and Tradition. ✝

The Criteria for Acceptance into the Canon

The leaders of the early Church, called *episcope* (Greek for "overseers"), or bishops, decided what writings to include in the New Testament. This was one way they exercised, and still exercise, their role as the teaching authority in the Church, and thus preserved the teachings of the Apostles in a continuous line of succession. The bishops, relying on Apostolic Tradition, confirmed what the Holy Spirit had inspired in the worshipping community through the use and acceptance of these books. Within this Tradition these four criteria were used, and a book had to meet all four to be included:

1. **Apostolic** A book had to be based on the preaching and teaching of the Apostles and their closest companions and disciples.

2. **Community acceptance** The Christians of an important Christian community had accepted a book as valid and consistent with their beliefs and practices.

3. **Liturgical** Early Christians were using this book in their liturgical celebrations—most importantly, the Eucharist.

4. **Consistent** A book's message had to be consistent with Hebrew, or Jewish, writings and other Christian writings; it could not contradict what was already accepted as the Word of God.

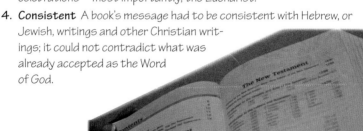

Part Review

1. Why was the conversion of Saint Paul such a significant event for the Church?

2. How did Jewish Christians react to the entry of Gentiles into the Church?

3. What problem was presented to the Council of Jerusalem and what was its resolution?

4. Why did Saint Paul write letters to his Gentile converts?

5. What factors or events prepared Saint Peter to favor the admission of Gentiles into the Church?

6. Explain the three broad stages in the development of the New Testament.

7. Explain the relationship among Sacred Scripture, Sacred Tradition, and the Magisterium of the Church.

Part 3

Growth and Persecution in Apostolic Times

"I am the resurrection and the life; whoever believes in me, even if he dies, will live. . . . Do you believe this?" (John 11:25–26). These words of Jesus could well have been recalled by the early Christians who faced persecution for believing in Jesus Christ, the Son of God, rather than in the divinity of the Roman gods, including the Roman emperor.

But, from the Roman viewpoint, it was worship of the gods and of the emperor that held the state together. And surely the state must be held together at all costs—even the cost of human life.

But the Church survived this threat to its very existence, and even thrived when the courage and integrity of the martyred Christians—who proclaimed their faith by giving up their lives—became known to all.

"The blood of martyrs is the seed of Christians"[1] (*CCC*, 852) wrote Tertullian, the first Father of the Church, and in these early centuries, that seed took root, blossomed, and bore fruit in true worship of the one, true God and in and service to all—then and today.

The articles in this part address the following topics:

Article 7 Persecutions and Progress

martyrdom
Witness to the saving message of Christ through the sacrifice of one's life.

Paul's missionary journeys, along with the work of the other Apostles, brought the message of Jesus to the known world. Under the guidance of the Holy Spirit, the Church grew quickly. But along the way there were persecutions, organized programs of oppression, imprisonment, and cruelty against Christians, often resulting in death by martyrdom. Before his conversion Saint Paul cooperated in persecutions led by Jewish leaders who considered the followers of Jesus to be a threat to the Jewish faith.

But, periodically, the Romans also considered the Christians a threat to the established order. The Roman government had a religious and governmental system in place that mandated the worship of many gods, including the emperor, the leader of the Roman Empire. When the Romans took over Israel, the Jewish leaders asked for and received an exemption from this requirement. But, when the Christians—now spread from Jerusalem into Gentile lands—could no longer be identified as a subset of the Jews and could claim a religious identity of their own, the exemption no longer applied to them. With their refusal to worship the emperor or offer sacrifices to Roman gods, Christians became easy scapegoats when Rome found itself in turmoil. Roman cruelty found an outlet in the torture and death of Christians who suffered **martyrdom** rather than renounce their faith.

Tales of public executions where Christians were shot with arrows or torn apart by wild beasts may seem like fiction today, but accounts from the time relate that many Christians faced these atrocities with courage.

The Blood of Martyrs

Under the Roman emperors Nero, Diocletian, Decius, and Domitian—whose names struck terror into the hearts of Christians—thousands paid the ultimate price for their faith. We have evidence from the Jewish historian Josephus, as well as from Roman writers (Tacitus, Suetonius, and Pliny), that Christians were thought to be atheistic (because they did not believe in Roman gods), subversive (because they refused state orders to worship the gods or the emperor, a unifying factor in the Roman Empire), and practitioners of cannibalism (because they partook of the Eucharist). Christians were blamed for natural disasters like plagues and earthquakes, because these were seen as punishments from the gods for Christian failure to appease the deities and support the Roman way of life.

In the year AD 64, Emperor Nero, who was blamed for starting a fire that burned Rome, deflected that blame onto the Christians and began a persecution that took the life of Saint Peter. In the second persecution led by Nero, Saint Paul was beheaded. In his cruelty Nero displayed the sufferings and deaths of Christians as public recreation.

Other persecutions followed in waves, including a severe one under Emperor Domitian (AD 81–96). Under Emperor Trajan (98–117), Christianity was punishable by death if discovered, but this emperor did not hunt down Christians on a wide scale, as others had done. After ceasing for some years under Emperor Hadrian (117–138), persecutions resumed under Marcus Aurelius (161–180). Septimius Severus (193–211), who sought to establish a single religion for the empire, decreed death for anyone converting to Judaism or Christianity. Saints Perpetua, Felicity, and Irenaeus were put to death under his reign.

Emperor Decius (249–251) required all citizens to carry written proof, in the form of a certificate, that they had offered sacrifice to the pagan gods of the empire. But perhaps the worst persecution was the last, under Diocletian (284–305), who had decided to uproot Christianity from the Empire. To that end he confiscated the property of Christians (including churches and sacred books), sentenced them to hard labor, and put them to death.

The Cruelty of Nero

In the year 64, most of Rome was destroyed in the Great Fire of Rome. It is thought that Nero had started the fire in order to obtain for himself a small parcel of land. The historian Tacitus relates what happened as a result:

> To kill the rumors [that Nero had started the fires that destroyed much of Rome], Nero charged and tortured some people known for their evil practices, the group popularly known as "Christians."
>
> In their deaths they were made a mockery. They were covered with the skin of beasts, they were torn to death by dogs, crucified, or set on fire to illuminate the night when daylight failed. Nero had thrown open the gardens for the spectacle. . . . Hence, although they were guilty of being Christian there arose a feeling of compassion for them; for it was not, as it seemed, for the public good, but [to] glut one man's cruelty, that they were being punished.

The Seed of the Church

Yet, as Tertullian has said, "The blood of martyrs is the seed of Christians"[2] (*CCC*, 852). The courage and conviction of the martyred Christians won hearts. During these first centuries, the Church thrived. One reason, as Tertullian states, is that those who found the faith worth dying for inspired others. In the midst of a corrupt society, capable of such cruelty, the lives of the Christians stood out in their love for one another and their care for those living on the margins of life, outside the Roman mainstream: the poor, slaves, and women. The basic goodness of the Christian way of life also appealed to intellectuals and others of good will who were looking for spiritual values in their lives as an alternative to cruelty as entertainment and to the worship of sadistic and corrupt emperors.

The Growth of Christianity

There were practical social and political reasons for the spread of Christianity as well. Because the Jews had spread out from the land of Israel and had established pockets of population, along with synagogues, in Gentile areas, it was easy for Christian evangelists to find their way to these same population centers and preach the Gospel to the Jews. Even though the message was usually rejected, the Gentiles in the area would be the next logical audience. And the Gentiles were open to the message of Jesus and this new way of life.

The Roman Empire shared a common language (Greek and then later Latin) as well as a common culture. Roman roads were maintained and often guarded from robbers by Roman troops. Ships made constant voyages from one Mediterranean town to the next, thus simplifying travel. (Comforts were not provided. Travelers brought their own food and bedding.)

Most of all, the lands around the Mediterranean Sea were united by the *Pax Romana,* or Roman peace. This peace, imposed by the empire for about two centuries after the birth of Christ, meant that although persecutions could terrorize Christians, the spread of their message and way of life was not continually disrupted by war.

Article 8 Early Christian Worship

Imagine that you are an early Christian in the first century, say, a Greek-speaking Gentile somewhere in Antioch, where the followers of the Way were first called Christians (see Acts of the Apostles 11:26.) It is Sunday and you have just put in a hard day selling dates and figs in the marketplace. (On Saturday the Jews observed a day of rest, but Sunday would not be an official day of rest for Christians until Emperor Constantine came to power.)

But Sunday is the Christian day of worship, in honor of the Resurrection of Christ, and the Eucharist is at the heart of Christian worship. So this evening you are on your way to the weekly gathering of Christians at the home of a neighbor. Your little community has been growing, and the people (your assembly, in Greek *ekklesia,* leading to the German and

© DeA Picture Library / Art Resource, NY

In the early Church, Christians gathered in homes to avoid unwanted attention.

Old English *kirche*, to today's English *church*) crowd together into the open courtyard of the home, called an atrium.

The Liturgy of the Word

You listen as the readings begin, usually from the Old Testament. Often a psalm is sung. Then selections from a letter from the Apostle Paul or another Apostle are read aloud. Some in your community had known elders who had known Paul, and you always look forward to hearing something from his writings, which have been copied over and over and treasured. These readings are followed by a talk from the presider, who reminds the assembly to act on what they have heard.

Saint Justin Martyr (of whom we will hear more in article 9, "The Early Apologists") describes the next part of the liturgy:

> Then we all rise together and offer prayers for ourselves . . . and for all others, wherever they may be, so that we may be found righteous by our life and actions, and faithful to the commandments, so as to obtain eternal salvation.
>
> When the prayers are concluded we exchange the kiss.[3]
>
> (*CCC*, 1345)

Live It!

The Mass: Then and Now

The basic structure of the Mass has remained the same since the time of the early Christians. Now, as then, we are called to full, active, and conscious participation in the Liturgy. Here are some tips for doing so:

1. **Pay attention to the words.** Be still and quiet, especially during the words of consecration. Allow the Holy Spirit to help you to pray the Mass. Bring your own life to Christ as you say your own personal "Amen" ("Yes, it is true!") to his life in yours.

2. **Pay attention to the actions.** Watch and be present. Stand, kneel, and sit with purpose and attention. We are a mind-body partnership: If the body slouches, the mind and spirit will too.

3. **Make a Mass intention.** Make your participation at Mass a prayer for someone else. Include your intention in the prayers of the Mass. Join your offering to the infinite prayer of Jesus Christ in the Eucharist.

Now that the assembly has exchanged the sign of peace, everyone is prepared to celebrate the Eucharist together as one.

The Liturgy of the Eucharist

Saint Justin Martyr continues:

> Then someone brings bread and a cup of water and wine mixed together to him who presides over the brethren.
>
> He takes them and offers praise and glory to the Father of the universe, through the name of the Son and of the Holy Spirit and for a considerable time he gives thanks (in Greek: *eucharistian*) that we have been judged worthy of these gifts. When he has concluded the prayers and thanksgivings, all present give voice to an acclamation by saying: "Amen."
>
> When he who presides has given thanks and the people have responded, those whom we call deacons give to those present the "eucharisted" bread, wine and water and take them to those who are absent.[4] (*CCC*, 1345)

The Collection

Saint Paul himself, in his letters, mentions collecting money for the poor, and this was one of the stipulations that the Council of Jerusalem imposed on the Gentiles—that they "be mindful of the poor," which, Saint Paul continues, "is the very thing I was eager to do" (Galatians 2:10).

At the time of the early Christians, the bread and wine for the Eucharist were brought by the assembly as their offering. What was not used for the Eucharist was given to the presider for his own sustenance, or to those who were poor. Other donations of both food and money were also accepted as offerings. Saint Justin Martyr further explains the importance of this collection:

> Those who are well off, and who are also willing, give as each chooses. What is gathered is given to him who presides to assist orphans and widows, those whom illness or any other cause has deprived of resources, prisoners, immigrants and, in a word, all who are in need.[5] (*CCC*, 1351)

The Roman Empire provided no pensions or retirement plans for those too old or too ill to work, or for widows. In these circumstances, if family members could not provide support, or if one had no family, the only recourse was begging. Now those on the fringes of society would receive help from their Christian community. Truly the early Christians took the words of Jesus to heart: "This is how all will know that you are my disciples, if you have love for one another" (John 13:35). This remains our Christian ideal today.

The Didache

The full English title of *The Didache* is *The Teaching of the Twelve Apostles.* (The word *didache*, pronounced DID-ah-kee, means "teaching" in Greek.) Most scholars believe that *The Didache* dates to the late first or early second century. Written anonymously for the Christian community, it is a pastoral manual of teachings and practices. *The Didache* was lost in the early centuries of the Church and then rediscovered in 1873.

Chapter 9 of *The Didache* gives instructions on the Eucharist. The form of the prayers of the Eucharist is taken from the Jewish prayer of thanksgiving called a *berakah* (BEAR-ah-kah). The blessing for the cup is given first: "We thank thee, our Father, for the holy vine of David Thy servant, which You madest known to us through Jesus Thy Servant, to thee be glory for ever"(translation, Roberts-Donaldson).

This is followed by the blessing of the bread: "We thank Thee, our Father, for the life and knowledge which You madest known to us through Jesus Thy Servant; to Thee be glory forever. Even as this broken bread was scattered over the hills, and was gathered together and became one, so let Thy Church be gathered together from the ends of the earth into Thy kingdom; for Thine is the glory and the power through Jesus Christ for ever" (Roberts-Donaldson).

Article 9 The Early Apologists

Throughout the first and second centuries, the Church continued to grow. Its influence cut across all classes of people, and gradually writers and philosophers were becoming Christian. Of course, they wanted to reach out to their colleagues and share with them the truth they had found in the teachings of Jesus and of the Apostles. In addition to strengthening the faith of the Christian community, these writers and philosophers carried on a dialogue with pagan philosophers and intellectuals, sometimes even with emperors. They wanted to show that Christianity was reasonable, creditable, and respectable—and that it should not be subject to persecution. Some used the ideas and vocabulary of pagan philosophy to show how these ideas were present and yet more fully developed in Christianity. These Christian writers and philosophers were called **apologists**.

apologist
One who speaks or writes in defense of someone or something.

An "apology" (from the Greek *apo*, which means "related to," and *logos*, which means "word") is a defense of something—a defense of a belief or of a way of life. The early Christian apologists used their knowledge of Greek and Roman philosophy to defend Christianity. Three of the most famous of these writers and apologists were Saint Ignatius of Antioch, Saint Justin Martyr, and Saint Irenaeus.

© Zvonimir Atletic/Shutterstock.com

Early apologists not only argued for the reasonableness of their faith, they risked their lives rather than deny their beliefs.

Saint Ignatius of Antioch (ca. 35–107)

Consecrated the second bishop of Antioch around the year 69, Ignatius was dearly loved by his people. When he refused to renounce the Christian faith, he was taken under guard from Antioch to Rome and was told that the wild beasts in the Coliseum awaited him. Along the way he wrote seven letters of encouragement and instruction to the Christians of Asia Minor and Greece. The content of these letters has been handed down to us today. In his letters Ignatius urged Christians to remain faithful to the apostolic teaching and to their bishops, the successors of the Apostles. Saint Ignatius, on his way to death, used Eucharistic symbolism to explain to his fellow Christians that he was ready to give up his life and be with God:

> My love of this life has been crucified, and there is no yearning in me for any earthly thing. Rather within me is the living water which says deep inside me: "Come to the Father." I no longer take pleasure in perishable food or in the delights of this world. I want only God's bread, which is the flesh of Jesus Christ, formed of the seed of David, and for drink I crave his blood, which is love that cannot perish.
>
> *(Liturgy of the Hours,* volume IV, page 1491)

Saint Justin Martyr (ca. 100–165)

In the preceding article, we read a portion of Saint Justin Martyr's work, his description of the Eucharist. (See article 8, "Early Christian Worship.") Saint Justin Martyr was a Gentile from Samaria who became Christian around age thirty. In his *First Apology*, *Second Apology*, and *Dialogue with the Jew Tryphon,* he includes details of his life to make certain points. Because of this we know a little more about Saint Justin Martyr than we do about other early saints.

He seems to have studied under various philosophers but was most influenced by Stoicism and Platonism, two of the popular philosophies of the time. In his works he recounts two more powerful influences that led to his conversion to Christianity. Walking along the seashore, he met an old man who told him that human knowledge alone cannot lead to God. Instruction is needed from the prophets, who, inspired by the Holy Spirit, could make God known to us. In his *Second Apology*, he also relates, "When I was a disciple of Plato, hearing the accusations made against the Christians and seeing them intrepid in the face of death and of all that men fear, I said to myself that it was impossible that they should be living in evil and in the love of pleasure." Justin himself was later martyred, with several companions, for refusing to offer sacrifices to pagan gods.

Saint Irenaeus (ca. 130–200)

Saint Irenaeus was born in Smyrna in Asia Minor and studied in Rome. As a priest he went to Gaul (present-day France) to serve at a church in Lyons. In 177 he was sent to carry a message to Rome. While he was there, the Church in Lyons suffered a severe persecution, and his bishop, Saint Pothinus, was martyred. When Irenaeus returned to Lyons, he was its second bishop.

But in Lyons he faced another kind of disturbance. The philosophy of Christian Gnosticism was spreading. This heresy held that knowledge would earn us salvation, and, furthermore, this mysterious knowledge could be known by only the favored few. The Gnostics held that the physical world was inferior to the spiritual world, and this conviction led to the denial of the human nature of Christ and to various other distortions of the Christian message.

Much of the writings of Irenaeus have been lost, but his work combating this heresy has survived. This treatise, *Against Heresies,* written in five books, exposed the errors of Gnosticism and contrasted them with the teaching of the Apostles and Sacred Scripture. This widely circulated treatise is credited for the demise of Gnosticism in that era.

Saint Irenaeus is also credited with helping to settle a scriptural controversy of his time, concerning which of the four Gospels is the best. Various regions of the Christian world had their preferences, but Irenaeus asserted that all four were canonical and all four were important.

Pray It!

Formed by God

In this prayer attributed to Saint Irenaeus, we are compared to impressionable clay. (See Jeremiah 18:6 and 2 Corinthians 4:7 for similar comparisons.) Ask God to shape and form you into the work of art he wants you to be.

It is not you that shapes God;
it is God that shapes you.
If you are the work of God,
await the hand of the artist,
who does all things in due season.
Offer him your heart,
soft and tractable,
and keep the form
in which the artist has fashioned you.
Let your clay be moist,
lest you grow hard
and lose the imprint of his fingers.

Tertullian

Tertullian (ca. 160–220) was an early Christian writer and theologian from Carthage, in Africa. During Tertullian's lifetime, Carthage was a province of the Roman Empire. Tertullian was a scholar, was trained as a lawyer, and was an excellent orator. He was a convert to Christianity and was married. Two of his books are addressed to his wife. He wrote extensively about Christian

doctrine and was the first Christian writer to write in Latin (rather than Greek).

Unfortunately, Tertullian came under the influence of Montanism, a sect whose adherents called themselves spiritual people (while they considered others to be carnal people). This seems to have caused a break with the Church, but Tertullian continued to write against heresies, especially Gnosticism.

Irenaeus was buried under the altar of his church in Lyons. Sadly this church, with his tomb, was destroyed by the Calvinists in 1562.

Article 10 Authority in the Church

Christ established and sustains the Church on earth, as a community of faith, hope, and charity, and as a visible organization through which he communicates truth and grace to all people. (See *CCC*, 771.) When those whom God calls to lead his Church respond with the help of the Holy Spirit, the results are amazing, and the Good News of Jesus Christ spreads throughout the world. To illustrate this truth, we will take a close look at authority in the early Church through the lives of Saint Peter, the first Pope; Timothy, a disciple of Saint Paul; and the writings of Saint Ignatius of Antioch, whom we discussed in article 9, "The Early Apologists."

college of bishops
The assembly of bishops, headed by the Pope, that holds the teaching authority and responsibility in the Church.

Peter, the First Pope

When Peter and Paul were hard at work spreading the Gospel—Peter mainly to the Jews and Paul to the Gentiles—the Gospels had not yet been written. The Acts of the Apostles had not yet been written. (See article 7.) Peter could not point to Matthew 16:18 to prove that Jesus had called him to be the Rock of the Church. Yet the Christians of Peter's time knew that Jesus had made Peter the visible foundation, the Rock, of the Church and had entrusted the "keys" (symbol of authority) to him. Peter was their leader, and later the many references to his leadership in the Gospels and the Acts of the Apostles would witness to this fact.

As the Church began to acquire a formalized structure, Peter emerged as the bishop of Rome. Because the church of Rome had primacy among the other churches that were centers of Christianity at that time (Antioch and Constantinople, for example), Peter, as Bishop of Rome, came to have primacy over other bishops. Thus Rome became the See (from the Latin *sedes*, meaning "seat") of Peter. Every Bishop of Rome is the successor to Saint Peter and the head of the **college of bishops**, the Vicar of Christ, and Pastor (Shepherd)

Catholic Wisdom

The Wisdom of the Early Apologists

The apologists explained the Catholic faith. Here are some of their words.

"The glory of God is man fully alive." (Saint Irenaeus)

"We . . . pray for our enemies, and endeavor to persuade those who hate us unjustly to live conformably to the good precepts of Christ, to the end that they may become partakers with us of the same joyful hope of a reward from God the ruler of all." (Saint Justin Martyr)

"Wherever the bishop shall appear, there let the multitude of the people also be; even as, wherever Jesus Christ is, there is the Catholic Church." (Saint Ignatius of Antioch)

© Georg Zinsler/Demotix/Corbis

Pope Francis, elected in 2013, is the 266th successor of Peter. This photo was taken on the day of his formal Inauguration Mass.

presbyter

A synonym for "elder" in the Acts of the Apostles and an alternative word for "priest" today.

of the universal Church. Eventually the Bishops of Rome came to be called Popes (from the Latin *papa* and the Greek *pappas*, both a familiar form of *father*). The Pope has "supreme, full, immediate, and universal power in the care of souls" (*Christus Dominus* 2) (*CCC*, 937).

Even when Emperor Constantine decided to move the capital of the Roman Empire to Constantinople (see article 11), the headquarters of the Catholic Church and the seat of its leadership remained in Rome.

Timothy: A Bishop of the Early Church

We learn much about Timothy from the First and Second Letters to Timothy. To understand how Timothy become a pastor (a shepherd of a congregation), and his role, it is helpful to know the following.

By the time the Letters to Timothy were written (about AD 100), the Church had achieved, by the early second century, a certain organizational structure that included bishops, **presbyters** (or priests), and deacons. These letters were written to instruct these Church leaders on their various tasks within the Church.

There were no seminaries at this time. Timothy prepared for his roles as a presbyter and then a pastor (probably a bishop) by learning from his family, whose faith was praised (see 2 Timothy 1:5), and from teachers like Paul (see 3:10–17). At a certain point in Timothy's life, when Paul and the community judged him ready, Paul conferred on him an ecclesiastical office through the laying on of hands (see 2 Timothy 1:6). This is the same as the laying on of hands through which bishops, priests, and deacons are ordained in the Sacrament of Holy Orders today.

The Roles of Bishops and Presbyters

Christ gave the Apostles and their successors, the bishops, a share in his own mission: to proclaim the faith and to plant his kingdom on earth. From Christ they receive the power of acting in his very person. We can learn much about the role of bishops from the Letters to Timothy (see 1 Timothy 3:1–7). Having received their office from the laying on of hands, bishops, in turn, delegate their helpers (presbyters, or priests) for service in the same way (see 5:17–23.) "Individual bishops are the visible source and foundation of unity in their own particular churches. . . . It is in and from these that the one and unique catholic church exists" (*Dogmatic Constitution on the Church*, 23).

Both presbyters and deacons share in the mission of the bishops but do not have their authority and are not considered successors to the Apostles. Only the bishops, in union with the Pope, have that role in the Church. In summary,

Deacons in the Church

The role of deacon in the Church began with a need: the distribution of food for widows and others who were in need. The Apostles asked that seven reputable men filled with the Spirit and wisdom be chosen to take charge of this distribution. Stephen, who became the first Christian martyr, was chosen as the first deacon of the Church, followed by six others. The Apostles prayed and laid hands on them (see the Acts of the Apostles 6:1–7.)

Gradually the office of deacon was inserted as one of the ministries along the path to ordination, and thus it became a temporary office. The reforms of the Second Vatican Council (1962–1965) restored the permanent diaconate in which men are ordained as deacons for life.

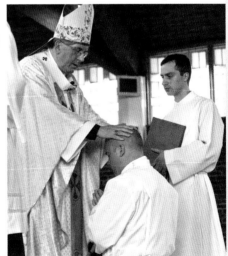

© Bill Wittman/www.wpwittman.com

bishops are obligated to teach the faith; to celebrate divine worship, above all the Eucharist; and to guide their churches as true pastors. They are also, in communion with and under the guidance of the Pope, to share responsibility for the leadership of the Church.

Part Review

1. Tertullian has said, "The blood of martyrs is the seed of Christians"[6] (*CCC*, 852). Explain how this statement is borne out in the early history of the Church.

2. Briefly summarize some of the practical social and political factors that contributed to the spread of Christianity.

3. Compare the Liturgy of the Word and the Liturgy of the Eucharist in the early Christian Liturgy and in the Mass today.

4. What is *The Didache,* when was it written, and what teachings does it contain?

5. Choose one of the early apologists and give a brief summary of his work and teachings.

6. Explain the roles of bishops and presbyters in the early Church? How does the role of bishops remain unchanged?

7. Why is Rome called the See of Peter? Why does it have a place of eminence in the Church?

Part 4

Age of the Fathers

During the first three centuries of Christianity, the Church grew and the faith spread throughout the Mediterranean world. However, as we have learned, this often came at a high price. Followers of Christ faced periodic persecutions and even martyrdom. In the fourth century, this all began to change. As you will learn in this part of the student book, this turn in the tide began with an act of Emperor Constantine, who legalized Christianity in 313. Christians no longer had to worship in secret or live in fear of retribution.

The fourth century also brought a wave of heresies, such as Arianism, that challenged the Church's beliefs. In response, the leaders of the Church gathered at Ecumenical Councils where Church teaching was clarified and affirmed. The Church Fathers also responded to these heresies with rich and brilliant writings that defended the faith and addressed other important subjects. As you will see, with the growth of the Church, new challenges developed, yet the Church was becoming stronger and more formally organized, and thus better able to respond to the challenges.

This change was particularly beneficial to Christians and to all the citizens of the Western Roman Empire when, in 476, the empire collapsed and a leadership void was created. The Church was able to provide leadership, governance, and aid to citizens that the empire no longer could.

The articles in this part address the following topics:

- Article 11: Constantine and the *Edict of Milan* (page 52)

- Article 12: The Fathers of the Church (page 55)

- Article 13: Church Councils and Doctrinal Development (page 59)

- Article 14: The Collapse of the Roman Empire of the West (page 63)

Article 11 Constantine and the *Edict of Milan*

Despite persecutions, heresies, and countless challenges, the Church had survived for three centuries. In fact, the Church thrived and grew, extending to new parts of the Roman Empire. By the start of the fourth century, Christianity had taken root in parts of North Africa, Asia Minor and the Arabian Peninsula, and as far north as Gaul (in modern-day France). However, the followers of Christ had endured much suffering and were challenged to remain steadfast in their faith in the face of profound hardships. But this was about to change. Christians, who had been an often persecuted and despised minority in the Roman Empire, were about to find a protector whose support of their faith, customs, and worship would have an enduring effect on the Roman Empire and the Church, and the relationship between them.

Emperor Constantine

When Emperor Constantius died in 306, the Roman troops chose Constantine (ca. 272–337) to be emperor. When Constantine reached Rome to take power, he faced the forces of a rival emperor and found himself and his troops engaged in a critical battle outside Rome. The Church historian Eusebius tells of the events that led to Constantine's

Pray It!

The Exaltation of the Holy Cross

We have seen what inspiration the image of the cross provided to Constantine. His mother, Saint Helena, was intent on discovering the holy places in Israel touched by the life of Jesus. On the hill traditionally believed to be the hill of Calvary, the Romans had built a temple to the goddess Aphrodite. Saint Helena had the temple razed, and under it was found three crosses—one of which was discovered to be the cross of Christ. Constantine later had the Church of the Holy Sepulcher built over this site.

The Feast of the Exaltation of the Holy Cross is celebrated on September 14, the anniversary of the dedication of the Basilica of the Holy Sepulcher in 335. This short prayer has long been associated with the holy cross and is often prayed during the Stations of the Cross during Lent: "We adore you, O Christ, and we bless you, because by your holy cross you have redeemed the world."

conversion: Before the battle, Constantine had a dream in which he was told that if he placed the Chi-Rho, the first two letters of Christ's name in Greek, on his troops' banners and shields, he would be triumphant. Constantine did as he was instructed. He won the battle and was named emperor of the Western Roman Empire.

Christianity Is Legalized

In 313, shortly after assuming power, Constantine, along with Licinius, his counterpart from the Eastern Empire, issued the **Edict of Milan**, which proclaimed religious toleration in the Roman Empire. After centuries of oppression and persecution, Christians could now worship freely. In addition to this newfound freedom, the Christians of the empire gained new privileges: Clergy were exempt from paying taxes, Christian property that had been confiscated was being returned, and Constantine was commissioning the building of churches in many parts of the empire, especially in Rome and Palestine.

Edict of Milan
A decree signed by emperors Constantine and Licinius in AD 313 proclaiming religious toleration in the Roman Empire, thereby ending the persecution of Christians.

Changes in Worship

It is easy to imagine some of the effects the legalization of Christianity had on the lives of Christians. After centuries of being hunted, punished, and killed for being followers of Christ, of having to gather and worship in secret, they were suddenly able to openly proclaim their faith. Now instead of having to gather in secret for fear of retribution, they could worship publicly. Eucharistic celebrations were no longer small gatherings in private homes. Instead, churches, often modeled after the basilicas—or official buildings of the Roman Empire—were being built and becoming the centers for worship where Christians could gather for liturgical celebrations. ✝

© Gerard Degeorge / The Bridgeman Art Library International

As the ruins of this fourth-century Christian basilica show, basilicas of this period had vaulted aisles on the sides of the main church and an apse, or rounded recess, at one end. Arched windows let in plenty of light.

Worship in East and West

When, in 324, Constantine defeated Licinius, he became the sole emperor, ruling over a now unified empire. He moved the seat of government from Rome to Byzantium, renaming it Constantinople, in what is today Istanbul, Turkey. There were now two major centers of the empire—the East and the West. In each, the Church developed different styles of celebrating the liturgy and the Sacraments, as well as different styles of church architecture.

In the East large worship spaces covered by a large dome, representing the heavens, were common. In the West church buildings were long with a semicircular structure on the end. Despite differences in architectural styles, in both cultures, churches were built to convey God's transcendence, expressed through the grandeur of the buildings.

Worship practices also evolved differently in the East and the West. For example, in the East the Eucharistic liturgy was focused on God's Kingdom at the end of time; in the West Christ's sacrifice was especially emphasized, with the altar a focal point during the liturgy. In churches in the East, a wall separates the altar from the rest of the church. Although in the early history of the Church and today the prayers and rituals that make up the liturgy can differ to reflect the many cultures in which Christians live, the essential elements of the liturgy do not change.

Article 12 The Fathers of the Church

Following Constantine's legalization of Christianity in the Roman Empire, the Church entered a new period in her history known as the Age of the Fathers, so called because of the men whose holiness and intellectual contributions greatly shaped the direction of the Church for the future. Although their contributions differed, with some known for their work on Sacred Scripture, some for clarifying Church doctrine, and others for strengthening the papacy, all share some basic characteristics, including the following: The Fathers of the Church are generally recognized for maintaining theological positions within accepted doctrinal boundaries, and often helped to set those boundaries. Second, they lived holy lives, some to an exceptional degree. Finally, their writings and teachings have been approved by the Church and have helped shape her teaching (adapted from John Vidmar, *The Catholic Church Through the Ages*, pp. 46, 48).

In this article we look at some of the **Fathers of the Church (Church Fathers)** and **Doctors of the Church** who have made the most outstanding contributions.

Saint Athanasius, Bishop of Alexandria (ca. 297–373)

Athanasius is best known for his defense against **Arianism**, a heresy developed by Arius (ca. 250–336), a priest from Alexandria. Arius claimed that Jesus Christ was not fully God and that he was a created being who was greater than humans but subordinate to God. Athanasius instead supported the doctrine of the Council of Nicaea (325), which stated that the Son of God is one in being, or of one substance, with the Father. His writings include *On the Incarnation of the Word* and *The Life of Anthony*, about Saint Anthony of the Desert (see article 15, "Western Monasticism," in section 2).

Saint Basil the Great (ca. 330–379)

Like Athanasius, Basil supported the teachings of the Council of Nicaea and stood in opposition to Arianism. Along with his theological contributions, Basil is also known for his

Fathers of the Church (Church Fathers)
During the early centuries of the Church, those teachers whose writings extended the Tradition of the Apostles and who continue to be important for the Church's teachings.

Doctor of the Church
A title officially bestowed by the Church on those saints who are highly esteemed for their theological writings, as well as their personal holiness.

Arianism
A heresy developed in the late third century that denied Christ's full divinity, stating that Christ was a created being who was superior to human beings but inferior to God.

care for the poor and for his contributions to the development of monasticism in the East.

Saint Gregory of Nazianzus (ca. 329–390)

Gregory of Nazianzus was archbishop of Constantinople. He was a classically trained philosopher and orator, and brought Hellenism, or classical Greek thought, into the early Church. His preaching brought many to the Church. Gregory made an important contribution to the theology of the Trinity, influencing theologians of both the East and the West, in the early Church and today.

Saint Ambrose, Bishop of Milan (ca. 339–397)

As bishop of Milan, Ambrose opposed Arianism and attempts to revive paganism. In addition, he strongly promoted the authority of the Church over the wishes of the emperor. Ambrose read Greek fluently and brought the wisdom of the Greek Fathers into the West. His best known writings include numerous sermons and letters as well as *On the Duties of the Clergy* and *On the Sacraments.* Ambrose is also known for his influence on Saint Augustine, which led to Augustine's conversion.

Live It!

The Spirit of Saint Basil

Under Saint Basil's guidance, Eastern monks and nuns gathered in communities (rather than living separately) to live in harmony. When Basil became bishop of Caesarea, he gave his entire inheritance to support those in need and started a soup kitchen to distribute food during a time of famine.

In the Greek tradition, it is Saint Basil who brings gifts to children on January 1 (Saint Basil's Day in the Eastern Churches), and an extra place at table is set for him. Thus, in Greece, Saint Basil is the original Father Christmas.

How can we live in the spirit of Saint Basil? Here are some ideas:

1. Learn to live with others in harmony, in your family and among your friends.

2. Help your neighbor in times of need.

3. Take special care of those who are weak and vulnerable.

4. Be a gift giver by sharing your time, talent, and treasure with those around you.

Many of the Church Fathers were bishops, who, along with the Pope, are the authoritative teachers in the Church.

Saint Augustine, Bishop of Hippo (354–430)

Of all the early Church Fathers and Doctors of the Church, perhaps the best known is Augustine of Hippo. Although he became one of the most influential thinkers and greatly admired saints in the Church's history, Augustine's early life was far from focused on Christ or his Church. Instead Augustine lived the life of a pleasure seeker, indulging his senses and neglecting his soul. After meeting and learning from Saint Ambrose, Augustine gradually came to realize that all his searching for answers, for pleasure, and for knowledge was a search for God. He was baptized by Ambrose in 387. In 391 he was ordained a priest in Hippo, North Africa. He became that city's bishop a few years later.

After his conversion Augustine dedicated his life fully to God. He wrote prolifically, and his extensive writings have had a profound influence on Christian thought. He clarified the theology of Original Sin and taught about the necessity of divine grace for salvation. His best-known works include *Confessions*, which tells of his conversion and the role of grace in his life, and *City of God*, which tells of the origin and destiny of the City of God (those who are united in love of God) and the City of Man (those who prefer the self to God).

Saint Jerome (ca. 347–420)

Jerome, a monk who lived as a hermit, made a tremendous contribution to the life of the Church through his scholarship, especially his study and translation of the Bible. From 386 on, Jerome lived in a monastery that he founded in Bethlehem. This is where he carried out his work of translating the Bible from its original Hebrew and Greek into Latin, the language of the people of the Western Roman Empire. This work formed the major part of what came to be known as the **Vulgate**, which is still the Church's official translation of the Bible.

Vulgate

The version of the Bible translated from Hebrew and Greek into Latin by Saint Jerome and which became the definitive version and officially promulgated by the Church.

Saint John Chrysostom (ca. 349–407)

John was archbishop of Constantinople. He is known for his desire for reform and his denunciation of abuse of authority, by both ecclesiastical and political leaders, for his austere lifestyle, and for his preaching. His preaching earned him the name *chrysostomos*, meaning "golden mouthed." His sermons are said to have shown an understanding of the lives of ordinary Christians. Orthodox and Eastern Catholic Churches count him—along with Basil the Great and Gregory Nazianzus—among the Three Holy Hierarchs.

Saint Leo the Great (Pope 440–461)

Leo I was Pope in a politically turbulent time, during which he greatly increased the authority of the Church. He stressed that the authority of the Church was given to her by Christ, passed on through Peter to all the Popes, and emphasized that the Pope, and not the emperor, has jurisdiction in ecclesial matters. In his *Tome* he declared Christ's oneness in two natures—human and divine, a teaching accepted and promulgated by the Council of Chalcedon in 451.

Gregory the Great (Pope 590–604)

In the leadership void created by the collapse of the Western Roman Empire, Gregory established papal authority in the temporal realm. He developed a system for providing charitable relief for the poor, oversaw the development of schools for the education of priests, and introduced far-reaching

liturgical reforms that still influence the Church's celebration of the liturgy. Pope Gregory is also remembered for the missions he sponsored to evangelize the Anglos and Saxons, Germanic tribes settled in Great Britain, which brought about the Christianization of those lands. For all these contributions to the Church, and for his writings, which included *Dialogues*, a collection of four books recounting miracles and the lives of the saints, Pope Gregory I is recognized as one of the Church's greatest Popes and is named a Doctor of the Church. ✝

Ecumenical Council

A gathering of the Church's bishops from around the world convened by the Pope or approved by him to address pressing issues in the Church.

¹³ Church Councils and Doctrinal Development

As the Church grew and the followers of Christ spread throughout the Mediterranean world, conflicts over important beliefs became more common and, at times, threatened the unity of the Church and its faithfulness to Christ's teachings. Thus the fourth and fifth centuries became a time for the Church to clarify and define key beliefs—including beliefs about Jesus' divinity and humanity, the Holy Trinity, and the Blessed Virgin Mary, especially her real and perpetual virginity.

Emperor Constantine was so committed to the teachings handed down from the Apostles that he ordered that all books written by Arius should be burned.

© Gianni Dagli Orti / The Art Archive at Art Resource, NY

The Council of Nicaea (AD 325)

In 325 Emperor Constantine convened the Council of Nicaea, the Church's first **Ecumenical Council**, in response to Arianism, which denied Jesus' full divinity. One critical implication of this false teaching was that if Jesus is not fully divine, then he is not God and thus cannot redeem us, because only God has the power to redeem. Arius could not be persuaded of the error of his teaching, and the heresy spread.

consubstantial
Having the same nature or essence.

Theotokos
A Greek title for Mary meaning "God bearer."

Logos
A Greek word meaning "Word." *Logos* is a title of Jesus Christ found in the Gospel of John that illuminates the relationship between the three Divine Persons of the Holy Trinity. (See John 1:1,14.)

The Council of Nicaea brought together approximately three hundred bishops who denounced Arius's teaching and set to work on a creed that would spell out key Church doctrine, including on who Jesus is. The creed they developed, which was further developed and then promulgated at the Council of Constantinople, and is now commonly known as the Nicene Creed, professed Jesus' divinity with these words: "the Only Begotten Son of God. . . . Light from Light, true God from true God, begotten, not made, **consubstantial** with the Father" (*Roman Missal*). We pray these words when we recite the Nicene Creed at Mass today.

The Council of Constantinople (AD 381)

The Council of Nicaea did not bring an end to the Arian heresy. Arius and his supporters continued to teach Arianism. Saint Athanasius of Alexandria (ca. 297–373) and Saint Ambrose of Milan (ca. 339–397), whom we read about in article 12, "The Fathers of the Church," were instrumental in defending the Church against Arius's teachings. In 381 the Council of Constantinople was convened, and here the teachings of the Council of Nicaea were confirmed and Jesus' full divinity was affirmed.

The Council of Constantinople also addressed another controversy. Because the Council of Nicaea had not clarified the divinity of the Holy Spirit, the Third Divine Person of the Trinity, this became a source of conflict within the Church. Much like the followers of Arius denied the divinity of Christ, another sect, called the Macedonians, denied that the Holy Spirit had a divine nature. This group taught that while the Father and the Son were divine, the Holy Spirit was a creation of the Son and a servant of the Father and the Son. The Council of Constantinople firmly taught the divinity of the Holy Spirit.

The Councils of Ephesus (431) and Chalcedon (451)

Nestorius, the patriarch of Constantinople (428–431), gave rise to a Christological heresy known as Nestorianism when he rejected the widely used title *Theotokos* ("God-bearer" or "Mother of God") for the Virgin Mary. He held that Mary gave birth to the human Jesus, not the divine *Logos*, who had existed for all time. Nestorius's position was faulted for splitting Jesus into two distinct persons, one human and one divine. Nestorius and his teachings were eventually condemned as heretical at the Council of Ephesus in 431 and at the Council of Chalcedon in 451. The Council of Ephesus decreed that Mary is *Theotokos* because her Son, Jesus, is both God and man. The Council of Chalcedon, convened by Pope Leo I (Leo the Great), also developed the theology of the **hypostatic union** of the inseparable human and divine natures in the one Divine Person of Jesus Christ. Some Eastern churches began separating over doctrinal disputes arising out of the Councils of Ephesus and Chalcedon.

hypostatic union
The union of Jesus Christ's divine and human natures in one Divine Person.

The Council of Chalcedon and East–West Relations

In addition to these doctrinal disputes, another decision of the Council of Chalcedon would have far-reaching effects on the relations between the Churches in the East and West. The bishops at the Council declared that the Bishop of Rome was preeminent in authority, and that the patriarch (bishop) of Constantinople was second in authority. Formerly, the bishops of Antioch (in Syria) and Alexandria (in Egypt) were considered the two highest authorities after the Bishop of Rome, the Pope.

Pope Leo objected to elevating Constantinople in authority, because this would mean that the Eastern emperor could interfere more in religious matters. This change in custom would lead to six centuries of disputes between Christians in the West, led by the Pope, and Christians in the East, led by the patriarch of Constantinople. Eventually there

Catholic Wisdom

Saint Ephrem and the Blessed Virgin Mary

Saint Ephrem (c. 306–373), a Father of the Church, spurned the teachings of those who rejected the doctrine of the hypostatic union. He affirmed the unity of the human and divine natures of Christ, writing this: "He was one in divinity and humanity without distinction. Believe that our humanity was spiritual in him who clothed himself with a body, and that he is not two but one, from the Father and from Mary. He who divides him in two will not enjoy Eden with him."

The Development of the Eastern Patriarchates

In the Old Testament, a patriarch is the father or head of a clan or tribe. Old Testament patriarchs include Abraham, Isaac, Jacob, and Jacob's twelve sons. In the Church the word *patriarch* refers to the Pope and some bishops.

The early Church identified three patriarchs: The Bishop of Rome, the bishop of Alexandria, and the bishop of Antioch. The Patriarch of Rome governed the whole Church in the West; the patriarch of Alexandria governed the area of Egypt and Palestine; and the patriarch of Antioch governed Syria, Asia Minor, Greece, and the remainder of the Church in the East. In 325 the Council of Nicaea recognized these three patriarchates as having a supreme place in the Church's hierarchy.

At the Council of Constantinople (381), the bishop of Constantinople was added as a patriarch. Then, because of the increasing importance of the

Holy Land—in part because of the rise in pilgrimages to its holy sites—and its bishop, the Council of Chalcedon (451) formed the patriarchate of Jerusalem, assigning to it Palestine and parts of the Antioch patriarchate.

By the sixth century, these five had been established as the only patriarchates in the Church. Today there are six patriarchs in the Eastern Catholic Churches. Each is the head of those who belong to his rite. These patriarchs are all under the authority of the Pope.

would be a complete break between the Churches of the East and West. We will learn more about this break, or schism, in article 19, "The Eastern Schism" in section 2.

An Ongoing Work

Throughout history the Church has responded to the needs of the times by expressing articles of faith in creeds and professions of faith. The Nicene Creed, a product of two Ecumenical Councils, is one example. In the early centuries especially, the Church clarified her Trinitarian faith, defending against errors that were distorting it. This clarification was the work of the early Church Fathers, under the guidance of the Holy Spirit. It was sustained by the faith of the people. There have been twenty-one Ecumenical Councils. The most recent, Vatican Council II, was held from 1962 to 1965 and, among other issues, addressed the Church's relationship to the modern world. The Eastern Orthodox, now separated from the Catholic Church, accept the authority of the first seven Ecumenical Councils: Nicaea I (325) to Nicaea II (781). ✝

Article 14 The Collapse of the Roman Empire of the West

For centuries following 27 BC—a date commonly identified as the start of the Roman Empire—the empire thrived and was a center for learning, culture, material comforts and, often, excesses. Citizens of the empire felt secure with the

© Charles Plante Fine Arts / The Bridgeman Art Library International

Invasions by Visigoths left the city of Rome in ruins. The Church was able to meet many needs that arose as an entire civilization crumbled.

empire's military supremacy and believed in their superiority. They saw their empire, as the name Mediterranean indicates, as the "center of the earth." In the fourth century, however, all this began to change.

The Shifting Tide

Ever since Constantine had moved his capital to Constantinople, formerly Byzantium, the Eastern Roman Empire continued to grow in power and influence. During the same period, the Western Empire faced continuing decline, often under the leadership of ineffective or corrupt emperors. Waves of barbarian invasions put great economic, social, and political pressures on the empire. The Roman emperors were unable to thwart the invasions.

In 395 Emperor Theodosius died, and the leaders that followed were generally figureheads, and often military strongmen. The future of the Western Empire became bleaker than ever. Growing social and moral decay, a weakened military, an ever-expanding empire that was harder to govern and protect, and growing economic hardships left the empire vulnerable to attack. In 410 Rome was sacked by the Visigoths, a tribe of Germanic people who had lived to the north for several centuries. (It was in response to this event that Saint Augustine wrote *City of God*, to help Christians see that they were building something good even in the midst of a crumbling earthly empire.) The city fell in 455, and in 476, a barbarian chieftain, Odaecer, deposed Romulus Augustus, the last emperor of the Western Empire. This is the date traditionally associated with the collapse of the Roman Empire in the West.

The Empire in the East

After the fall of Rome, the Eastern Empire continued to exist and thrive as the Byzantine Empire. Under Emperor Justinian (527–565), barbarian tribes in North Africa, Italy, and Spain were defeated. This brought about a partial restoration of the Western Empire. Justinian's reign marked a blossoming of Byzantine culture, with the commissioning of the building of churches, including the magnificent *Hagia Sophia* (Holy Wisdom). Emperor Justinian's reign also brought the lasting legacy of the systematic reform and codification of Roman law, which provided the basis of European civil law.

Justinian's reign was followed by a succession of weak leaders. They frequently provoked disputes between the patriarch of Constantinople and the Pope. Under these emperors, the tension between the papacy and the patriarch of the Eastern Empire grew, contributing to the East–West Schism of 1054.

Though it was becoming increasingly weakened, the Eastern Empire survived until 1453, when Constantinople was captured by the Ottoman Turks.

Leo the Great

Pope Leo I (440–461), or Leo the Great, as he became known, stands out for shaping the role of the papacy into a force for leadership in the Western world. Leo was intelligent, tough, and courageous—qualities that would serve him well in facing the challenges of his time, with the Roman Empire under constant attack and the Church facing challenges to her beliefs.

Before becoming Pope, Leo had already gained experience as a mediator and leader by settling a dispute between a Roman general and the Roman governor of Gaul. The beleaguered Western emperor, Valentinian III, asked Leo, after he had become Pope, to intervene and make peace with Attila the Hun, the fierce leader of a barbarian tribe who was threatening Italy. Leo traveled two hundred miles to meet Attila face-to-face. No record exists of what Leo and Attila said to each other. What is known, however, is that the Huns turned back, and Rome was saved.

Leo's contributions to strengthening the Church earned him the designation of Doctor of the Church. He stressed that the authority of the Church was given to her by Christ, passed on through Peter to all the popes. Leo is also credited with contributing to the affirmation by the Council of Chalcedon in 451 that Jesus Christ is one Person with two natures, human and divine.

The Contributions of the Papacy and the Church

With the sack of Rome in 410 and the progressive decline of the Western Empire, a leadership vacuum was created and the needs of the citizens were often either neglected or simply impossible to meet. Gradually the Church would begin to fill the leadership void because it was the one stable and generally respected institution that could provide governance and protection for civilians. The Church also became a provider of the basic needs of citizens. Having, from her earliest days, provided for the needs of the poor, the Church now developed an organized system of charitable relief for the poor in Rome. Much of this charitable work was supported by donations from noble families and profits and food from Church-owned farms. The Church also began to establish schools for the clergy that also provided instruction to the laity. Often these church schools were the only sources of education for the laity. ✝

Part Review

1. What changes did the *Edict of Milan* bring into the lives of Christians in the Roman Empire?

2. Describe some common contributions and characteristics of the Church Fathers.

3. Name two Fathers of the Church and describe the contributions of each.

4. In what ways did the Church fill the leadership void created by the fall of the Western Empire?

5. What were some of Pope Leo the Great's specific contributions to building up the Church?

6. Explain one important teaching of the Council of Ephesus and one of the Council of Chalcedon.

7. The Council of Nicaea was the Church's first Ecumenical Council. What important doctrines did it define or clarify?

The Church in the Middle Ages

Part 1

The Early Medieval Period

Following the fall of the Roman Empire in the West in 476, Europe was plunged into a period of social change and, at times, chaos. With the power vacuum created by the absence of Roman rule, barbaric tribes accelerated their invasions into lands formerly controlled by Rome. It is in this landscape of repeated invasions by Germanic and Scandinavian peoples, tribal rule, and social instability that lasting changes developed in Europe, many with an impact that endures to this day. In this part we will look at some of these developments. The earliest among them is the birth of monasticism in the West, led by the vision of Saint Benedict of Nursia, "the father of Western monasticism." Even as monasticism spread and contributed to the expansion and stability of Christianity and the Church, competing ideologies and interests posed challenges to this stability. In Arabia a nascent religion called Islam was taking root and expanding east, west, and north, eventually claiming Christian lands and peoples throughout these regions. Even within the Christian world, conflicting secular and ecclesial interests threatened the Pope's position as spiritual authority and the leader of the People of God.

The articles in this part address the following topics:

Article 15 Western Monasticism

The founding of Christian monasticism is traditionally attributed to Saint Anthony of Egypt (251–356). Around age twenty, Anthony withdrew from society to live as a **hermit**, practicing a life of prayer, meditation, and penance in a desert cave in Egypt. As Anthony's reputation spread, other men sought him out and took up their own lives of solitary prayer and penance in nearby huts and caves. Eventually such groupings of monks centered around a spiritual leader like Anthony spread throughout the deserts of Egypt and Asia Minor. Although all these monks shared a common goal of growing in holiness and giving up worldly comforts for Christ, they did not have a formal structure or organizing principle.

As the number of monks grew and the movement spread, one of Anthony's contemporaries, a man named Pachomius (292–346), recognized the need for some sort of order and uniformity within the movement. Pachomius organized the first monasteries in 320. In these monastic communities, a group of men or women would follow a common rule stressing prayer, celibacy, poverty, and obedience to a superior, called an **abbot** or **abbess**. Unlike the earlier monasteries, Pachomius's were organized into walled communities, where the monks typically lived in communal houses.

hermit
A person who lives a solitary life in order to commit himself or herself more fully to prayer and in some cases to be completely free for service to others.

abbot, abbess
The superior and spiritual leader of a monastery (masculine: abbot; feminine: abbess).

Pray It!

Monastic Prayer

The heart of monastic life is liturgical prayer. This public prayer of the Church includes the Mass and the Liturgy of the Hours.

In addition to this public prayer, monks and nuns pray privately, even while they are working. Thus their entire lives become a prayer. Arrow prayers—short, to-the-point prayers—that "pierce the heavens" like an arrow are often used: "Lord, have mercy"; "Jesus"; "Peace." Another prayer, from the Eastern tradition, is "The Jesus Prayer": "Lord Jesus Christ, son of the living God, have mercy on me, a sinner." These short prayers focus the mind and heart.

Try praying some parts of the Liturgy of the Hours. Books are available. Try using a word or phrase as an arrow prayer when you have a few moments of free time.

illuminated manuscript

A manuscript in which the text is supplemented with artwork such as decorated initials, borders, and illustrations, often using gold and silver. During the Middle Ages, manuscripts were copied and illuminated by hand, work often done by monks.

The Development of Western Monasticism

The ideals of Eastern monasticism soon spread to the West, promoted in large part by *The Life of Anthony,* written by Saint Athanasius (ca. 297–373) while he was exiled in Germany during the Arian controversies. This work quickly drew a large following and attracted westerners to the monastic life.

In France, Saint Martin of Tours (316–397) established monasteries with a particular mission to evangelize barbarians. Saint Patrick (ca. 389–461), as bishop, established monasteries all over Ireland. Similarly, Saint Brigid (ca. 453–525) established several convents, or monasteries for women, in Ireland. Most remarkably, Brigid founded Kildare, a double monastery—one for men and one for women—and a center for learning and evangelization.

During the sixth and seven centuries, when barbarian invasions in Europe were threatening the survival of early Church writings, monks in Ireland devoted their lives to preserving Western learning by hand copying and illustrating manuscripts. Many of these texts, called **illuminated manuscripts**, remain to this day treasures of the Church.

From Ireland, monasticism and Christianity spread to Scotland through the work of Saint Columba (ca. 521–597), an Irish missionary monk, who established a monastery on the Scottish island of Iona in 563. From here monasticism spread further still, eventually reaching back to the European continent.

Saint Benedict of Nursia

Although many holy people made important contributions to the growth of Christian monasticism, Saint Benedict of Nursia (ca. 480–550) in particular is recognized for the growth of the monastic movement and for establishing it as an enduring force in the Church. Like Anthony and others who had gone to the desert two centuries before, Benedict wanted to seek God in the solitude and silence of the countryside. After some time living as a hermit in a cave, Benedict began to attract followers who also wanted to live a life dedicated to God. A group of these men formed the community that would be Benedict's famous monastery at Monte Cassino.

In 529 Benedict and his monks built their monastery on the top of a mountain halfway between Rome and Naples. The community within the monastery was nearly a complete economic unit, supplying itself with food, clothing, and shelter. Eventually a group of women seeking the monastic life formed a community not far from Monte Cassino, led by Saint Scholastica, Benedict's twin sister. Benedict and Scholastica taught the monks and nuns to read so that they could read and understand Scripture and their daily prayers. Life for the monks was simple and well ordered, balanced between prayer and work (*ora et labora*).

© Abbey of Monte Cassino, Cassino, Italy / Alinari / The Bridgeman Art Library International

Saint Benedict originated his Rule here at Monte Cassino. The simple life of work and prayer, which the Rule embodies, reflects the teaching of the Gospel.

At Monte Cassino, Benedict developed a rule for his monks (the Rule of Saint Benedict). The Rule was based on moderation in all things. For example, rather than extreme fasting, a monk was expected to eat two meals a day; rather than giving up wine altogether, a monk was to drink just a small amount. Benedict also called on his monks to take vows of chastity, poverty, and obedience. Benedict's guidelines for monastic life eventually became the standard for Western monasticism and provided the model for religious life in the Church.

Monastic Contributions to the Church and Society

The monasteries established throughout Europe in the Early Medieval Period influenced the Church and society for centuries to come. Their contributions included the following:

- The monasteries Christianized Europe, bringing Christ to countless people.
- They preserved Western knowledge and learning by promoting learning for the monks and by copying the great secular and religious writings of earlier centuries.
- The monks developed great art, architecture, and music that endure to this day.

- Monastic communities developed new and effective agricultural, wool production, and vine-growing techniques.
- When a formal system for education collapsed with the fall of the Western Empire, monasteries became local centers for learning and provided education through the establishment of monastery schools. ✝

Medieval Manuscripts

During the Middle Ages, important texts were preserved through hand copying. Monastic scribes—or medieval monks dedicated to the work of hand copying texts—working in the scriptorium of a medieval monastery would spend many hours a day painstakingly copying the Bible, the writings of the Church Fathers, and other important works. Often the manuscripts they produced were illuminated, or decorated with ornate lettering, borders, and miniature illustrations, frequently using gold and silver.

© Pabkov/Shutterstock.com

Article 16 The Development of Islam

In the seventh century, while Christianity continued to spread throughout Western Europe, polytheism was still the common religious norm in many parts of the world. This was true of the Arabian Peninsula, a vast desert to the south of Palestine, and home to a nomadic and tribal people. It was in this culture that Islam developed, founded by Mohammed.

Mohammed was born in Mecca, on the Arabian Peninsula, in AD 570. In the year 610, Mohammed had a prophetic call. Islamic tradition holds that the angel Gabriel visited Mohammed and brought him revelations from God,

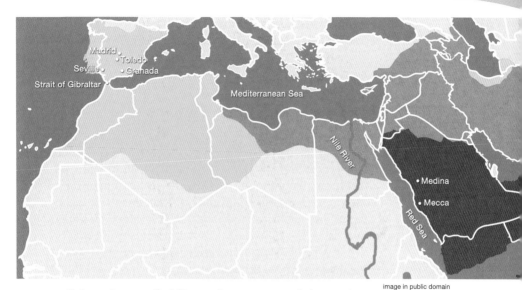

image in public domain

or Allah. Mohammed's followers began to record the revelations, and these recordings formed what became known as the Koran. These teachings became the basis for Islam.

A key tenet of Islam, and one that separated it from the culture in which it originated, is monotheism—that is, the belief that there is only one God. Yet although Islam borrowed some ideas from Christianity and espoused a belief in one God just as Christianity did, Islamic theology differed

Islam spread throughout the Mediterranean region, covering the same area where Christianity had its origins.

Live It!

Islam and You

In a visit to the country of Jordan, Pope Benedict XVI met with both Christian and Muslim leaders. He said:

> Muslims and Christians, precisely because of the burden of our common history so often marked by misunderstanding, must today strive to be known and recognized as worshippers of God faithful to prayer, eager to uphold and live by the Almighty's decrees, merciful and compassionate, consistent in bearing witness to all that is true and good, and ever mindful of the common origin and dignity of all human persons. ("Meeting with Muslim Religious Leaders," May 9, 2009)

How can you meet this challenge? Begin by educating yourself about Islam and other religions. Take time to get to know neighbors or classmates who may seem "foreign" to you because of their religion. And always be prayerful, merciful, compassionate, and respect the human dignity of all.

from Christianity in one important way: Islam accepted Jesus as a prophet sent by God, but contended that Christ was not divine and that his humanity and divinity could not be a reconcilable truth.

The Rise and Spread of Islam

Following his religious experience, Mohammed remained in Mecca, where he preached and brought a growing number of followers to his faith, called Islam, which is an Arabic word that means "submission." But growing persecution by the Meccan authorities led him and his followers to take flight. In 622 they left Mecca and emigrated to Medina. This migration, called the *hijra*, marks year one of the Muslim era.

In Medina, Mohammed established his religious and political authority. He raised an army, which engaged in raids on Meccan caravans. Eventually, Mohammed was allowed back to Mecca and the inhabitants converted to Islam. By the time of his death in 632, Mohammed had succeeded in unifying all of the Arabian Peninsula both religiously and militarily.

Following Mohammed's death, his successors took up the cause of spreading the faith and Islam expanded rapidly. The army grew and marched onward in battle, spreading the Islamic faith eastward and westward. Previously Christian areas were overcome, and many fell to Muslim control. The first major Christian cities to fall were Damascus and Antioch in Syria, in 636 and 637, followed by Jerusalem in 638 and Alexandria in 642. Iraq and Persia also fell under Muslim control in 642. Throughout the seventh century, Muslim armies continued their march west through North Africa and east toward Byzantium. In 711 Muslim armies crossed the Strait of Gibraltar and invaded the Iberian Peninsula, beginning a northward campaign that resulted in the collapse of the Visigothic Kingdom in Spain. Over the following decade, nearly all of the Iberian Peninsula was brought under Muslim control.

The march continued northward and eastward. In 717 Byzantine Emperor Leo Isaurian halted Eastern expansion by defeating the Muslims at the gates to Constantinople. In 732 in a key battle now known to us as the Battle of Tours, Charles Martel, the king of the Franks, turned back Muslim invaders and halted Muslim expansion in Europe. Thus, although most of Iberia had fallen into Muslim hands, the Christian identity of the lands north of the Pyrenees Mountains was preserved.

What Accounts for Islam's Success?

The reasons for the successful spread of Islam are numerous and complex. Islam did not force conquered civilizations to convert and even gave Christians and Jews special protection as "people of the book"—that is, as adherents of the Old Testament. Heavy taxation on non-Muslims as well as exclusion from government jobs and other privileges, however, were often compelling incentives to convert. Furthermore, in non-Christian regions, where tribal divisions and warfare were often the norm, Islam offered order and stability. Turning the tide once Islam took hold proved to be a challenge for the Church. Unlike barbarian cultures that had been converted, Islam offered its adherents a cohesive cultural, political, and theological system that did not leave a void for the Church to fill.

© Guenter Rossenbach/Corbis

Consequences for Christendom

Less than a century after the founding of Islam, Islamic conquests had altered the political and religious composition of all of Arabia and North Africa, of the Iberian Peninsula to

feudalism
A system that evolved in Western Europe in the eighth and ninth centuries in which society was ordered around relationships derived from the holding of land in exchange for service and protection.

Franks
A Germanic tribe that inhabited the Roman provinces of Gaul (roughly coinciding with modern-day France) starting in the sixth century.

Papal States
An independent country ruled by the Pope until 1870, covering a wide strip of land in the middle of the Italian Peninsula. The Papal States were awarded to the papacy in 756 in a formal deed called the Donation of Pepin.

the north, and of parts of Asia to the east. The consequences for the Church were catastrophic. The Mediterranean region, where Christianity had firmly taken root, was now under Muslim control. Jerusalem, Antioch, and Alexandria, the three ancient patriarchates, had fallen, and had thus lost their influence. In the West the center of secular power shifted from Rome in the south to the Frankish kings in the north, where **feudalism** developed. The Church, which had been able to thrive in the Mediterranean, now lived with the constant threat of a new and capable enemy. In the Eastern Empire, although Muslim invaders had been successfully turned away, Constantinople never recovered from the damage that had been done. Though it survived for another seven hundred years, Constantinople never regained its former glory. ✝

Article 17 Charlemagne: Holy Roman Emperor

As Islam continued to pose a threat to the Church, the Lombards, a Germanic tribe, pursued expansion into northern Italy. The Byzantine emperor, who ruled both the Eastern and Western Empires from Constantinople, was growing less and less effective in protecting Rome. Thus the Church sought the help of the **Franks**. At first the Pope turned to Charles Martel, but Martel saw no advantage in an alliance with the Pope. However, his successor, Pepin, saw things differently and was eager to ally himself with the papacy.

Pepin had seized control of the throne from the descendants of another Frankish king, Clovis, and declared himself the King of the Franks. He believed that an alliance with the Pope would legitimize his rule. He petitioned Pope Zachary (741–752) to declare him the legitimate ruler, and the Pope consented. In 751, at the Pope's direction, Boniface (675–754), a Benedictine monk and bishop, crowned Pepin. This act signaled a growing relationship between the Church and secular rulers.

In subsequent years, Pepin's forces defeated the Lombards and returned to the Pope territories that the Lombards had captured. In 756 the Pope was granted his own territory. This formal deed, known as the Donation of Pepin, granted the Pope a wide strip of land in the middle of the Italian Peninsula. The territory became known as the **Papal States**, with

the Pope as its ruler. The Papal States remained an independent country under the rule of the papacy until 1870.

Charlemagne and the Roman Empire

After Pepin's death in 768, his son Charlemagne (French
for "Charles the Great") emerged as a powerful king, rising
to the position in 771, following his brother's brief rule.
Charlemagne was a devout Christian but also an ambitious
ruler and a strong military leader. In 774 Charlemagne
defeated the Lombards. For
this the Pope gave him the
title Protector of the Papacy.
The Pope was growing more
indebted to, and dependent on,
Charlemagne and increasingly
compliant in responding to his
instructions on how to rule the
Papal States.

Christendom
The Church's sphere
of power and authority,
both politically and
spiritually, during the
Middle Ages.

© Bibliotheque Municipale, Castres, France / Giraudon / The Bridgeman Art Library

    Charlemagne carried out
military campaigns throughout Western Europe and
often forced the conversion
of conquered peoples. By the
year 800, Charlemagne had
created a vast empire in the
West—and the most power-
ful since the Roman Empire.
Pope Leo III recognized Charlemagne's importance to
Christendom. At Christmas Mass in Rome in 800, the Pope
crowned him Holy Roman Emperor. The appointment of a
Roman emperor in the West created tension between Rome
and Byzantium in that it signaled a break between Rome and
the Eastern Empire.

    For the next four hundred years, the Pope would crown
the Holy Roman Emperor, an act signaling the unity of
Christianity and politics, the oneness of Church and society
in Christendom.

    Under Charlemagne, what became known as the
Carolingian Renaissance brought enlightenment to the
West. Charlemagne placed a high emphasis on learning and
appointed educated men—mostly priests, monks, and bishops—to government positions. At his palace in Aachen, in

At the time of
Charlemagne's
coronation as Holy
Roman Emperor, his
lands included all of
modern-day France,
Switzerland, Belgium,
and The Netherlands,
most of Germany,
northern Italy, west-
ern Austria, and part
of Spain.

Germany, he started a school that attracted the best teachers from his empire.

Despite Charlemagne's political and military achievements, his empire did not endure. Following his death in 814, the empire was split up by his sons and suffered from renewed **Viking** invasions and ineffective leadership. The empire officially ended with the death of Charlemagne's grandson Charles the Fat in 888. ✝

Christianizing the Vikings and the Slavs

In the 800s Viking invasions spread throughout Europe. The Vikings traveled along seacoasts and rivers from Norway and Denmark into the British Isles, attacking and destroying monasteries and their libraries. Soon the Norsemen, or "men from the north," controlled England, Ireland, and Scotland. The Norseman also took control of a region of France that became known as Normandy.

Gradually, however, the Vikings were converted to Christianity, in part through intermarriage and treaties and in part because of the work of Christian missionaries who traveled north to the Vikings' homelands.

In Eastern Europe the Slavs—ancestors of peoples we know today as Russian, Polish, Czech, and other Eastern Europeans—were also converting to Christianity, thanks in large part to the work of two Byzantine Greek missionaries, brothers Cyril and Methodius. The brothers developed a Slavic alphabet (call Cyrillic) and translated the Gospels into the newly devised language. Now the Slavs could hear and read the Good News in their own language, and many conversions followed.

18 Gregorian Reform

Article

In the period following Charlemagne's rule, feudalism grew as a way to provide political and economic order in a weak empire. However, feudalism also promoted chaos, because every estate was, in a sense, a kingdom. During the feudal period, secular control of Church offices had become commonplace. Civil rulers at various levels often had the final word on the appointment of bishops, and bishops and abbots often served as government officials because they were educated and had charge of Church lands. Worse, a rich man could buy himself the office of bishop, even though the Church condemned this as a sin of **simony**. Some bishops passed their religious offices to relatives, based on nepotism, rather than on fitness for the office.

Also during this time, as you may recall from article 17, "Charlemagne: The Holy Roman Emperor," the Church had acquired the Papal States. Although this appeared to be a great step forward for the Church, control of the Papal States also meant dependence on kings and emperors and an understanding of the Pope as a ruler of land as well as a spiritual leader.

The Lay Investiture Crisis

When Gregory VII (1073–1085), also called Hildebrand, became Pope, he campaigned against simony, clerical marriage, and lay investiture. The latter is the practice by which a high ranking person, such as an emperor, king, count, or lord could appoint bishops or abbots, "investing" them with power and requiring their loyalty. As a monk of the Cluny

Vikings
The Scandinavian explorers, merchants, and warriors who invaded and settled in Europe from the late eighth to the eleventh centuries.

simony
Buying or selling something spiritual, such as a grace, a Sacrament, or a relic.

papal bull
An official letter or charter issued by the Pope, named for the *bulla*, or wax seal, that was used to authenticate it.

antipope
A person claiming to be Pope in opposition to the Pope chosen in accordance with Church law.

Catholic Wisdom

In Nomine Domini

In Nomine Domini is the name of a **papal bull** (an official document sealed with a red wax seal known as a *bulla*) of Pope Nicholas II (1058–1061) promulgated in 1059, establishing the cardinal-bishops as the sole electors of the Pope. The bull replaced the right of nomination of the Holy Roman Emperor. The bull further stated that any **antipope** should be treated as an invader and a destroyer of all Christianity, and subjected to a perpetual anathema.

Cluniac Reforms

With abbots and bishops answering to local secular powers, maintaining a commitment to the Gospel and the Church's mission grew increasingly difficult. However, in the 900s a breakthrough in the organization of monasteries led the way for reform. A duke began a Benedictine monastery in Cluny, France. The monastery's charter was unusual for the time in that it specified that the monastery be independent of any secular ruler.

A succession of wise and holy abbots at Cluny brought about a renewal of the original Benedictine spirit. The monks at Cluny lived simply, prayed long and devoutly, performed charitable works for the poor, and inspired others to take the Gospel message seriously. Soon hundreds of monasteries across Europe adopted the Cluniac Reforms. This spiritual renewal was possible because Cluny was governed not by a secular ruler but by a monk committed to the ideals of monasticism.

movement, Gregory saw the clergy's independence from civil powers as crucial to any reform in the Church.

The German emperor Henry IV objected to the Pope's ruling. The struggle between the two worsened. In 1076 the emperor convoked a synod in which Gregory was deposed. Gregory in turn deposed and excommunicated Henry and declared that Henry's subjects did not need to obey him any longer. Fearing that the German nobles would exploit the situation, Henry asked Pope Gregory for forgiveness. The two were reconciled after Henry performed public penance in 1077. However, Henry's repentance was short lived, and he failed to carry out promises he made to the Pope. Gregory again excommunicated and deposed Henry in 1080. In response, Henry set siege to Rome and deposed Gregory and appointed a pope of his own choosing. Though Gregory was rescued from the attack, he died in exile a short while later.

In 1122 the controversy over lay investiture was resolved with the Concordat at Worms (in Worms, Germany), whereby the emperor agreed that rulers would no longer have the right to appoint bishops. All bishops would be elected and consecrated by Church authority. ✝

Emperor Henry IV and Pope Gregory VII engaged in a conflict whose dramatic episodes included efforts to oust each other, public penance, excommunication, and even the appointment of a new Pope by a secular authority.

Part Review

1. Describe the origins of monasticism, making sure to identify the key "fathers" of monasticism.

2. Describe at least three ways Western monasticism influenced the Church and society in medieval Europe.

3. What was the area of expansion for Islam in the seventh and eighth centuries, and what were the means?

4. What were the consequences of the rise of Islam for the Church?

5. What were some of the effects of the Pope's appointment of Charlemagne as Holy Roman Emperor?

6. Briefly describe the Cluniac Reforms and their effect on monasticism.

7. What was the investiture crisis? What were some of the negative consequences of lay investiture for the medieval Church?

Part 2

Threats from Within and Without

Every period in the Church's history can be identified by some key events and changes that give the period its overall identity. For example, the early centuries of the Church have been labeled the age of persecution, and the period following the fall of Rome, when monasteries were established throughout Europe, is often called the monastic period. In a similar way, the period in the Church's history that follows the start of the second millennium can be identified by the conflicts that shaped it. Following the year 1000, the start of the period called the High Middle Ages, the Church became caught up in a series of disputes and conflicts that tested her resolve and resilience. The first of these was the break with the Church of Constantinople. After centuries of tension between East and West—including the separation of some Eastern Churches in 431 and 451—a lasting break between the two Churches took place in 1054, the effects of which last to this day. Then, in the late eleventh century, the call for the First Crusade ushered in two centuries of recurring battles between Christendom and Islam for control of the Holy Land and other Christian territories. Finally, in the thirteenth century, a struggle provoked by those entrusted with the leadership and care of the Church led to division within the Church and threatened her stability and brought into question her authority to guide the faithful.

The articles in this part address the following topics:

83

Article 19 The Eastern Schism

As we have seen throughout this course, for many centuries, as far back as the Councils of Ephesus (431) and Chalcedon (451), tension had been building between the Eastern, or Greek-speaking, Church and the Western, or Latin-speaking, Church. In 1054 these tensions reached a breaking point, in an event that is today called the Eastern Schism. Before we get to that decisive event, however, let's take a look at the growing differences and tensions that led to this break between the Byzantine and Latin Churches.

Tensions and Disagreements

Theological differences had plagued the Eastern and Western Churches since the Arian heresy (see article 12, "The Fathers of the Church," and article 13, "Church Councils and Doctrinal Development," in section 1). When the Councils of Ephesus and Chalcedon condemned the Nestorian heresy, which denied Mary's role as the Mother of God, some East-

Pray It!

For the Unity of Christians

As we will learn when we study the Church in the modern era, our modern popes, including Pope Francis, have worked and prayed for the unity of all Christians. In this they unite with the prayer of Jesus, who, after the Last Supper, prayed not only for his disciples but for all of his followers through the ages: "So that they may all be one, as you, Father, are in me and I in you, that they also may be in us" (John 17:21).

Prayer for Christian unity is the responsibility of all Christians. You might like to pray for unity, using the Opening Prayer (or Collect) of the Mass for the Unity of Christians:

> Attend with favor to the prayers of your people,
> we ask, O Lord,
> and grant that the hearts of believers
> may be united in your praise and in repentance together,
> so that, with division among Christians overcome,
> we may hasten with joy to your eternal Kingdom
> in the perfect communion of the Church.
>
> *(Roman Missal)*

ern Churches who followed the teaching of Nestorius began to separate from the Western Church.

The Council of Chalcedon also judged that the See of Constantinople should be ranked after Rome, because the bishops viewed Constantinople as "the New Rome." Accordingly, in canon 28 the Council elevated the See of Constantinople to a position second only to Rome in eminence and power, ahead of the Sees of Alexandria and Antioch, which had been historically considered the highest authorities after Rome. Pope Leo rejected this decision. However, fearing that withholding approval for canon 28 might be interpreted as rejecting the entire Council, in 453 he confirmed the Council's canons with a protest against canon 28. This decision by the Council led to centuries of disputes between Christian communities loyal to the Pope and those loyal to the patriarch of Constantinople.

The two Churches also differed in their views of the relationship between the Church and the state. The Eastern Church accepted the emperor's dominance over it. In fact, in the East, the emperor was seen as the Vicar of Christ (a title that in the Roman Church is reserved for the Pope). As such, it was his responsibility to call Church Councils and assist them in settling doctrinal disputes and to name the **patriarch** of Constantinople. In the West, however, the relationship between the Church and emperors was just the opposite: the Pope had primacy over the Church and was the only one who could call a Council. And he asserted authority over government and society.

During the 700s a controversy raged in the Eastern Church over the use of icons in liturgy. This was known as the Iconoclast Controversy. In 726 the Byzantine emperor Leo III condemned the veneration of sacred images, believing this was a form of idolatry. He ordered the destruction of all icons, an act known as **iconoclasm**, and attempted to impose a policy against the use of icons and sacred images on the worldwide Church. The Pope stood in opposition to the emperor

patriarch (Eastern)
In the Old Testament, a patriarch is the father of a group or tribe. In the Eastern (or Greek) Church, a patriarch is a spiritual father. The title is given to the highest ranking bishops in the Church.

iconoclasm
The deliberate destruction of religious icons and symbols.

Church architecture in the Eastern Church typically features a central dome surrounded by a cross-shaped building lining up with the points of the compass, sometimes topped with smaller domes.

© Nikolay Mikhalchenko/Shutterstock.com

filioque

Latin for "and from the Son," this phrase was added to the Nicene Creed in the Roman Church to express that the Holy Spirit descended from the Father and the Son, rather than *from* the Father and *through* the Son, as the Byzantine Church expressed.

and defended the veneration of icons as an important part of Christian piety. In 787 the Second Council of Nicaea supported the Pope's position, an outcome that further fueled tensions between the East and the West.

Another dispute between the two Churches arose in the ninth century when Emperor Photius condemned the Latin Church's inclusion of the word **filioque** (meaning "and from the Son") in the Nicene Creed, accusing the Church of heresy. The term differs from the Eastern Church's teaching that the Holy Spirit descended from the Father *through* the Son. *Filioque* was not part of the creed developed at the Councils of Nicaea and Constantinople and was first added to the Latin creed in the sixth century, and its inclusion spread. (It was adopted in liturgical celebrations in the eleventh century.) The word *filioque* continues to be one difference between the Eastern and Latin Churches.

The Final Break

In 1054 the decisive split between the Eastern and Latin Churches occurred. The two Churches accepted the Pope, the Bishop of Rome, as the successor of Saint Peter. However, the Byzantine Church felt that this authority had been taken too far when, in the eleventh century, popes began to declare and assert their authority over the whole Church, including the Eastern Church, taking power away from the patriarch of Constantinople. Thus in 1054 Patriarch Michael Cerularius of Constantinople publicly declared that because of their differences, the two Churches could not be in union.

To reach an understanding, Pope Leo IX (1049–1054) sent legates to meet with Patriarch Cerularius. Unfortunately, the two sides could not come to an understanding. The crisis peaked when Cerularius closed all Latin churches in Constantinople, excommunicated all priests who continued to follow the Latin tradition, and halted the use of the *filioque* in the Nicene Creed.

Pope Leo sent an envoy to Constantinople to issue a papal bull demanding Cerularius's submission to the Pope. When Cerularius refused, the envoy, though he had no authority to do so, excommunicated him. In turn, Michael Cerularius called a synod to condemn the actions of the Pope's representative and to excommunicate the Pope. He

East–West Relations after the Schism

Although the Eastern Schism of 1054 is seen as the official break between the Greek and Latin Churches, this event did not dramatically change relations between the two Churches. Instead it was the events of 1204 that led to a deep and lasting division.

In that year, following the Byzantine emperor's call for aid from the Western Church when his city was besieged by Muslims, Crusaders sent to assist Constantinople sacked and looted the city and its churches and drove out its citizens (see article 20, "The Crusades"). They proclaimed the Western emperor king and installed a Latin bishop. Any hope for unity dissipated. Future attempts at reconciliation failed. In 1453 Constantinople fell to the Turks—bringing an end to the Roman Empire in the East—and attempts at healing stalled for centuries.

Hope for reconciliation was revived in 1976 when Pope Paul VI (1963–1978) and Patriarch Athenagorus I lifted the mutual excommunications of 1054. Ecumenical efforts continued, keeping alive the hope for eventual unity between the Catholic and Orthodox Churches.

© Bettmann/CORBIS

further declared that he was solely in charge of the Byzantine Church. Most Eastern churches sided with the patriarch. Following the Eastern Schism, the Christian world was divided into the Roman Church of the West and the Orthodox, or Greek, Church of the East. ✝

Article 20 The Crusades

Not too many years after the schism between the Latin Church and the Greek (or Eastern) Church, an urgent request for help was sent by the Byzantine emperor to Pope Urban II (1088–1099). The Greeks were seeking protection against the Turkish Muslims who had invaded their territory and had made inroads into parts of Asia Minor formerly under Byzantine control. Constantinople was under serious threat, and Nicaea, its closest fortified neighbor, had fallen to the Turks in 1084.

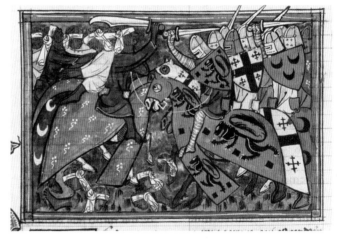

This fourteenth-century manuscript shows crusaders inflicting fatal wounds on their Muslim enemies. Crusaders and Turks alike were driven by religious zeal, each regarding the other as "infidels."

© The Gallery Collection/Corbis

The Roman Church responded swiftly and affirmed a willingness to help, because despite bitter feelings between the East and the West, the two shared a common foe. In 1009 the Turks had besieged Jerusalem, and their caliph, or leader, had ordered the destruction of the Church of the Holy Sepulcher in Jerusalem. Within just a few years, countless churches had been pillaged and destroyed, often with mosques built in their place. A campaign of subjugation began against Christians in Jerusalem. Their movement was restricted, and they were forced to wear distinctive clothing to identify them as "infidels." Pilgrimage routes to Jerusalem were now blocked and Christian pilgrims were prevented from visiting the Holy City.

For all of Christendom, this assault on Jerusalem was an outrage and an affront that required a swift and uncompromising response.

The First Crusade

In 1095 Pope Urban turned to his homeland of France to recruit men for an expedition against the Turks. At the Council of Clermont, a large crowd of military men, French nobles, and clergy gathered to hear his call in a rousing sermon that detailed the fantastic atrocities being committed against pilgrims and Christians in Jerusalem and in the East.

So with the Pope's blessing, the First Crusade set off in 1096 to help the Byzantine Church and to take back Jerusalem. The campaign was a mix of gains and losses, both material and moral. In Byzantium some territories were recovered, but the knights' motives were meeting growing suspicion among the Greeks, and tensions grew. Upon reaching Jerusalem, the Crusaders, driven by misguided zeal to regain control of the city, massacred Jews and Muslims alike. Nevertheless, militarily the Crusade was a success. In 1099 Jerusalem was back in Christian hands.

The knights who returned from the First Crusade were honored as defenders of the faith. They were also granted **indulgences**. Many received tangible rewards too, in the form of loot or by staying on in the conquered territories and establishing feudal estates.

The Second and Later Crusades

The Second Crusade (1145–1149) was initiated after some territories won by the Christians in the First Crusade fell back to the Muslims. The Crusade failed disastrously. Before too long the Muslims had recaptured Jerusalem and all the lands taken by the knights in the First Crusade.

The Third Crusade (1189–1192) was launched under the joint leadership of King Richard (the "Lion-Hearted") of England, Philip II of France, and Emperor Frederick Barbarossa of Germany. This crusade failed to recapture

indulgence
The means by which the Church takes away the punishment that a person would receive in Purgatory.

The Fourth Crusade

When Pope Innocent III (1198–1216) rallied nobles to undertake a new crusade early in his papacy, his intention was to renew efforts to address the problem of Muslim influence in the Holy Land. Crusaders had chosen the Mediterranean Sea route to Jerusalem. However, to raise funds to cover the cost of the ships required to transport them, the knights agreed to a "side trip" to Constantinople, where they would be compensated handsomely for regaining the throne by force for a Byzantine emperor who had been deposed by a rival.

The Crusaders sailed to Constantinople. After a siege of the city, the Crusaders broke the city walls and spilled into the streets of Constantinople. What was intended to be a simple military coup turned into an attack on the citizens of Constantinople and a pillaging frenzy. Crusaders broke into churches and stole or destroyed precious icons, relics, and adornments. Beautiful churches and the holiest of shrines were vandalized, and the most vibrant Christian city in the world was left in ruins.

When Pope Innocent III learned of the sack of Constantinople, he railed against the Crusaders:

> How, indeed, will the church of the Greeks, no matter how severely she is beset with afflictions and persecutions, return into ecclesiastical union and to a devotion for the Apostolic See, when she has seen in the Latins only an example of perdition and the works of darkness, so that she now, and with reason, detests the Latins more than dogs? (translated in James Brundage, *The Crusades*)

Indeed the wounds inflicted by the Fourth Crusade were slow to heal. Though later leaders of the Byzantine Church would seek compromise with the Western Church, the people of the Eastern Church would not forget the suffering inflicted upon them by their fellow Christians. Following the Fourth Crusade, the split between the East and the West seemed irrevocable.

Jerusalem but gained the right for Christians to visit the city. In 1204 the Fourth Crusade was launched, with devastating results.

Later Crusades

Smaller crusades followed, including the so-called Children's Crusade (1212), in which thousands of children marched along the coast of Italy to set sail for the Holy Land, only to face death from disease or starvation. Those who survived were abducted and sold into slavery. Other crusades also failed to meet their intended goal, and in 1291, Acre, the last Christian stronghold in Muslim territory, fell, bringing to an end Christian control of the Holy Land.

Outcomes of the Crusades

Militarily the Crusades had only very minor successes. Jerusalem and Asia Minor were still in Muslim hands. The Crusades did, however, bring about some gains for the West. Crusaders brought back to Europe many goods and inventions. Through contact with Muslim scholars, they learned of advances in astronomy, mathematics, and science. They also brought back the works of Greek philosophers, which influenced the scholastics of the twelfth and thirteenth

Live It!

Christians and Muslims Today

The study of history can bring about greater understanding. Just as it would not be reasonable to try to understand Christianity based on the events of the Crusades, it would not be fair to base an understanding of Islam on the beliefs and actions of the extremists who claim that their cruelty is willed by God.

Each year the Pontifical Council for Interreligious Dialogue highlights the end of Ramadan, the great fast of Islam, with a message to Muslims. The latest message, in 2011, noted, "Christians and Muslims, beyond their differences, recognise the dignity of the human person" ("Message for the End of Ramadan, 2011," 3). The greeting ended, "We are spiritually very close to you, dear Friends, asking God to give you renewed spiritual energy and send you our very best wishes for peace and happiness" (6).

How can your study of history bring greater peace to the world?

centuries, including Thomas Aquinas (see article 24, "Scholastics and Medieval Universities"). These discoveries would bring about profound changes, eventually leading to the period in Western history called the Renaissance. ✝

Article

21 Challenges to the Papacy

Following the reign of Pope Innocent III in the early thirteenth century, the temporal power of the papacy gradually declined. In the fourteenth century, two Catholic nations, England and France, entered into a struggle over territory that would last nearly one hundred years. National identity was beginning to draw the allegiance of the Christian populace, and nations and kings were growing stronger in their ability to command their subjects' loyalty, even over the Church.

The Decline of the Papacy

Many historians see the reign of Pope Boniface VIII (1294–1303) as the start of the decline of the power of the papacy. Strong leaders and the forces of nationalism were beginning to assert themselves in new ways. In particular, two capable and powerful kings, Edward I of England and Philip II of France, sought to assert authority over the Church by taxing the clergy. The Pope issued a bull forbidding taxation of the clergy and threatening excommunication for those collecting such taxes. The response was swift. King Philip sent troops to Italy to arrest the Pope. The Pope was eventually rescued (but died a month later). Nevertheless the event signaled that the papacy was becoming weakened by nationalism. The situation grew worse when two years later, the college of cardinals, which included a number of French cardinals, elected a French Pope, Clement V.

The Avignon Papacy

Pope Clement (1305–1315) was a weak pope who was dominated by the French king. The Pope created ten cardinals in 1305; nine of them were French. In 1309 he moved the Church's headquarters from Rome to Avignon, in the South

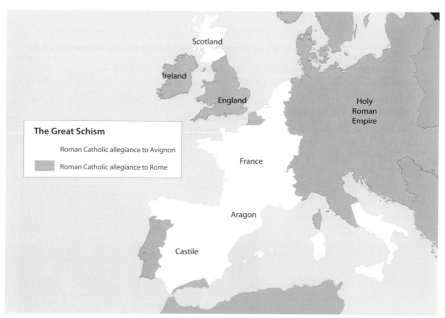

The Great Schism

Roman Catholic allegiance to Avignon

Roman Catholic allegiance to Rome

Scotland

Ireland

England

France

Aragon

Castile

Holy
Roman
Empire

©Alfonso de Tomas/Shutterstock.com

of France. The papal court in Avignon was a place of sumptuous wealth and material comforts.

Besides being concerned about the affluent lifestyle of the Avignon popes, Christians in Europe, especially outside of France, believed that the Pope, as the successor of Peter and the Bishop of Rome, should live there. Also, during the Hundred Years' War (1337–1453), it seemed problematic for the Pope to align himself with the French cause. Further, the arrangement deprived the papacy of military and financial independence.

Moving the Church's headquarters to Avignon in France would have disastrous consequences nearly 70 years later, when two men, one in Rome and one in Avignon, both claimed to be the rightly elected Pope.

Catherine of Siena's Plea

The Avignon Papacy dragged on for more than seventy years. The seventh Avignon Pope, Pope Gregory XI, had hopes of returning to Rome. Catherine of Siena (1347–1380), one of the great medieval **mystics**, is credited with persuading him to follow through on this idea. In 1376 she took the bold step of visiting the Pope in Avignon and urging his return to Rome. Catherine's message to the Pope was direct: She condemned the greed, materialism, and pride of the papal court and urged Gregory XI to return to Rome to serve as shepherd to his flock. The following is from a letter Catherine wrote to Pope Gregory XI:

mystic

A person who regularly has an intense experience of the presence and power of God, resulting in a deep sense of union with him.

Be the true successor to Saint Gregory; love God, have no attachments either to kinsfolk, or friends, or temporal necessity. Do not fear the present storm, nor the spoilt members who have rebelled against your authority. . . .

No longer resist the will of God, for the starving sheep wait for you to return to the see of Saint Peter. You are the

The Black Death

During the Avignon Papacy, a terrible catastrophe struck Europe. Called the Black Death or bubonic plague, this epidemic is estimated to have killed one-third of the European population, or about twenty million people. Cities were especially hard hit, some losing more than half of their population. Two-thirds of Venetians, for example, are believed to have died from the plague.

The Black Death arrived in Europe in 1347 by way of Sicily. At the time, people

© Walters Art Museum, Baltimore, USA / The Bridgeman Art Library

had no idea what caused the disease. Today we know that the bacteria of the plague was brought to Italy by merchant ships and was likely spread by fleas from shipboard rats.

The Black Death permeated the psyche of the medieval populace. It became the subject of folklore, art, and music, which often reflected a sense of impending doom. Yet despite all the suffering and seemingly endless misery, solace could be found in the acts of kindness and mercy of those who ministered to the sick. Even in Avignon, where the papal court continued to reside in luxury, aid was offered to plague victims and sanctuary was offered to Jews who had become the scapegoat for the plague.

For the Church, the Black Death brought a drastic loss of clergy, many having succumbed to the disease, which they likely acquired while tending to the sick. The Church scrambled to replace the lost clergy, resulting at times in the ordination of men ill-prepared for the calling.

Vicar of Jesus; you must resume your proper seat. Come without fear, for God will be with you. . . . Be bold; save the Church from division and iniquity.

Catherine had a deep respect for the papacy and wanted the men occupying the office to be worthy of the calling. Not long after Catherine's visit to Avignon, Pope Gregory XI returned the papal court to Rome.

The Great Western Schism

Pope Gregory XI's return to Rome 1377 did not bring an end to the troubles facing the papacy. When Gregory died in 1378, pressure from Roman mobs helped elect an Italian, Urban VI. Not long after the election, French cardinals claimed to have been pressured into electing Urban. They returned to France, deposed him, and elected a Frenchman to replace him. The new Pope took the name Clement VII and reestablished a papal court in Avignon. Neither man would give up his claim to the office. The **Great Western Schism** resulted, causing confusion for faithful Christians and political maneuvering as governments took sides along political lines.

A Church council was called to resolve the situation and declare the rightful Pope. Instead it deposed both popes and named a third Pope, Alexander V. Alexander died on his way

Great Western Schism

A split within the Church that lasted from 1378 to 1417, when there were two or three claimants to the papacy at once. Also called the Papal Schism.

Catholic Wisdom

The Imitation of Christ

The Imitation of Christ, by Thomas à Kempis (c. 1380–1471), a late medieval monk, promoted a simple message: Even though life is precarious, you can live with the hope of salvation if you follow Christ. Here are two brief passages from the book:

"Oh, if we never sought after fleeting joys or never busied ourselves chasing after possessions and status, what a good conscience we would keep!"

"In everything you do, think of how your life will end and of how you will stand before God."

For a people living in the shadow of the Black Death, this message struck home. But not only for them. Since its writing, *The Imitation of Christ* has been an enduringly popular work of Christian devotion.

Conciliar movement

A reform movement that emerged in the Church in the fourteenth century that held that final authority in spiritual matters rested with church councils, not with the Pope. Conciliarism emerged in response to the Avignon Papacy.

to Rome, leading to yet another election, this time resulting in the appointment of John XXIII. There were still three popes. The papacy had degenerated into a battle for temporal power and influence, played out in an increasingly absurd drama. This drama of popes and antipopes, often three claimants to the office at a given time, continued until 1417, when the Council of Constance (1414–1418) elected Martin V as the new Pope, ending the schism. However, competing papal claimants did not fully abate until 1429, when Clement VIII (1423–1429) resigned. It should be noted that the twentieth-century Pope John XXIII (1958–1963) was permitted to take this name because the first Pope John XXIII was later deposed as an antipope.

The Cost to the Church

Even from the distance of several hundred years, we can see how disorienting and unsettling this drama of popes and antipopes struggling to claim the Chair of Peter was. For the Church at the time, the Great Western Schism had a devastating effect. The papacy lost its dignity and authority and came to be viewed with cynicism. Because excommunication was a penalty leveled freely and recklessly by popes and antipopes against their foes, it lost influence as a legitimate measure to correct serious sins. Finally, the **Conciliar movement**, which gave Church councils—at times convened by secular rulers—supremacy over popes, further depleted the power of the papacy. Conciliarism thrived until the mid-fourteenth century, when Pope Pius II (1458–1464) formally condemned it and reestablished papal primacy. ✝

Part Review

1. Describe two of the disagreements that created division between the Churches of the East and West.

2. What was the effect of the Great Western Schism on the Church and on Christendom?

3. What were some of the negative outcomes of the Crusades?

4. Briefly summarize the events of the Avignon Papacy, including its resolution.

5. What is the current state of relations between the Roman Catholic Church and the Greek Orthodox Church?

6. Overall, did the Crusades produce more successes or failures? Explain your answer.

7. Explain the Conciliar movement and its origin.

Part 3

The High Middle Ages

The High Middle Ages, the period starting around AD 1000, was a period of intense activity in all parts of European society, and in the life of the Church. In the Church the eleventh century brought a renewal to monastic life, building on reforms that had begun in the preceding century. Existing monastic orders established and enforced strict rules for their monks. In addition, new monastic orders were founded and spread across the continent, building up the Church and Western society. New building techniques led to the development of churches the likes of which had never been imagined, in a style that today we call Gothic architecture. As town populations grew around these Gothic cathedrals, the seeds of the university system began to take root, and the scholastic movement was born. Scholastic theologians like Thomas Aquinas, drawing on the newly rediscovered works of Aristotle, produced writings that enriched the Church and clarified her teaching.

Church teaching was also strengthened and affirmed in the documents of Lateran Council IV. Of particular importance was the Council's teaching on the Eucharist. Finally, the Medieval Inquisition, the first of two inquisitions in the Medieval period, quelled heresies against the Eucharist and defended Church teaching.

These articles in this part address the following topics:

Article 22 New Religious Orders

The High Middle Ages, the period beginning about the year 1000 and lasting until about 1300, was a time of new developments in religious life. Among the key events of the time were the renewal of Benedictine monasticism, the introduction of new religious orders, and the appearance of religious orders for women.

Renewal of Benedictine Monasticism

The reforms of the High Middle Ages began to take form in the tenth century, having their origins in Cluny, in central France. In 909 a Benedictine monastery was founded at Cluny. Here a return to the rule and spirit of Saint Benedict was stressed, with emphasis on true Christian discipleship, poverty and simplicity, and freedom from lay influence. Cluny became the leader of Western monasticism. By the middle of the eleventh century, the reforms begun at Cluny had spread to other Benedictine monasteries, including Monte Cassino, the first monastery established by Saint Benedict, in 529.

In addition to reform of the Benedictine monasteries, new monastic orders were also established in the eleventh century. Among these were the Carthusians and the Cistercians. Both of these new orders relied on the Rule of Saint Benedict; however, the rule was drastically modified, and an even greater emphasis was placed on sacrifice and poverty. The Carthusians emphasized a life of austerity, in which monks lived a hermitic life, meeting in community only on feast days. The Cistercians, founded in 1098 at Cîteaux, in France, also stressed solitude, though not to the same degree as the Carthusians, along with manual labor and poverty. In 1115 Saint Bernard, a Cistercian monk and prominent theologian, was sent to Clairveaux, outside of Paris, to found a monastery. Through his influence the order attracted a rapidly growing number of followers; by the time of his death in 1153, the order had grown to nearly 350 houses. With their focus on work and discipline, Cistercian abbeys became leaders in technological knowledge—about agricultural techniques, metal working, and textiles, for example—and were an important contributor to France's economy throughout the medieval period.

Mendicant Orders

mendicants

Members of religious orders that rely on charity for support.

As new monastic orders and reforms were bringing a renewal to monastic life, with a strengthened emphasis on separation from the material world and on true discipleship, new orders were emerging with a focus on reforms beyond the monastic walls. The mendicant (or "beggar") orders— the Order of Preachers (the Dominicans), and the Order of Friars Minor (the Franciscans)—in particular stand out in this regard. Unlike monks who sought to bring salvation to others through a life of prayer and sacrifice apart from the world, the **mendicants** involved themselves in the world, preaching and teaching and serving the poor. They traveled from town to town, relying on charity for their basic needs.

The Franciscans

Also known as the Order of Friars Minor, the Franciscans were a mendicant order founded by Francis of Assisi (1181–1226).

Pray It!

Praying with Saint Francis of Assisi

This prayer has long been attributed to Saint Francis of Assisi (1181–1226), and reflects his spirit of peace and joy:

Lord, make me an instrument of your peace:
where there is hatred, let me sow love;
where there is injury, pardon;
where there is doubt, faith;
where there is despair, hope;
where there is darkness, light;
where there is sadness, joy.

O Divine Master,
grant that I may not so much seek to be consoled
as to console,
to be understood as to understand,
to be loved as to love.
For it is in giving that we receive,
it is in pardoning that we are pardoned,
it is in dying that we are born to eternal life.
Amen.

As the son of a wealthy silk merchant in Assisi, Italy, the young Francis pursued a life of pleasure and material comforts. He squandered money and sought adventure by fighting in the small battles that occasionally erupted between his town and neighboring Perugia.

Around age twenty-five, Francis's life changed dramatically. A series of spiritual events led him away from the life of a wealthy merchant's son and from military life. Francis had an encounter with a leper whom he identified with the crucified Christ. Then, while praying in a small chapel in San Damiano, Francis heard Christ speak to him from the crucifix that hung above the altar. Christ's plea to Francis was, "Repair my house." At first Francis responded to this by rebuilding churches. Then, upon hearing the Gospel message in which Jesus sent his disciples out without money or possessions (see Mark 6:8–9), Francis understood that Christ was calling him to a different kind of service. He took up a life of complete poverty, committed to strengthening the Church by preaching the Good News. Before long Francis attracted a group of likeminded men. He formed a religious community that lived under a rule first approved by Pope Innocent III in 1209. However, the Franciscan **Friars** were not connected to a particular monastery. Instead they became the first mendicant order, begging for their sustenance.

A central theme of Franciscan spirituality was the imitation of Christ and of his poverty. The preaching of Saint Francis and his brother friars was a powerful voice for renewal in the medieval Church. The legacy of Saint Francis resonates today in the Church, most recently expressed in the name of our current Pope, Pope Francis. After his election in March 2013, he revealed that his choice of name reflected his concern for the poor and for the environment.

The Dominicans

While traveling in France as a young priest, Dominic de Guzman (1170–1221) encountered the Albigensians, a heretical sect active in France in the eleventh and twelfth centuries. Dominic envisioned a religious order dedicated to combating the heresies through preaching. He wanted his order to live the monastic ideals outside of the confines of a

© Hermitage, St. Petersburg, Russia / Giraudon / The Bridgeman Art Library

The Order of Preachers, founded by Saint Dominic, offered systematic education to its members, training them to preach the Gospel to ordinary people in the local languages.

friars

Members of religious orders of men who serve the Church through teaching or preaching.

The Poor Clares

Men were not the only ones attracted to Francis's life and proclamation of the Gospel message. Soon after Francis founded his religious order, Saint Clare became a devoted follower of his way of life. Clare wanted to belong to a religious order like that founded by Francis. In 1212, under Francis's guidance, she established a convent for herself and several other women. Unlike the Franciscan Friars, who moved about the countryside to preach, Saint Clare's sisters lived in a monastery. Their life consisted of manual work and prayer. Saint Clare wrote the order's rule, the first monastic rule known to have been written by a woman. Clare's rule was patterned on that of Saint Francis and emphasized apostolic poverty.

Following Clare's death, the order she founded was renamed in her honor as the Order of Saint Clare, commonly referred to today as the Poor Clares.

© Santa Chiara, Assisi, Umbria, Italy / The Bridgeman Art Library

monastery, traveling through the countryside to teach and preach against the heresies. Dominic also wanted a well-educated clergy, capable of defending the Church against heresies. Dominic gathered a group of young men who were willing to take up this life of poverty and dedicate themselves to preaching. Soon he and his followers spread throughout Europe, teaching and preaching the Good News.

In 1215 Pope Innocent III formally recognized Dominic's community as an order of preachers. The order began to spread rapidly throughout Western and Central Europe. Eventually, the Dominicans, or Black Friars (so called because of their habit—a white robe covered with a black cloak), lived in communal houses. From the beginning Dominic had emphasized the importance of theological study in the service of teaching, believing that an educated friar would be of the greatest service to the Church, able to illustrate the truth of the Gospels and the wisdom of the Church's Tradition. Dominican houses were established in Paris, Bologna, and other university towns, and Dominicans joined the university faculties. The Dominicans were among the greatest intellectuals of the period, with Saint Thomas Aquinas their most famous son (see article 24, "Scholastics and Medieval Universities"). ✝

Article 23 Medieval Cathedrals: Works of Beauty and Inspiration

In the days of the early Church, Christians gathered in their homes for the celebration of the liturgy, often fearful of unwanted attention and persecution. Over time the gathering place for worship became more formal, and simple stone churches were built in the Roman Empire. When Constantine legalized Christianity in the Roman Empire in 313, new, grander churches were built, often modeled after the basilicas—government buildings of the Roman Empire. In subsequent centuries church architecture varied by region but remained mostly unchanged, until the High Middle Ages. That era ushered in a period of magnificent church architecture that inspires us to this day.

© abadesign/Shutterstock.com

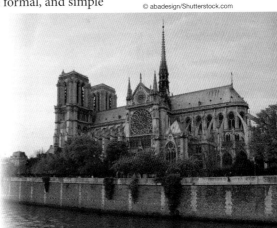

Notre Dame Cathedral on the Île de la Cité in Paris was begun in 1163 and not fully completed until 1345, over 180 years later.

Gothic Grandeur

The cathedrals that sprang up in cities and towns across Europe, from Paris to Milan to Salisbury, England, were an important development in the Church's life during the Middle Ages. In towns across Europe, grand cathedrals were built with spires that rose to the heavens. The cathedrals were built in part because of the influx of people from the

Mass in the Cathedral

Imagine yourself in a small medieval town, say in northern France in the thirteenth century. You wake on a Sunday morning to the sound of church bells. You tend to your household chores and prepare yourself to attend Mass. As you leave your small cottage and step outside, your eyes are drawn to the grand spire of the cathedral rising up over the rooftops.

As you reach the cathedral, you are surrounded by other worshippers arriving from town and from the countryside. When you enter you are again overcome with the wonder you felt upon first entering this awe-inspiring church. You take your place in the nave, reaching near the front, to be as close to the main altar as possible. All around, light streams in through the stained glass windows that masterfully retell the Gospel stories in pictures. The monks lift their voices in song and the smell of incense fills the air. You are lifted up in prayer as you hear the words of the priest, offering the sacrifice of the Mass to God on behalf of his people. Humbled in the presence of the Lord and awed at the lofty grandeur of the cathedral, a magnificent expression of praise to God, you join your prayers with those of the assembly: "*Benedicam dominum in omni tempore. . . .*"

countryside to towns and cities; in turn, however, these churches spurred the growth of towns and cities, attracting master craftsmen and laborers alike.

The cathedrals were the work of master artisans who carved images and designs into stone, and who developed techniques for hoisting huge stone blocks hundreds of feet into the air and fit them together to construct the cathedrals, all with manual tools and without engines or cranes. It took decades, even centuries, to construct a cathedral, and even longer to furnish it completely. Money often ran out and new revenue had to be raised from the bishop and from the king and local lords.

The grand cathedrals and abbey churches built in the eleventh through fourteenth centuries were of two distinct styles—Romanesque and Gothic. Although architecturally distinct, they share some common characteristics.

The first type, named after the Roman style of building, employed massive pillars with rounded arches to hold up stone roofs, replacing the flammable wood-beamed churches of the past. These churches resembled fortresses, with thick walls and small windows to let in light.

Gothic cathedrals, unlike their "stocky" Romanesque counterparts, were perhaps most notable for their height, amplified by their tall spires that reached to the heavens, and their graceful airiness. In addition, these cathedrals had high, thin walls; rib-vaulted ceilings; and flying buttresses—concrete arches that help to hold up the walls from

Live It!

Gothic Architecture Lives

Look around your town and diocese and plan a tour of the Gothic churches you find. Look for high, pointed ceilings; pointed arches; and a round "rose window" of stained glass. You may find one or more tall thin towers. You might also see flying buttresses and gargoyles (fantastic creatures poised along the roof or gutters). According to legend, gargoyles are placed on the church to chase the devil away.

You may also find churches in the Carpenter Gothic style. These are churches made of wood but with some Gothic features, like high ceilings and pointed arches over the windows.

Take photos and make a display of your findings. Look for opportunities to visit Gothic churches away from home when you travel.

nave

The main body of a church or cathedral, where the assembly gathers.

chancel

The part of a cathedral that contains the high altar.

Divine Office

Also known as the Liturgy of the Hours, the official public, daily prayer of the Catholic Church. The Divine Office provides standard prayers, Scripture readings, and reflections at regular hours throughout the day.

the outside. Flying buttresses were a major architectural innovation that allowed cathedrals to reach new heights. Another key distinctive characteristic of the Gothic cathedral is the abundant use of stained glass, often with a rose window as the centerpiece, situated at the west end of the **nave**. For a population that was largely illiterate, the intricate detail of the stained glass, which often depicted events from Sacred Scripture, was a tool for religious instruction and inspiration.

Inside the Cathedral, the front enclosure—the choir or **chancel**—contained the high altar, from which the Eucharistic sacrifice would be offered; the bishop's cathedra (chair), symbolizing his teaching authority and power; and stalls for the priests or monks, who several times a day sang or recited the **Divine Office**. Along the side walls of the cathedral were side altars or chapels from which a priest could celebrate private Masses. In some of the chapels, saints and kings were buried beneath the stone floors. The central area of the church, the nave, was used for the people's Mass. Most cathedrals also had high pulpits, from which long Sunday sermons were given—an important source of religions education for the people. ✝

Article 24 Scholastics and Medieval Universities

As a high school student, especially if you are in your junior or senior year, you no doubt have given a lot of thought to your plans after high school. You may now be pondering the question of which

These students are training to be priests or monks, as evidenced by the tonsure, the shaved area on their heads.

college to go to—Catholic or secular, public or private, in a city or another setting, and so on. Let's stop for a short while to look back at the predecessors of the many colleges and universities available to you today.

The Formation of Medieval Universities

In the Early Middle Ages, as far back as the sixth century, education was often provided by cathedral or monastery schools, in which monks and nuns taught classes, with a primary focus on the training of the clergy. These schools were often the only places for learning, both for the formation of the clergy and the children of the nobles and the villagers. With the steady growth of European society and the rise of towns that began in the twelfth century, a transition began from this system of education to one centered on universities, such as those that sprang up in Europe's major cities.

The universities grew out of the cathedral schools. Teachers and students began to group together to study the liberal arts—astronomy, music, grammar, rhetoric, logic, mathematics, and geometry—as well as the sciences—theology, law, and medicine. For the mutual protection of students and masters, these gatherings formed a *universitas*, a type of corporation modeled on the craftsmen's guilds of the period. As in a guild, the masters had to earn a license and the students had to earn degrees recognizing their completed studies.

Students (males only) could enter the university at age fourteen. Study of the liberal arts typically took six years. Further study, in medicine, law, or theology, could take an additional twelve years, culminating in a master's or doctoral degree.

Universities of the North and South

The University of Bologna was the first university to be chartered, in 1088. It was followed by the University of Paris (1150) and the University of Oxford (1167). By the start of the fourteenth century, more than eighty universities had been founded throughout Europe, including at Cambridge (England, 1209), Salamanca (Spain, 1218), Padua (Italy, 1222), and Coimbra (Portugal, 1290). Later universities, established in the fourteenth century, include Prague (Czech

scholasticism

The method of thinking, teaching, and writing devised in, and characteristic of, the medieval universities of Europe from about 1100 to 1500. Although concerned with all of scientific learning, scholasticism is most closely identified with knowledge about God.

Republic, 1348) and Cracow (Poland, 1364). Most of these universities are still a center for learning today.

Early in the history of the universities of Europe, two distinct branches emerged. In the south, schools modeled on the University of Bologna specialized in law and medicine. In the north, universities like Oxford, Cambridge, and Paris specialized in the liberal arts, canon law, and theology—the "queen of sciences."

Influential Scholars

The medieval universities established a method of learning known as **scholasticism**. Scholasticism emphasizes dialectical reasoning, in which two or more people holding different points of view about a subject arrive at the truth by dialogue, with reasoned arguments. Among its aims was to reconcile the newly rediscovered works of Aristotle with the truths of the Church. Though scholasticism has as its object all of scientific learning, it is most closely identified with knowledge about God. Scholasticism is based in the principle that faith and reason can be reconciled.

Several important figures are closely identified with the scholastic movement of the High Middle Ages. These include Saint Anselm of Canterbury (1033–1109), Peter Abelard (ca. 1079–1142), Saint Thomas Aquinas (1225–1274), and Blessed John Duns Scotus (ca. 1265–1308). Anselm promoted "faith seeking understanding" and encouraged Christians to inquire into the truths of Scripture. Similarly, Duns Scotus, a well-known philosopher and theologian, emphasized the importance of understanding Scripture. Peter Abelard became famous for his explorations of Aristotle's philosophy and perfected the technique of theological investigation with a method in which the *quaestio* (question) led to interrogation (an investigation), followed by *disputatio* (argument and final resolution). Among all the scholastics, none has left a mark as lasting as Thomas Aquinas, a Dominican friar from Italy. ✝

Thomas Aquinas and the *Summa Theologica*

Thomas Aquinas was a student of Albert the Great (c. 1206–1280), a German Dominican friar and scholar recognized for his comprehensive knowledge of and prolific writings on science and religion. Thomas was derided by his classmates as "The Dumb Ox" because of his slow movement and his quiet seriousness. The student misunderstood by his peers went on to become the greatest medieval theologian and one of the most influential scholars in the Church's history.

Thomas Aquinas was a prolific writer. His masterpiece is the *Summa Theologica*, a twenty-one volume work in which he shows the logical relationship between faith and reason. In the *Summa* Aquinas follows the method of medieval disputation (problem or question posed, objections addressed, resolution reached) to prove the existence of God and our relationship

with him. He further explains that although human reason can achieve brilliance, it can't grasp or explain everything, especially mysteries of our faith, such as the Incarnation and the Resurrection.

Aquinas's teachings and writings have greatly influenced Church teaching and have helped the Church to defend her teaching. Today Thomas Aquinas is honored as a Doctor of the Church.

Article 25 The Eucharist: Heresies, Teachings, and Devotions

We have already learned about some of the significant heresies of the early Church, such as the Arian heresy. In the Middle Ages, a sect known as the Albigensians posed a new threat to the Church. The Albigensians were a dualistic sect that saw all of the created world, including the human body, as evil. They were also antisacerdotal (opposed to the priesthood) and rejected the dogma of the Eucharist. In the trials against heretics that formed the Medieval Inquisition (see article 26, "Understanding the Inquisitions"), Dominican inquisitor Bernardo Gui (1262–1331) said this of the Albigensians:

> [T]hey attack and vituperate, in turn, against all the sacraments of the Church, especially the sacrament of the eucharist, saying that it cannot contain the body of Christ. . . . Of baptism, they assert that the water is material and corruptible . . . and cannot sanctify the soul. . . . [T]hey claim that confession made to the priests of the Roman Church is useless.

The Church took steps to combat the Albigensians, stating a key response to their attack against the Eucharist during Lateran Council IV.

Lateran Council IV and the Eucharist

Pope Innocent III (1198–1216), one of the most effective and powerful popes in the Church's history, convened the Fourth Lateran Council. The Council, one of the most important in the Church's history, was attended by more than twelve hundred bishops and leading churchmen, and established seventy canons, or Church laws. Among these were:

- the enforcement of clerical celibacy and the elimination of simony
- the seal of confession—that is, that sins revealed in the Sacrament of Penance and Reconciliation could not be revealed by the confessor
- a call for annual confession and the Easter Duty—receiving the Eucharist at Easter

- recognizing the number of Sacraments instituted by Christ as seven
- defining *Transubstantiation*—the "Real Presence" of Christ in the Eucharist through the transformation of the substance of bread and wine into the Body and Blood of Jesus Christ.

Transubstantiation

Although at the Consecration during the Liturgy the bread and wine retain their physical form, they are truly changed in substance into the Body and Blood of Christ by the power of the Holy Spirit. The Fathers of the Church affirmed the faith of the Church in the efficacy of the words of Christ, through the priest, to bring about this change. Saint John Chrysostom declared the following:

> It is not man that causes the things offered to become the Body and Blood of Christ, but he who was crucified for us, Christ himself. The priest, in the role of Christ, pronounces these words, but their power and grace are God's. This is my body, he says. This word transforms the things offered.[1] (*Catechism of the Catholic Church*, 1375)

The doctrine of transubstantiation was further clarified at the Council of Trent, in the sixteenth century (see article 30, "The Council of Trent," in section 3). Belief in the Real Presence of Christ in the Eucharist separates Catholics from most other Protestant Christians.

Catholic Wisdom

The Life of the Church

As Pope Saint John Paul II (1978–2005) wrote in his encyclical *On the Eucharist in Its Relationship to the Church (Ecclesia de Eucharistia)*, "the Church draws her life from the Eucharist." The Pope went on to say this:

> In a variety of ways [the Church] joyfully experiences the constant fulfillment of the promise: "Lo, I am with you always, to the close of the age" (Matthew 28:20), but in the Holy Eucharist, through the changing of bread and wine into the body and blood of the Lord, she rejoices in this presence with unique intensity. (1)

Eucharistic Adoration in the Middle Ages

The High Middle Ages, particularly the thirteenth century, saw a rise in devotion to the Blessed Sacrament. Two key devotions that emerged during this period were the Feast of Corpus Christi and Eucharistic Adoration. Let's take a look at the history and practice of each.

Feast of Corpus Christi

© VASILY FEDOSENKO/X00829/Reuters/Corbis

The Feast of Corpus Christi celebrates the Body of Christ, consecrated in the Mass. It is observed on the Thursday after Trinity Sunday or, in some places, on the following Sunday. At the request of Juliana of Liege (in Belgium), a thirteenth-century bishop of Liege convened a synod in 1246 to order a celebration of Corpus Christi to be held each year in his diocese. The devotion to Corpus Christi soon became widespread and, through a papal bull of Urban IV (1261–1264), became a feast day of the entire Church.

In many places today, the celebration of the Feast of Corpus Christi is marked by a procession carrying the Blessed Sacrament, with great reverence, out of the church and through the streets.

Eucharistic Adoration

Eucharistic Adoration is typically performed with the Blessed Sacrament in exposition, displayed in a monstrance. On Holy Thursday the Eucharist is not exposed for adoration but is placed on the altar in a ciborium.

Saint Francis of Assisi is credited with establishing the practice in Italy. The practice of lay adoration of the Blessed Sacrament can be traced to 1226 when, to give thanks for victory in the Albigensian Crusade, King Louis VIII (1187–1226), asked that the Blessed Sacrament be placed on display at the chapel of the Holy Cross. The practice of displaying and praying before the exposed Blessed Sacrament soon spread and became an established devotion in the medieval Church and continues to today. ✝

Saint Clare and the Eucharist

In classical art Saint Clare of Assisi (1194–1253) is often depicted carrying a monstrance containing the Blessed Sacrament. According to tradition, in 1240 Saracen (Muslim) invaders were warded off from attacking Clare's convent in Assisi, Italy, when she carried a monstrance containing the Eucharist to the monastery's entrance, where the assailants were about to attack. Here is an account of the incident, written by Tommaso da Celano, a thirteenth-century Franciscan friar:

© Elio Ciol/CORBIS

Bands of soldiers and Saracen archers numerous as bees were stationed by the imperial command to lay waste of fortified castles and to besiege cities. And when at one time their hostile fury was directed against Assisi, . . . the Saracens . . . rushed into the confines of S. Damiano. . . . Although she was ill, Clare with a stout heart directed that she be led to the door and placed before the enemy, a silver casket enclosed in ivory, in which the Body of the Holy of Holies was most devoutly kept, preceding her. . . . The boldness of [the invaders] being changed into fear, they quickly descended the walls they had scaled. (Fr. Paschal Robinson, translator and editor, *The Life of Saint Clare*)

Article 26 Understanding the Inquisitions

A phenomenon associated with the Church of the Middle Ages is that of inquisition. The term *inquisition* may be familiar to you and indeed has become part of everyday parlance as a word for an unfair trial. However, the reality is that this reflects a simplistic understanding of the inquisitions of the medieval Church, of their purpose, and of how they were conducted. For starters, we should clarify some basic history. During the Middle Ages, there were two distinct events that

Medieval Inquisition

An inquisition established by the Church in the thirteenth century aimed at rooting out heresies. Sometimes called the Papal Inquisition.

Spanish Inquisition

An inquisition process established in the late fifteenth century by the Spanish monarchs Ferdinand and Isabella intended to maintain Catholic orthodoxy in Spain.

fall under the "inquisition" label: the **Medieval Inquisition** (also called the Papal Inquisition), which addressed common heresies of the thirteenth century, and the **Spanish Inquisition**. The latter began in the late fifteenth century, some two hundred years after the Medieval Inquisition ended. This inquisition was essentially about adherence to Catholicism among those in Spain who had converted from other faiths. Let's take a closer look at each of these historical events.

The Medieval Inquisition

The practice of capturing and punishing heretics against the Christian faith began in the fourth century, with Emperor Constantine. During that time the pursuit of heretics was the purview of civil authorities. Penalties could include fines, imprisonment, corporal punishment, such as flogging, or even execution. The first heretic was executed in 350. As early as that time, the Pope and other leaders in the Church, such as Saint Ambrose, objected to this practice. They believed that the purpose of capturing a heretic should be conversion, not execution and therefore eternal damnation.

With the fall of the Roman Empire in the West and the barbarian rule that replaced Roman authority, the pursuit of heretics disappeared. At the start of the second millennium, religious fervor was on the rise. In this atmosphere several heretical groups emerged—including the Albigensians and the Waldensians, both of whom promoted doctrines and practices in conflict with the Church. The Church condemned these heretical groups. Then, in 1231, the Papal Inquisition was established by Pope Gregory IX to combat these and other heresies. The Papal Inquisition was active primarily in Germany, Italy, and France, where the major heretical groups of the time were centered.

Inquisitors were chosen mainly from the Dominican Order and the Franciscan Order, because they were well educated, devoted to the Pope, and free from alliances with secular leaders. The inquisitors—organized into a tribunal (a panel of three)—were both investigators and judges. When they arrived in a town, they first set out to determine, partly by speaking to townspeople, whether a heresy had occurred. If so, then the accused was given a list of charges, witnesses were summoned, and a trial followed, typically conducted in secret.

© Index, Barcelona, Spain / The Bridgeman Art Library International

Although the Medieval Inquisition is often remembered as a vicious hunt for anyone in opposition to Catholic orthodoxy, with references to "burning at the stake," the facts reflect a different reality. Most sentences were "canonical" penances, such as fasting, making pilgrimages, attending Mass more frequently, or wearing distinctive clothing. An estimated 1 percent of defendants found guilty of heresy were given over to the secular arm (civil authorities) to be put to death, and about 10 percent were sentenced to prison. This is not to say that the Medieval Inquisition was free of problems. Abuses did indeed take place, often resulting from overzealous inquisitors exceeding their authority. However, the provocative details must be balanced with the plainer ones, in which reasoned and compassionate sentences were handed out, with the aim of reuniting the sinner to the Church and to God.

The Inquisition essentially consisted of an investigation, or inquiry, into the religious beliefs of the accused. The court aimed to suppress doctrines that were inconsistent with Church teaching.

The Spanish Inquisition

Unlike the Medieval Inquisition, the Spanish Inquisition was under the authority of the kings of Spain, rather than directly under Church authority. Like the Medieval Inquisition, the facts of the Spanish Inquisition have been distorted by exaggeration and misinformation.

The Spanish Inquisition began in the fifteenth century, about two centuries after the Medieval Inquisition had almost ended, under the authority of King Ferdinand and Queen Isabella of Spain. To bolster their authority, the king and queen sought to stamp out any possible opposition to their leadership and to unite all of Spain, through conformity to Catholicism. The first inquisitors were appointed in 1481. In that year the first *auto da fe* (a ceremony at which the condemned were sentenced) was held, and six people were burned at the stake. Although Pope Sixtus IV (1471–1484) had authorized this inquisition, he objected to using Church courts in persecuting Jews. He demanded that the accused be allowed to appeal to Rome and to have legal counsel, and that personal enemies of the accused be disqualified as witnesses. King Ferdinand rejected these demands, and the Pope lost all control over the inquisition process.

The Spanish Inquisition targeted recent converts to the faith, particularly Jews and Muslims, because their conversions were suspected of being feigned, rather than a true acceptance of the faith. Other targets included those guilty of lesser offenses, such as blasphemy and sexual sins.

The first sixty years of the Spanish Inquisition concerned mostly converts, and led to most of the executions—with nearly three thousand *conversos* (Jewish and Muslim converts to the Catholic faith) executed. Over the next three hundred years, inquisition activity involved mostly trials for offenses against the faith and produced fewer executions, focusing on those suspected of Protestant sympathies (in the sixteenth century) and, in the New World, on ensuring "purity of blood" (European versus Indian and African blood) for those seeking ordination. The Spanish Inquisition was officially abolished in 1834. ✝

A Time Line of the Spanish Inquisition

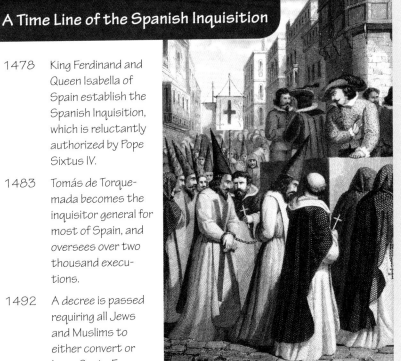

1478   King Ferdinand and Queen Isabella of Spain establish the Spanish Inquisition, which is reluctantly authorized by Pope Sixtus IV.

1483   Tomás de Torquemada becomes the inquisitor general for most of Spain, and oversees over two thousand executions.

1492   A decree is passed requiring all Jews and Muslims to either convert or leave Spain. Few Muslims were left, as they had been defeated in Granada earlier that year. Of the 100,000 or so Jews, about a third left the country.

1540   The Spanish Inquisition turns its focus to Protestants in Spain.

1548   Saint Ignatius of Loyola is briefly imprisoned by the Spanish Inquisition, after being found guilty of being an *alumbrado* (an "enlightened one" or a charismatic).

1781   The last execution is carried out.

1834   The Spanish Inquisition is formally abolished.

Part Review

1. Describe the monastic reforms of the High Middle Ages and their origins in the Benedictine monastery founded at Cluny in the tenth century.

2. In what ways did the new monastic orders of the High Middle Ages build up the Church and society?

3. Name the two mendicant orders founded in the thirteenth century and briefly describe the origins and purpose of each at its founding.

4. What key teaching about the Eucharist did Lateran Council IV promulgate?

5. What are some architectural characteristics that distinguished Gothic cathedrals from churches that preceded them?

6. Briefly summarize the scholastic model of learning and explain its primary aims and focus.

7. Describe the development and growth of the medieval university system.

8. Describe the Medieval Inquisition and the Spanish Inquisition, making sure to clarify the differences between the two.

9. What two devotions to the Eucharist developed in the thirteenth century? Provide a brief summary of each.

An Age of Renewal and Growth

Part 1

Renaissance and Reform

In the 1400s the Middle Ages, a period covering nearly a thousand years, was gradually fading and giving way to a new reality in the religious, social, and political realms. For the Church the crisis of popes and antipopes—the Papal Schism—and the Avignon Papacy left the papacy tarnished and weakened. Further, the papacy had become a target of cynicism because of some popes' focus on temporal power and riches. In the social and intellectual sphere, a movement was born that shed the religiosity and piety of the Middle Ages and focused instead on glorious human achievements. Thus the Renaissance began, and with it the humanist movement. Finally, as princes and monarchs began to assert their supreme authority over their subjects ahead of the Church, national identities began to replace the authority and unity once dominated by the Church. In this context the Protestant Reformation was born and the once united Christian world fractured into various denominations, or confessions.

The articles in this part address the following topics:

Article 27 The Renaissance

As the period known as the Middle Ages was drawing to a close, Europe was ushering in a new era known as the Renaissance. The Renaissance, a term that means "rebirth," represents a period of cultural awakening in which the ancient civilizations of Egypt, Greece, and Rome were rediscovered.

The Renaissance began in Florence, in Tuscany, in roughly the late fourteenth century. From there, it spread to the rest of Europe. A distinguishing characteristic of the period is **humanism**, a movement to revive classical learning, such as Latin and Greek literary and historical texts, and that focused on human achievements rather than on the divine. Humanism was expressed in scholarship, art, architecture, and music, which were often supported by wealthy patrons and by the Renaissance popes.

humanism
A cultural and intellectual movement that emphasized classical learning, such as Latin and Greek literary and historical texts, and that focused on human achievements rather than on the divine.

Humanist Scholarship

Most humanist scholars were Christian. Eminent among them is Erasmus of Rotterdam (1466–1536), who developed important new Latin and Greek translations of the New Testament. Erasmus and other Christian humanists encouraged the Church to return to the Gospel values, and were at times critical of what they saw as the excesses of the Renaissance Popes.

Scholarship in this period received a tremendous boost from the invention of the printing press, around 1440, by Johannes Gutenberg. Books could now be mechanically reproduced, thus also becoming widely available to greater numbers of people.

Art and Music

Some of history's greatest and most enduring achievements in the arts have their roots in the Renaissance. Master artists of this period celebrated the beauty of God's creation, especially visible in humanity. Supported by wealthy patrons, such as the Medicis of Florence, and by popes, these artists created works of immense beauty that stand to this day as a testament to human achievement, both in their subjects and in the genius of the works themselves. The most famous of these include Michelangelo's *Pieta* and scenes from Genesis on the ceiling of the Sistine Chapel; Da Vinci's *Last Supper*; and Botticelli's *Birth of Venus,* as well as works by Bernini, Giotto, Raphael, Donatello, and the Dominican friar Fra Angelico, who was beatified during the papacy of Saint John Paul II in 1982 and was later named the patron of Catholic artists.

Music also saw new developments during the Renaissance, with the emergence of new liturgical forms and sacred music. The best known composer of the period was Palestrina, whose musical compositions had a lasting influence on the development of liturgical music. Palestrina made such a favorable impression on Pope Julius III that he appointed him musical director of his chapel. In his youth, Palestrina was a spiritual disciple of Saint Philip Neri (1515–1595),

"the Apostle of Rome," and under his spiritual guidance gained an insight into the spirit of the liturgy that later influenced his music.

Despite the fact that Michelangelo was a sculptor and not a painter, he mastered difficult techniques of perspective, painting on curved surfaces to be viewed from 60 feet below.

© Sylvain Sonnet/Corbis

Pray It!

Praying with Art and Music

When we come before God in prayer, we come with all of our senses. Try some of these ideas to help you to use the senses of sight, sound, and touch in your praise of God: set one of your favorite Scripture quotes to a simple tune you can remember; use crayons or paints to express your prayer or your feelings to God, using various colors and abstract designs; find religious art (perhaps from books in the library) to look at and just "be" in God's presence with it; write a prayerful poem or song and set it to music. As the psalmist says, "Sing to the LORD a new song" (Psalm 96:1).

The Renaissance Popes

The ten popes of the Renaissance period (Nicholas V [1447–1455] to Leo X [1513–1521]) did much to advance the arts through their patronage of great artists and the grand building projects they initiated. These works still enrich the Church today. Still not all of the outcomes of these popes' efforts were positive. Further, at times their motivation was personal gain rather than the glory of God. The Renaissance popes frequently used their power to enrich themselves and their families, even appointing relatives to the **college of cardinals**. Pope Alexander VI (1492–1503), of the wealthy and powerful Borgia family and an infamous Renaissance pope, appointed at least eight relatives. Further, because these popes were in constant need of money to fund their lavish building and arts projects, they sought new sources of revenue. One of these sources was the sale of indulgences, a practice that led to the coming revolution in the Church that we now know as the Protestant Reformation. (We will learn more about this topic in article 28, "Luther's Complaint.")

Architecture

A visit through Italy today, particularly Rome and Florence, would reveal some of the greatest architectural achievements of the Renaissance. Located in Vatican City, in Rome, is Saint Peter's Basilica. Saint Peter's has the largest interior of any church in the world. Although there has been a church at the site since the fourth century, the current basilica was constructed in the sixteenth and seventeenth centuries, begun under the direction of Pope Julius II (1503–1513). It houses some of the Church's greatest artistic treasures, including works by Michelangelo and Bernini. The initial design for its dome was created by Bramante, but the dome was later redesigned and completed under Michelangelo. Renaissance

college of cardinals

A Church body made up of all the cardinals whose function is to advise the Pope about Church matters and to elect a successor following the death of a Pope.

churches can be found throughout Rome. Many of them also house the works of master artists.

Renaissance architecture abounds in Florence also. From the palaces of the Medicis to churches built under their patronage, a trip through Florence is like a walk back in time. The crowning glory of the city is the Basilica di Santa Maria del Fiore (Basilica of Saint Mary of the Flower), familiarly known as the *Duomo* (Italian for *cathedral*). This basilica was completed in 1436, with the dome engineered by Filippo Brunelleschi.

Of course, to note Saint Peter's Basilica and Florence's *Duomo* is like noting two stars in a constellation. Nevertheless these two examples point to the creative genius that flourished at this time and that still enriches the Church and the world today. ✝

Article 28 Luther's Complaint

© bpk, Berlin / Art Resource, NY

In the fifteenth century, images cut into the surface of a block of fruitwood were printed on hand presses. Some woodcuts showed scenes from daily life: this one depicts the sale of indulgences on the street.

By the start of the 1500s, the Church and politics in Europe were in a volatile state, a reality brought about by practices within the Church that left it vulnerable to criticism, and by the forces of nationalism. For the Church a scandal over indulgences proved to be the fuse that exploded the situation. A then-unknown German friar, Martin Luther, unwittingly put a match to that fuse. Before we look at Luther's actions and their consequences, let's consider the matter of indulgences as they were promoted in that time.

Indulgences

The original intent of indulgences was to offer Christians a way of doing good as penance for their sins. For instance, making a pilgrimage could merit a special indulgence, which took away punishment that would otherwise have been suffered after death in purgatory. Unfortunately, indulgences came to be seen as a kind of magic antidote to sin rather than as an element to support true Christian living. In this atmosphere indulgences could be bought and sold rather than earned through good works and prayer. Among some churchmen the selling of indulgences became a common practice. The Dominican friar Johan Tetzel is an infamous seller of indulgences, generating profits to fund papal building projects, including Saint Peter's Basilica.

Luther's *Ninety-five Theses* is not a list of grievances against the Church. It is an argument, or disputation, organized into numbered points, which opens with a call for debate on the statements in the document.

© Foto Marburg / Art Resource, NY

Martin Luther's Call for Reform

Martin Luther (1483–1546) was an Augustinian priest and monk and a scholar who had studied the Church Fathers and Scripture. Luther believed that only faith in God's love and mercy could justify sinners. This belief sharply contrasted with some of the exaggeratedly pious practices of the time, which at times were based in superstition rather than true faith in God. Luther sought to preach his views to others. On October 31, 1517, he posted his famous *Ninety-five Theses* on the door of the church in Wittenberg. Among other things, this document protested against the sale of indulgences. Luther hoped his statements would invite debate with other theologians. Instead his bold yet simple act began an upheaval that became the Protestant Reformation. Luther had not intended to begin a movement to break away from the Church of Rome, but his call for reform and the Church's response brought about just that outcome.

Catholic Wisdom

Justification by Faith Today

In 1999 the Lutheran World Federation and the Catholic Church, after serious dialogue, mutually agreed on the meaning of "justification by faith." They stated: "Together we confess: By grace alone, in faith in Christ's saving work and not because of any merit on our part, we are accepted by God and receive the Holy Spirit, who renews our hearts while equipping and calling us to good works" ("Joint Declaration on the Doctrine of Justification," 15).

Luther's Doctrine

When Luther was eventually called to Rome, he refused to go. Instead he further elaborated on the following teachings:

- *Sola Scriptura* In contrast with the Church's position that Sacred Scripture and Sacred Tradition together contain the Deposit of Faith, Luther stated that Scripture alone transmits Revelation.
- *Sola fide* Luther stated that humankind is justified by faith alone, rather than by both faith and good works, as the Catholic Church teaches.
- *Sola gratia* Luther rejected the understanding that our cooperation with God's grace is essential for our salvation and believed that salvation comes solely by divine grace, an unearned gift of God, and is not merited by the sinner.

Luther further taught that there are only two valid Sacraments—Baptism and the Eucharist—rather than seven.

The Church's Response

The Pope at the time, Leo X (1513–1521), did not initially become involved in the matter of Luther's *Ninety-five Theses*. Leo saw the situation as a quarrel among monks. However, in December 1520, Leo condemned forty-one of Luther's proposals and gave him sixty days to recant or be excommunicated. Luther gave no sign of changing his stand, and the excommunication became final in January 1521. According to the European law of the time, a secular ruler—in this case Charles V of Germany—had to arrest and punish heretics who did not recant their heretical beliefs. However, Luther was protected by his friend Duke Frederick of Saxony, who agreed to give him safe passage and to hide him. At home in Germany, support for Luther grew, fueled in part by German nationalism, the movement for a united and independent Germany. The Germans, tired of supporting a papacy now seen as corrupt, sought to promote the interests of their homeland instead.

While in hiding, Luther completed a German translation of the Bible. He also wrote catechisms explaining his ideas. With the aid of the printing press, invented a century or so earlier, his writings, as well as his translation of the Bible, had a wide reach.

By 1525 Luther had come out of exile and married. He had stressed the priesthood of all believers and rejected the position that priests should be required to be unmarried. Luther continued to attract a strong following, and his followers began to be called Lutherans. In 1530 his good friend and follower Philip Melanchthon composed the basic creed for Lutherans, calling it the Augsburg Confession. The Augsburg Confession is still the statement of faith for Lutherans, and the year 1530 is considered the beginning of Protestantism. Because Luther rejected ecclesiastical power, he entrusted princes with the organization of churches and their worship. As a result the Lutheran churches became national churches, with their organization differing from one state to another. ✝

Indulgences and Reform

Luther was right in reacting negatively to the sale of indulgences. He was not alone. Several other leading Catholic theologians, such as the humanists Erasmus and Saint Thomas More, were also critical of this Church abuse. Unlike Luther, however, they remained loyal to the Church.

Eventually Pope Leo X issued a document clarifying the meaning and purpose of indulgences. As a result the selling of indulgences declined and eventually stopped. Most of Luther's early concerns about the abuse of indulgences were incorporated into Church teaching at the Council of Trent, held later in the sixteenth century (see article 30, "The Council of Trent").

Article

29 Religious Confessions in Europe

Following Luther's break with the Catholic Church and his establishment of the Lutheran Church, Christianity in Europe further split into different branches, or confessions, as the new Protestant communities are often called. A new religious landscape was beginning to take shape across Europe.

Which confession a sixteenth-century Christian belonged to was largely a matter of geography. Secular rulers legislated religious practice, and dissenters were subject to persecution, exile, and even execution.

Germany

In Germany, even as Lutheranism continued to expand, splinter groups formed. One example is the Anabaptists of Münster, whose goal was to establish a church founded on the Apocalypse. Neither violence nor dialogue succeeded in bringing about religious unity in Germany, and conflicts of religion took place during the Thirty Years' War (1618–1648). The war ended with the signing of the Peace of Westphalia, which gave princes the freedom to choose the confession for their subjects by establishing the principle of *cuius regio, eius religio* ("whose realm, his religion").

Switzerland

In France a reformer named John Calvin (1509–1564) took Luther's ideas even further, and created his own version of Protestantism, which became known as Calvinism. Like Luther, Calvin believed in the supreme authority of Scripture, and Scripture alone. Unlike Luther, however, he denied Christ's presence in the Eucharistic elements. Calvin advocated very simple church worship, with none of the elaborate rituals, ornamentations, or statues. However, under threat of persecution, he fled France for Switzerland. There he wrote the *Institutes of Christian Religion*, which clearly outline his understanding of the Christian faith and practices.

When Calvin arrived in Switzerland in 1536, that country already had a religious revolution in progress, led by Ulrich Zwingli (1484–1531), with its center in Zurich. Like Calvin, Zwingli departed significantly from Luther's theology, with a significant new addition in the teaching of **predestination**. Protestants in Geneva asked Calvin to help implement reforms.

Calvin proved an able administrator. He founded a university at Geneva to train ministers. He preached almost daily and wrote extensively. Just as Zwingli had done in Zurich, Calvin established a **theocracy** in Geneva, with the Church dominating state affairs. Calvin enforced strict moral laws and established a system of complete intolerance of any religion other than his brand of Protestantism. Practicing beliefs opposed to Calvin's was punishable by death, often by public burning.

predestination
The belief that each person's fate after death is predetermined by God and that no one can do anything to change it.

theocracy
A form of government in which God is understood to be head of the state, ruling by divine guidance granted to its clergy or other ruling officials.

The British Isles

The origin of the conflict between England and the Church was the marriage of King Henry VIII. Henry, who reigned from 1509 to 1547, had been given the title Defender of

Live It!

Church Unity and You

Through the Pontifical Council for Promoting Christian Unity, the Church advocates for unity with all Christians according to the conciliar decree *Unitatis Redintegratio* (1964) and collaborates in dialogue with other churches and world communions. These include several of the Orthodox Churches, as well as the various faith communions of Lutheran, Reformed, Methodist, Baptist, Disciples of Christ, some Pentecostal groups, and others.

What can you do for Christian unity?

1. Pray the prayer of Jesus, "that all may be one" (John 17:21).
2. Learn about your faith so you will be able to share the truth about Catholicism with others.
3. In relationships with other Christians, seek to understand. Ask questions, and respond to questions, with thoughtfulness and gentleness.

the Faith by Pope Leo X, for his defense of the faith against Luther. Now Henry faced a personal dilemma. He wanted his marriage to Katherine of Aragon annulled, or declared invalid by the Church, because she had not given him a son to inherit the throne and ensure succession. Clement VII (1523–1534), who was Pope at the time, would not consent to the annulment.

Henry rebelled against the Pope. He declared himself head of the Church of England and required all English clergy to commit their loyalty to him. Those who remained loyal to Rome, such as Thomas More, were executed. He then ordered the archbishop of Canterbury to annul his marriage to Katherine so he could marry Anne Boleyn. (Incidentally Henry ordered Anne's beheading a few years later and went on to marry four more times.)

Henry dissolved the monasteries in England and seized their properties. In 1534 Parliament passed the Act of Supremacy, declaring the English monarch the head of the Catholic Church in England, or the Anglican Church. Despite the official break with the Catholic Church, Henry VIII rejected Lutheran teaching and never considered himself a Protestant. The Church of England retained many essentials of the Catholic faith in the Act of the Six Articles of 1539, an act that standardized Church practices.

Following Henry's death, some Calvinist ideas crept into Anglicanism. When Elizabeth I, who reigned for forty-five years (1558 to 1603), took the throne, she took the title Supreme Governor of the Realm in Matters Spiritual and Temporal. She promulgated the *Thirty-nine Articles of Religion* defining the Anglican faith and solidified the dominance of the Anglican Church. As dissenters sprang up and sought to follow a Calvinist "purist" religion, these Puritans became subject to persecution.

Scotland adopted Calvinism and the Scottish Reformed Church (Presbyterian) received official status in 1560. John Knox, who was strongly influenced by Calvin, was its organizer. Although England tried to impose reforms in Ireland, Ireland steadfastly refused and remained loyal to Rome.

The Execution of Saint Thomas More

Despite pleas and pressure from his friends and family, Thomas More (1478–1535), Lord Chancellor to Henry VIII, refused to recognize King Henry VIII as head of the Catholic Church in England. In 1534 he was arrested for treason and imprisoned in the Tower of London. On July 6, 1535, he was executed.

It is said that More refused to cower before his executioners and had a sense of humor to the very end. He is quoted as saying to his executioner: "I pray you, Master Lieutenant, see me safe up, and for my coming down let me shift for myself." And then: "Pluck up thy spirits, man, and be not afraid to do thine office, my neck is very short. Take heed therefore thou shoot not awry" (William Roper, *The Life of Sir Thomas More*). He also proclaimed that he was God's first, but also a good servant to the king.

© Galleria degli Uffizi, Florence, Italy / The Bridgeman Art Library

More was then executed by beheading. His body was given to his foster daughter for burial. As was the custom for traitors at the time, his head was fixed upon a pike over the London Bridge for a month. It was rescued by his daughter and today is believed to rest in Saint Dunstan's Church in Canterbury.

Protestantism Expands

Over the next two centuries, many Protestant communities were found across Europe. Almost all of them were derived from, or related to, the three main movements of Lutheranism, Calvinism, and the Church of England. ✝

Part Review

1. Describe the theocracy that Calvin established in Geneva.

2. What is predestination and how is this belief contradictory to the doctrine of free will?

3. Imagine living in a world before the invention of the printing press and after it. Describe some of the likely social and religious changes this technological change might have generated.

4. Briefly explain Luther's doctrines of *sola fide* and *sola gratia* and provide a Catholic response to each.

5. Explain the Church's teaching on indulgences and describe the abuses related to indulgences that provoked disagreement from Luther and other theologians of his time.

6. Explain the principle of *cuius regio, eius religio*. What might be some of the implications if this became a guiding principle for modern nations?

7. What was at the root of England's break with the Catholic Church? In what ways did the outcome differ from the break begun by Martin Luther?

Part 2

Catholic Renewal in the Sixteenth and Seventeenth Centuries

In 1517, when Martin Luther posted his *Ninety-five Theses* at the parish church in Wittenberg, Germany, Rome was slow to respond, believing that Luther's heretical attacks against the Church would soon blow over. Instead Luther's words of protest started a movement that within a decade had transformed the religious map of Europe. An official response from the Church was not just needed now but was overdue. Finally, an Ecumenical Council was ordered to convene in 1537. Delays stalled the Council's opening until December 1545. Despite its slow start and sometimes halting pace, the Council introduced into the Church important reforms and addressed articles of the faith on a scale not seen since Lateran IV (1215). The decrees of the Council brought a renewal into all levels of the Church's life.

The articles in this part address the following topics:

Article 30 The Council of Trent

As the Protestant Reformation was taking place and Luther and other reformers and their adherents were separating from Rome, many who remained loyal to the Catholic Church and the Pope were also seeking reform. Reform efforts led to the founding of new religious orders with an emphasis on simplicity and piety and confraternities with a focus on prayer and good works, especially among the poor. But the Church's official response came in the form of an Ecumenical Council, the Council of Trent.

© Bonhams, London, UK / The Bridgeman Art Library

The cardinal legates who presided at the Council of Trent faced the difficult task of resolving conflicts among attendees with differing national interests and philosophical perspectives.

The Council Opens

A call for a general Church Council began early in the Protestant Reformation. The call came from churchmen and the laity, both seeking an effective response to the heresies of Luther and other reformers. However, various factors, many of them political, made the popes reluctant to call a council. Finally, Pope Paul III (1534–1549), seeing that the Protestant Reformation had won over a number of princes, especially in Germany, deemed a Council beneficial. Despite initial opposition from the cardinals, the Council was eventually approved. Though set to begin in May 1537, the Council was delayed until December 1545. The Council was held in Trent, in the southern Alps in Italy.

Of the more than five hundred bishops of the Church at the time, less than half attended the sessions of the Council, with a majority of those in attendance being from Italy. Throughout the Council rumors of epidemics and wars caused panic and halted Council proceedings. In September 1549 the Council stalled, and proceedings halted. It was reopened in May 1551 by Pope Julius III (1550–1555) but was broken up again just one year later. The Council was finally reconvened for the last time by Pope Pius IV (1559–1565), meeting from January 1562 until its final adjournment in December 1563.

The Decisions of the Council

The Council of Trent brought about what is now called the Catholic Reformation (sometimes called the Counter-Reformation). The Council clarified and defined many points of the Church's doctrine that had not been precisely defined to this point. The Council also outlined reforms for all areas of pastoral care. Some of the Council's decisions were motivated by a pure desire to guide the laity and bring reforms to the Church's hierarchy; others were a reaction against Protestantism. Nevertheless the Council effected many critical reforms that shaped the worldwide Church for centuries to come. Let's examine some of the most critical canons and decrees of the Council.

Pray It!

"Ave Verum Corpus"

In affirming the Real Presence of Christ in the Eucharist, the Council of Trent was affirming what the Church had always believed. We can look to the Fathers of the Church, especially Saint Ignatius of Antioch, for evidence of this. In addition, the Church expressed her faith in the Eucharist through hymns. A popular hymn from the fourteenth century, set to music by various composers, is "Ave Verum Corpus" ("Hail, True Body"). It is often sung by trained choirs during Holy Week. You may want to pray this as a thanksgiving after Holy Communion. This is one English translation:

> Hail, true Body,
> born of the Virgin Mary,
> who, having truly suffered, was immolated
> on the cross for all people,
> from whose pierced side
> flowed water and blood:
> Be for us a foretaste [of the banquet in Heaven]
> in the trial of death.
> O sweet Jesus, O loving Jesus, O Jesus, son of Mary,
> have mercy on me. Amen.

deuterocanonical
Books of the Old Testament that do not appear in the Hebrew Scriptures but are accepted by the Church as part of the canon of Scripture.

apocrypha
Writings about Jesus or the Christian message not accepted as part of the canon of Sacred Scripture.

justification
Justification is an invitation toward conversion, which happens as a response to God through the active life of faith. It involves the removal of sin and the gift of God's sanctifying grace to renew holiness. Justification was accomplished by Christ's Paschal Mystery, in his sacrificial death for all humanity.

merit
God's reward to those who love him and by his grace do good works. We cannot "merit" justification or eternal life, which are a free gift of God. The source of any merit we have before God is due to the grace of Christ in us.

Canons and Decrees

The following points summarize some of the key decrees of the Council of Trent, with excerpts from the Council documents in some instances:

- **On the Creed** The Council ordains and decrees that, before all other things, a confession of faith is to be set forth. The Council affirmed the Nicene Creed, adopted for the Church at the Councils of Nicaea and Constantinople.

- **On Scripture** A decree was passed confirming that the **deuterocanonical** books were part of the canon of Scripture. This was a response to Luther's designation of these books as part of the *apocrypha*. Further, the Vulgate was affirmed as the authoritative text of Scripture.

- **On Original Sin** The doctrine of Original Sin was affirmed, as was Baptism's efficaciousness in remitting Original Sin.

- **On Justification** **Justification**, through which we are freed from sin and sanctified, is effected through God's grace, granted to us through the Sacrament of Baptism. Faith makes it possible for us to accept God's grace and to cooperate in his saving work by doing good works. However, we must always remember that we are saved through God's grace, not through any **merit** earned by our own efforts.

- **On the Sacraments** The Council affirmed the validity of the Seven Sacraments, a statement deemed necessary in part to respond to Luther's acceptance of only Baptism and the Eucharist as valid.

  > If any one saith [says], that the sacraments of the New Law were not all instituted by Jesus Christ, our Lord; or, that they are more, or less, than seven, to wit, Baptism, Confirmation, the Eucharist, Penance, Extreme Unction [Anointing of the Sick], Holy Orders, and Matrimony; or even that any one of these seven is not truly and properly a sacrament; let him be anathema. (Page 54)

- **On the Eucharist** The Council affirmed the doctrine of Transubstantiation and the True Presence of Christ in the Eucharist:

  > And because that Christ, our Redeemer, declared that which He offered under the species of bread to be truly His own body, therefore has it ever been a firm belief in the Church of God, and this holy Synod doth now declare it anew, that, by

the consecration of the bread and of the wine, a conversion is made of the whole substance of the bread into the substance of the body of Christ our Lord, and of the whole substance of the wine into the substance of His blood; which conversion is, by the holy Catholic Church, suitably and properly called Transubstantiation. (Page 78)

From the Council to the People

Following the Council of Trent, Pius IV published the decrees and began to take steps toward their implementation. After him, Pius V (1566—1572) began to publish manuals intended to ensure adherence to the decrees of the Council by clarifying them for the laity. Among these were the *Roman Catechism* (a text for priests, to help them to preach and explain the Catechism). This is sometimes called the Catechism of the Council of Trent. Pius V also revised and required the publication of the *Roman Breviary* (a book containing the public prayers of the Church, including the Liturgy of the Hours) and the *Roman Missal*, which standardized the celebration of the Liturgy. Pius made this missal mandatory for all Latin Rite churches (with the exception of liturgies where a rite dating from before 1370 was in use). The Rite of the Mass laid out in this *Roman Missal* remained almost unchanged until the 1970 revision of the *Roman Missal*. The English translation of the *Roman Missal* was revised most recently in 2011.

- **On the Mass** The Council affirmed that the Mass is truly a sacrifice, because it makes present the sacrifice of the cross. It is a memorial of Christ's Passover, and makes present his unique sacrifice. It is the work of salvation accomplished by the Paschal Mystery, a work made present in the liturgical action.

  [Christ] declaring Himself constituted a priest for ever, according to the order of Melchisedech, He offered up to God the Father His own body and blood under the species of bread and wine; and, under the symbols of those same things, He delivered (His own body and blood) to be received by His apostles, whom He then constituted priests of the New Testament; and by those words, Do this in commemoration of me, He commanded them and their successors in the priesthood, to offer (them); even as the Catholic Church has always understood and taught. (Page 153)

- **On the Priesthood** The Sacrament of Holy Orders was defined to imprint an indelible mark on the soul of the ordained. Further, the requirements for priestly celibacy were upheld.

- **On the Founding of Seminaries** Acknowledging the importance of a well-educated and well-trained clergy, the council required dioceses to establish seminaries for the proper formation of priests.

  [T]he holy Synod ordains, that all cathedral, metropolitan, and other churches greater than these, shall be bound, each according to its means and the extent of the diocese, to maintain, to educate religiously, and to train in ecclesiastical discipline, a certain number of youths of their city and diocese, or, if that number cannot be met with there, of that province, in a college to be chosen by the bishop for this purpose near the said churches, or in some other suitable place. (Page 187)

- **On Marriage** The council stipulated that marriages must be witnessed by a priest, with a minimum of two witnesses:

  Those who shall attempt to contract marriage otherwise than in the presence of the parish priest, or of some other priest by permission of the said parish priest, or of the Ordinary, and in the presence of two or three witnesses; the holy Synod renders such wholly incapable of thus contracting and declares such contracts invalid and null. (Page 197) ✝

^{Article}
31 The Catholic Reformation and New Religious Orders

Although the Council of Trent had little effect in unseating Protestantism in countries where it had taken hold as the established branch of Christianity, the Council yielded much fruit for the Church. Among the positive outcomes were the religious orders that emerged following the Council, whose missions and members were shaped by the mandates of the Council. These include the Jesuits, Saint Teresa's reformed Carmelites, the Discalceds, and others.

Ignatius of Loyola and the Jesuits

Among the new religious orders of the sixteenth century was the Society of Jesus, or the Jesuits. The Jesuits were founded by Saint Ignatius of Loyola (1491–1556).

As a young man, Ignatius was a soldier, with thoughts of fighting heroic battles. When a serious injury left him bedridden for a period of time, Ignatius began to examine his life. With time on his hands, he began reading about the lives of the saints, such as Saint Francis and Saint Dominic. Gradually Ignatius began to realize that only a life lived for God had any meaning for him. Following the example of

Live It!

How to Make a Good Choice

During his conversion process, Saint Ignatius of Loyola wrote down his thoughts and feelings. Later he composed the Spiritual Exercises, outlining a path to making decisions about one's life. This is a short summary of the process of making a good choice:

1. A good choice can be made only if all the alternatives are good and positive ones.
2. A good choice must be a free choice; that is, we must set aside preferences and preconceptions, as well as any other pressures (like peer pressure). This is called detachment.
3. A good choice requires effort. We must truly want what God wants for us. We must trust our feelings to indicate what decision will bring us closer to Jesus. But this is only possible if we have been following Jesus in a consistent way.

Saint Francis, he abandoned his military life and committed himself to a life of labor for God. He began to study to become a priest.

In the 1530s Ignatius organized a group of six of his fellow students at the University of Paris into a religious fraternity. He began to lead them in a process of conversion based on his Spiritual Exercises. In 1534 the group professed vows of poverty, chastity, and later obedience, including obedience to the Pope. The group's main purpose was to spread the Christian message by preaching and teaching. The Society of Jesus, as the followers of Ignatius were now known, was approved by Pope Paul III in 1540.

Throughout their history the Jesuits have placed a great emphasis on education and have made significant contributions to the education of the laity and ordained ministers by founding universities and seminaries. In addition, the Spiritual Exercises of Saint Ignatius have contributed to the religious formation of countless Christians. Our current Pope, Pope Francis, is a member of the Society of Jesus.

Teresa of Ávila and the Carmelites

Saint Teresa of Ávila is one of three women who have been named Doctors of the Church. This title signifies that her contribution to Christian doctrine has benefited the entire Church.

© Javier García Blanco/iStockphoto.com

Teresa of Ávila entered the convent at a young age. However, she soon realized that the monastery that was supposed to be a place for contemplation and prayer was instead a place of materialism and superficial preoccupations. Teresa recognized that her convent, like many others in the years before the Catholic Reformation, had lost its focus on God. Her attempts at reforming the convent met much opposition. Teresa eventually decided to establish her own convent in Ávila, Spain. Her convent was a place of poverty and simplicity. The women who joined Teresa were encouraged to make Jesus the center of their lives. These sisters became known as the Discalced (meaning "without shoes") Carmelites—named for the simplicity of their footwear. Teresa eventually started other reformed Carmelite monasteries throughout Spain.

In her travels Teresa met Saint John of the Cross (1542–1591), the Spanish Carmelite friar and mystic. She convinced

John to bring her reforms to the men's religious houses. Teresa and John kept up a correspondence that leaves us with a rich treasure of their spiritual reflections. Both have also written works that continue to influence Christian spirituality today. Teresa's *The Interior Castle* describes how one can come to know and love God through prayer; Saint John of the Cross's *Dark Night of the Soul* is a poem that narrates the journey of the soul as it reaches union with God.

Other Saints and Reformers

As the teachings of the Council of Trent became absorbed into the life of the Church, many holy people took up the call to make real the Council's reforms at all levels of the Church. Let's take a look at a few key figures.

Saint Peter Canisius

Peter Canisius (1521–1597) made an important contribution to the Catholic Reformation in Germany. Soon after completing his university studies, he joined the Jesuits. In 1546 he was ordained. He traveled throughout Europe, especially Germany, to promote Catholic reforms. He attended several sessions of the Council of Trent and was later assigned to implement some of the Council's decrees. Peter provided counsel to princes and bishops. He founded universities and published several successful catechisms.

Saint Charles Borromeo

Charles Borromeo (1538–1584) was archbishop of Milan. During the Counter-Reformation he was responsible for a number of important reforms in the Church. Borromeo

Catholic Wisdom

The Wisdom of Saint Francis de Sales

Saint Francis de Sales was a wise spiritual director. Here are a few of his counsels:

"Have patience with all things, but first of all with yourself."

"Nothing is so strong as gentleness, nothing so gentle as real strength."

"Be who you are and be that well."

Because of his writings, Saint Francis de Sales is honored as the patron of writers, editors, and journalists.

believed that abuses in the Church often stemmed from clerical ignorance. Among his most important contributions to the Church were the seminaries he established for the education of priests.

Saint Robert Bellarmine

Another important figure in the Counter-Reformation was Robert Bellarmine (1542–1621). Bellarmine was an Italian Jesuit and a cardinal. He put into effect some of the reforms of the Council of Trent and wrote about the importance of the residence of bishops in their dioceses, a reform called for by the Council. In his writings Bellarmine attempted to

Cultural Developments after Trent

The Protestant Reformation and the Counter-Reformation brought about a number of cultural and artistic changes. In architecture, Renaissance art gave way to a new art form known as Baroque, a style known for its dramatic and exuberant detail. The style was in part a product of the Council of Trent and reflected the post-Reformation confidence of the Church while standing in opposition to the minimalist Protestant ethos.

In the eighteenth century, the Baroque style developed into an exaggeratedly ornate form called Rococo. For the Church, music in the post-Reformation focused on the Latin texts of the Mass. The high point of the period is seen in the works of Palestrina (1526–1594), a late Renaissance composer whose works have had a lasting influence on liturgical music.

systemize conflicting and controversial religious ideas of the time.

Saint Francis de Sales

Francis de Sales (1567–1622) was Bishop of Geneva, a Protestant stronghold with intense anti-Catholic sentiments. Francis was an accomplished preacher who used his oratory skills to win Protestants back to the Church. He is known for his spiritual writings. His *Introduction to the Devout Life* tells Christians in all walks of life of the importance of prayer and devotion to God, and stresses the importance of the Sacraments as a means of grace.

Saint Jane Frances de Chantal

Inspired by Saint Francis de Sales, whom she met while he was preaching in Dijon, Jane of Chantal (1572–1641) founded a religious order for women, the Order of the Visitation of Holy Mary, after the death of her husband. ♱

Part Review

1. Briefly state the Council of Trent's teaching on the Sacraments.

2. Briefly state the Council's teaching on the Eucharist.

3. In what ways did the Church's reforms of the sixteenth century lead to the founding of new religious orders, and how did those religious orders promote the reforms in response?

4. What important reforms related to the priesthood did the Council of Trent bring about?

5. How did the Society of Jesus contribute to the Church's reforms?

6. What important texts were published after the Council of Trent to bring some of the Council's teachings to the laity?

Part 3

The Church in the New World

Every student who has studied American history knows the date 1492. This, of course, is the year when Christopher Columbus arrived in the New World, claiming territory for the Spanish crown. This event and date that are so embedded into the fabric of our national history and identity heralded what was to become the Age of Exploration, a period lasting from the early fifteenth century to the late seventeenth century. During this time scientific discoveries of the scholastics and humanists enabled explorers to cross the oceans from Europe into new worlds. Monarchs often sponsored such expeditions in search of riches, such as gold and spices, and new colonies. These expeditions usually included a spiritual mission as well, to evangelize the natives of these foreign lands and to lead them to salvation. Jesuit, Dominican, and Franciscan missionaries often accompanied the explorers, and set out to bring the Good News to the indigenous populations. The sixteenth- and seventeenth-century missions to Latin America, Asia, and North America and their effects and outcomes are the focus of the next three articles.

The articles in this part address the following topics:

32 Missions to Latin America

The year Columbus arrived in the New World on an expedition for the Spanish crown was a high point in Spain's Catholic history. This was the year that the Muslims had been defeated in Granada, in Southern Spain. The country was once again, for the first time since Muslims had first crossed into Iberia in 711, a wholly Christian nation. At this time Spain was the most powerful country in Europe and was looking outward, seeking to cultivate its growing wealth and influence in foreign lands, through exploration, conquest, and evangelization.

conquistadors
Spanish for "conquerors," the name for the Spanish soldiers and explorers who brought much of the Americas under Spanish rule in the fifteenth and sixteenth centuries.

Explorers and Conquerors

In the 1500s when the Spaniards arrived in Mexico and South America, they encountered thriving native civilizations. In Mexico the Aztecs had built an advanced and sophisticated empire, with an impressive civil structure and building projects. Similarly, in Peru and the Andes, in South America, the Incas had a flourishing and vibrant civilization.

Despite their achievements, the Incas and the Aztecs were no match for the Spanish **conquistadors**. In Mexico, Hernando Cortés and his band of conquistadors massacred the Aztecs and looted their cities in search of gold. In Peru, Francisco Pizzaro led an expedition against the Incas and stole their treasures. Among the native peoples of both cultures, many of those not massacred were either enslaved or fell victim to disease, particularly small pox. By the middle of the sixteenth century, the formerly powerful Aztec and Incan empires had fallen, and their citizens were subject to Spanish colonial rule.

Missionaries and Holy People

Often exploring expeditions brought with them Catholic missionaries. These priests and friars, often Dominican and Franciscan, were to bring the native peoples into the Catholic fold through evangelization and Baptism. For the Spanish crown, this desire was motivated by two goals. First, the monarch of Spain, a country with deep ties and loyalty to the Catholic Church, had a true desire to bring the salvation

© Private Collection / Index / The Bridgeman Art Library International

Missionaries persuaded the Spanish State Council to adopt new policies regarding the indigenous people of South America. Practices didn't change though: most conquistadors were more interested in gold than in justice.

won by the cross of Christ to the unbaptized. The second and perhaps sometimes greater goal was adherence of the natives to the faith (and the culture) of their conquerors, which would ensure their cooperation and submission.

The missionaries who accompanied the colonizers frequently protested against the conquistadors' treatment of the native peoples. Rather than a quest for gold and riches, the missionaries were on a quest to save souls.

Bartolomé de las Casas

The Dominican friars were often the most outspoken—and sometimes the only—defenders of the Indians. One Dominican in particular, Bartolomé de las Casas (1484–1566), committed his life to this work. He appealed to the Spanish crown to end the system of *encomienda* and slavery. *Encomienda* was a system in which a person, usually associated with the conquering Spaniards, was entrusted with the care of a group of Indians, in exchange for their labor. In effect,

Live It!

The Church in Latin America Today

The people of Latin America have borne a turbulent history. Although much progress has been made, many of the people still live in great poverty. The United States Conference of Catholic Bishops (USCCB) has established a Subcommittee on the Church in Latin America, and each year, on the fourth Sunday in January, a special collection is taken up for the Church in Latin America. As chairman of the subcommittee, Archbishop José H. Gomez said, "From Caracas to Cochabamba, from Argentina to the Antilles, the Collection for the Church in Latin America helps to strengthen communion within the Church in the American continent, which is home to half the world's Catholics" (USCCB news release, April 28, 2010).

How can you contribute to the support and care of the Church in Latin America?

this became a form of slavery. Las Casas wrote and preached extensively in defense of the rights of the Indians.

To the other Christian evangelizers, his message was simple: You will win over many more converts to Christ if you treat them with respect and dignity. This is what Bartolomé de las Casas said himself:

> The safest way to proceed, the only rule which Christians should observe when they are in pagan countries, is to give a good example by virtuous works, in such a way that, according to the words of our redeemer, "seeing your works, they may praise and glorify your Father" and may think that a God who has such worshippers can only be good and true.

Las Casas depicted the horrors inflicted by the conquistadors in *A Very Brief Narrative of the Destruction of the Indians*. In 1542 King Charles V of Spain passed the New Laws, which did away with the *encomienda*. However, Las Casas's struggle to defend the Indians' rights continued throughout his lifetime.

Saint Martin de Porres

Martin de Porres (1579–1639) was the illegitimate son of a freed slave and a Spanish nobleman. As a young man, he experienced the cruel treatment inflicted on the lower classes of society in his native Peru. When Martin joined the Dominicans as a lay brother, he dedicated his life to the care of the poor and mistreated, tending to the slaves arriving on ships from Africa, and aiding the poor and the sick in the streets of Lima.

Saint Rose of Lima

Like Saint Martin de Porres, Rose of Lima (1586–1617) brought many to the Christian faith in Lima, Peru. Rose was a member of the Third Order of Dominicans and dedicated her life to fasting and prayer. Her reputation for holiness during her lifetime and the many miracles attributed to her following her death brought many believers to the Church. Together, Saint Rose of Lima and Saint Martin de Porres are the patron saints of Peru.

Saint Peter Claver

When Saint Peter Claver (1580–1654) arrived in Cartagena, Colombia, in 1610, from his native Spain, the city was the principal slave market of the New World. Thousands of enslaved people from Africa were brought there each month aboard slave ships in unspeakable conditions. Chained in the cargo hold, with disease and hunger rampant, many did not survive the journey.

Our Lady of Guadalupe

The Basilica of Our Lady of Guadalupe in Mexico City is the second most visited Christian shrine in the world today (after Lourdes, in France). The basilica and its history are a national treasure of the people of Mexico.

On December 9, 1531, the Virgin Mary appeared to a peasant named Juan Diego when he was on his way to Mass in the countryside near what is today Mexico City. Mary appeared as a young, pregnant native woman and spoke to Juan Diego in his native language. She asked him to ask the bishop to build a church on Tepeyac Hill, where she appeared. Juan did as Mary requested but was directed by the bishop to provide a sign that his message was truly from Mary.

Before Juan Diego could travel back to the Tepeyac Hill to ask Mary for a sign, he journeyed to visit a dying uncle. He encountered Mary along the way, and she assured him that his uncle was cured, and asked him to go instead to the bishop and to bring him flowers from the hillside. Juan Diego did as Mary asked of him. When he unfolded his cloak to reveal the flowers to the bishop, he and the bishop were astonished to see Mary's image imprinted on the cloak, just as Juan had seen her.

The bishop had the sign he needed and did as Mary instructed. As word of the miraculous events spread, the apparition site became a place of prayer and pilgrimage. In the years that followed, millions of Mexico's native peoples were baptized. Today Mexico remains a predominantly Catholic nation, with nearly 85 percent of its population belonging to the Catholic Church.

After his ordination in 1616, Saint Peter Claver dedicated himself to the care of the African slaves. He would board slave ships upon their arrival and tend to those who were dying and sick. In addition to ministering to the physical needs of the enslaved Africans, Claver defended their rights and often preached a message of Christian charity in the city square. Through Claver's acts of Christian charity and his preaching, thousands of people were converted and baptized. ✝

enculturation

The process of learning the requirements of a new or adopted culture and acquiring values and behaviors appropriate or necessary to live within that culture.

Article 33 Missions in the Far East

Around the time Spanish explorers arrived in South America, and missionary activity began on that continent, missionaries were also arriving in the Far East—in India, China, and Japan.

Missionaries in India

Saint Francis Xavier (1506–1552) was a driving force for the spread of the Gospel in India. In 1542 Francis and a small group of Jesuits arrived in Goa, on the west coast of India. Xavier reached out to the natives with gentleness and kindness. He would gather locals around him and teach them the Commandments, the Lord's Prayer, and the Hail Mary, and would explain Jesus' message of love and mercy. Thousands converted and were baptized. Xavier and his fellow missionaries later moved on to Ceylon (known today as Sri Lanka), an island off India's southern coast. Here too many converted and were baptized, and missionary schools and churches were established.

A later figure who played an important role in the evangelizing of India is Robert de Nobili (1577–1656), another Jesuit. De Nobili tried to adapt Christianity to the Indian culture. He believed that by respecting Indian traditions he could lead the Indians to acceptance of the Gospel message.

De Nobili's emphasis on **enculturation** carried over into the ordination and education of clergy. In India and Ceylon, native Indians were ordained into the priesthood to carry on the work of the Jesuit missionaries.

By the mid 1700s, the Church was well established in one state of India, and scores of churches had been opened in Ceylon. By 1900 Catholicism, though still a minority religion in predominantly Hindu nation, had spread throughout India and Ceylon.

Japan: Faith Amid Persecution

During his travels Francis Xavier met and converted a young Japanese man who persuaded him to bring the Christian faith to Japan. Xavier and his companions arrived in Japan in 1549 and began their work of spreading the Gospel.

Gradually the Jesuits constructed small churches among the Buddhist and Shinto temples of southern Japan. Soon more Jesuits, and later Franciscans and Dominicans, arrived in Japan and continued to covert and baptize. Within thirty or so years of the arrival of Francis Xavier and the first group of missionaries, nearly 200,000 Japanese had been baptized.

Unfortunately, the tide was about to turn. The Japanese ruler grew increasingly suspicious of the new faith, and persecutions began. In 1597 twenty-six Christians—Franciscan and Jesuit missionaries along with seventeen laymen—were executed by crucifixion in Nagasaki. Persecutions continued sporadically. In 1614 Christianity was officially banned. In the ensuing years, dozens of foreign missionaries and more than thirty thousand Japanese Christians were killed.

Saint Mary's Cathedral in Tokyo illustrates how the local aesthetic influences church art and architecture around the world.

© Barry Cronin/ZUMA/Corbis

Catholic Wisdom

Patrons of the Missions

The two patrons of the missions are Saint Francis Xavier and Saint Thérèse of Lisieux (1873–1897). Although Saint Thérèse volunteered for a Carmelite monastery in Hanoi, Vietnam, ill health prevented her going. However, she supported two missionary priests through her letters and prayers. From her cloister, her prayers went out to the entire world: "I would be a missionary . . . from the beginning of creation until the consummation of the ages" (*Story of a Soul*, page 193).

The faith continued to be practiced in secret and was kept alive in hiding for more than two hundred years. When French missionaries arrived in Nagasaki in the 1860s, they were astonished to find Japanese already declaring themselves as Christian. Without priests, elders had led Sunday prayers, baptized, and passed the faith on to the next generations. Despite a period of brief persecution in the 1860s, the faith continued to grow. Today there are about half a million Catholics in Japan, with Nagasaki home to the largest Catholic community.

The Church in China

Although Jesuit, Dominican, and Franciscan missionaries had previously attempted to gain entry into China, missionaries were not able to make inroads into the country until the Italian Jesuit Matteo Ricci (1552–1610) gained entry into China's imperial court. Ricci's knowledge of astronomy and other sciences, sought after by the Chinese, provided a way in. As he became known in imperial circles, he began to introduce his religion.

Ricci adopted the language and dress of his host country. He respected Chinese civilization and tradition and tried to show how Christianity could complement those traditions. Ricci translated Western texts on science into Chinese and wrote books about Christianity in a way that would appeal to Chinese scholars.

Ricci's respect for Chinese culture was adopted in the missionary work of other Jesuits who followed into China. Soon the liturgy in China was offered in Chinese rather than Latin.

By the mid-seventeenth century, nearly 150,000 Chinese people had been baptized into the Christian faith. In 1692 the emperor issued an edict tolerating Christianity, and the Jesuits continued their ministry in China.

Although the **Congregation for the Propagation of the Faith** initially endorsed the Jesuits' method of ministry, the Spanish friars had repeatedly voiced objection. In 1704 the Pope sided with the friars and banned the Chinese-language Mass and approved the notion that native people in missionary lands should adopt Western customs along with the Christian faith.

Congregation for the Propagation of the Faith
A Vatican office created in 1622 by Pope Gregory XV to coordinate and oversee foreign missionary activity.

Because of this the emperor became suspicious of the missionaries' motives, believing they wanted to subject the Chinese people to Western rule. He outlawed all Christian missionary work and expelled all missionaries. Chinese Catholics were now subject to persecution. Some who did not renounce their faith were executed as traitors. China opened up to the West again in the mid-1800s. Catholic missionaries, including women's religious orders, such as the

The Church in China Today

When Chairman Mao established the People's Republic of China in 1949, all religious activity other than that led by government-sponsored organizations was banned. Therefore today in China the Catholic faith can be practiced only under state supervision, with liturgical services conducted in state-approved churches, under the authority of the Chinese Catholic Patriot Association (CCPA). The CCPA does not accept the primacy of the Pope.

Since the founding of the People's Republic, clergy who resisted China's policy were subject to imprisonment, torture, and even martyrdom. In 2000 Cardinal Kung of Shanghai died after spending thirty years in prison for defying China's claim to authority over the Catholic Church in China. Today Catholics who are loyal to the Pope must worship in secret, for fear of persecution. It is estimated that nearly eight million Catholics in China are part of this underground Church. Another five million or so belong to the Church controlled by the CCPA.

© Fritz Hoffmann/In Pictures/Corbis

Daughters of Charity, again entered the country. By the early twentieth century, nearly half a million Chinese people had been baptized into the Church. ✟

Article 34 Missions to North America

Missions were established in America primarily by the Spanish and the French, with the Spanish dominating three regions—modern-day Florida; the southwest (Texas and New Mexico); and California. Texas and New Mexico, however, were settled by Spaniards from Mexico rather than from Europe. For the French, successes (albeit short-lived) were limited to the northern territories (New York and Maine) and Canada.

Before looking at mission settlements by region, let's take a brief look at the nature of mission settlements in general.

Missions in America

Missions in America were intended to fulfill a variety of functions, some economic, others religious. Along with a desire to spread the faith and to convert natives, specifically Indians, missionaries sought to "civilize" the natives. They did this by introducing the natives to European agricultural techniques, as well as Western learning and language, and by influencing them to abandon their native and tribal customs. A mission was typically a self-sustaining community where the priests or friars worked, farmed, and taught. From here the missionaries could evangelize and educate the native population. Often the natives were encouraged to establish settlements near the missions.

Mission life was often fraught with challenges and hardships. Sometimes the mission communities were unable to sustain themselves and lived with scarcity. The greatest threat, however, often came from the missionaries' interaction with the Indians. Despite some successes many Indian tribes rejected the advances of the Christian missionaries, seeing them as a tool of suppression or exploitation. At times Indian response was unpredictable, with initial acceptance followed by violent rebellion. Friars and priests, along with other European settlers, were sometimes violently mas-sacred. Of course, there were often grave consequences for the Indians too. A particularly insidious threat was exposure to European disease, which at times swept through native populations in epidemic proportions. Thus for both the evangelizers and the evangelized, the history of missions in North America is a poignant one.

Missions in Florida and the Southwest

Spain established the first missions in Florida in the second half of the sixteenth century. The spiritual motive was to convert the Indian natives to the Christian faith. However, as with missionary activity elsewhere in the new world, a desire to claim territory was also a factor. Beginning with Saint Augustine in 1565, Spain eventually established twenty-one missions in the Florida territory. Although the first missions were founded by the Jesuits, it was the Franciscans who had the more lasting presence in Florida. Both, however, faced chronic hostility from the Seminole Indians, often resulting in massacres of the missionaries. The challenges of retaining the missions in Florida became untenable over time, and by 1769 no missions remained in the territory.

In the Southwest, it was the Franciscans who founded the missions that spread throughout parts of Texas and New Mexico. In Texas the Franciscans founded twenty-one mis-sions, with several concentrated in San Antonio. Today the most famous of these, established in 1718 as San Antonio de Valero, is more commonly known as the Alamo, a key battle site in the Mexican-American War. In New Mexico, more than forty missions were founded. The most notable of these is Santa Fe. Mission activity in the Southwest declined throughout the eighteenth century and had all but ceased by the start of the nineteenth century.

Missions in California

As elsewhere the missions in California were established to Christianize the natives but also to protect Spain's interest in the territory.

The missions, founded by the Franciscans, became economic centers where Indians were taught the trades, such as carpentry and masonry, as well as farming techniques.

Yet not all the practices of the missions favored or suited the Indians. Cooperation was often strictly enforced. After Baptism the Indians were no longer considered free to leave the mission. They had to participate in the mission's work and worship under the supervision of the priests. Attempting escape and minor infractions would be met with severe penalties such as flogging.

The mission way of life did not find a receptive audience with the Indians, and many attempted to escape. Occasionally the Indians responded through rebellions and bloody uprisings. Tens of thousands of Indian Baptisms are recorded in California during the mission years, yet the marriage of European culture and Indian customs never reached a comfortable level. For this and other reasons, mission activity

This map, believed to have been published in 1718, represents in pink the extent of French settlement of the New World. The southern portion of the continent, marked here as "La Louissiane," was a French colony.

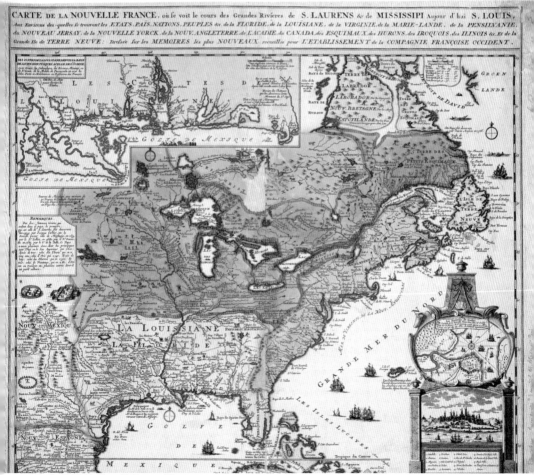

CARTE DE LA NOUVELLE FRANCE, où se voit le cours des Grandes Rivieres de S. LAURENS & de MISSISIPI Aujour d'hui S. LOUIS, Aux Environs des-quelles se trouvent les ETATS, PAIS, NATIONS, PEUPLES &c de la FLORIDE, de la LOUISIANE, de la VIRGINIE, de la MARIE-LANDE, de la PENSILVANIE, du NOUVEAU JERSAY, de la NOUVELLE YORCK, de la NOUV. ANGLETERRE de L'ACADIE, du CANADA, des ESQUIMAUX des HURONS, des IROQUOIS, des ILINOIS &c. Et de la Grande Ile de TERRE NEUVE: Dressée sur les MEMOIRES les plus NOUVEAUX, recueillis pour L'ETABLISSEMENT de la COMPAGNIE FRANÇOISE OCCIDENT.

Blessed Junipero Serra

More so than in any other time and place, the missions in California are closely identified with the work of one man in particular—the Franciscan Junipero Serra, appointed head of the Franciscans in California by the Spanish governor. Blessed Junipero Serra, though already fifty years old at the time of his appointment, led the founding of the Mission San Diego de Alcalá in 1769, and went on to personally establish eight other missions, including Mission San Luis Obispo and Mission San Juan Capistrano. By the time of his death in 1784, twenty-one missions were operating in California.

Today Blessed Junipero Serra is honored for his vast contribution to California's history. Throughout the state, streets and freeways bear his name, and statues stand in tribute to him. In the National Statuary Hall in the U.S. Capitol, a statue of Brother Junipero Serra is one of two statues representing the state of California.

waned within decades of the founding of the first mission, and by 1832 no active missions remained in California.

French Missions

Whereas Spanish missionary work began in Latin America and then expanded northward, France's missionary activity began in North America. It was the Franciscans who first arrived in Canada, in 1615. But their mission efforts faltered. They were succeeded by the Jesuits, who first arrived in Quebec in 1625. The Jesuits began their work with the French settlers, traders, and nearby Indians. Over time they extended their missionary activities west to the Huron nation, situated about a hundred miles north of present-day Toronto, where they established a settlement in 1639. A French presence soon extended into New York.

The Jesuits met success in evangelizing the Hurons and made many converts, but they faced an increasing threat from the Iroquois nation to the southeast. In New York State, the French Jesuits found themselves caught in the hostilities between the Huron nation and the Five Nations of the Iroquois. The Jesuits became a target of Iroquois aggression, and in the 1640s, several were martyred, including Isaac Jogues, Jean de Brebeuf, and others. These Jesuits have become known as the North American Martyrs, and were canonized in the 1930s. ✝

Pray It!

A Huron Christmas Carol

This carol was written by Saint Jean de Brebeuf in the Huron language, and this is a literal English translation. As we pray it, we are reminded that Jesus comes for all of us, of every time and culture.

Have courage, you who are human beings: Jesus, he is born.
The oki spirit who enslaved us has fled.
Don't listen to him for he corrupts the spirits of our thoughts.
Jesus, he is born.

Three men of great authority have left for the place of his birth.
Tichion, the star appearing over the horizon leads them there.
That star will walk first on the path to guide them.
Jesus, he is born.

They say, "Let us place his name in a position of honor.
Let us act reverently towards him for he comes to show us mercy."
It is the will of the spirits that you love us, Jesus,
and we wish that we may be adopted into your family.
Jesus, he is born.

(Translated by John Steckley)

Part Review

1. What were some injustices inflicted on the native peoples in the New World and what steps did the missionaries take to defend the natives' rights?

2. Bartolomé de las Casas's missionary philosophy was essentially that one can win over many more converts to Christ through an attitude of respect and dignity. How can you apply this approach in your own life today?

3. Summarize the history of the missions in California and the work of Blessed Junipero Serra in establishing the missions.

4. Describe the practice of enculturation as it was applied by Matteo Ricci and Robert de Nobili and tell why this approach can lead to successful evangelization.

5. Summarize the history of the Catholic Church in China and describe the situation for the Church in China today.

6. What were some of the challenges and hardships faced by the missionaries to North America working with the Native Americans?

7. Saint Francis Xavier is often called the Apostle of the Indies. Describe the missionary work that earned Saint Francis this title.

The Church in the Modern Era

Part 1

The Church in the Age of Reason and Revolution

During the medieval period, the Church and faith in God were foremost in the lives of the people of Europe. During the Renaissance humanist thought began to take root, and a new emphasis was placed on the value of human abilities and contributions, replacing, in some spheres, the view that God was the source of all good that existed in the world. Then came the Age of Reason. During this period, in the seventeenth and eighteenth centuries, God was not just relegated to a sometimes secondary place in relation to the human experience; he was marginalized by an influential group of philosophers, many of whom went so far as to attempt to prove that God did not exist.

The Age of Reason, also called the Enlightenment, and its aftermath, particularly in the form of the revolution in France, brought about significant and lasting changes for European society and for the Church. As we will see in this part, some of these changes had positive outcomes, gained at a terrible price.

The articles in this part address the following topics:

- Article 35: The Age of Reason (page 161)

- Article 36: The French Revolution (page 164)

- Article 37: The Effects of the Enlightenment and the French Revolution (page 168)

Article 35 The Age of Reason

As Europe and the Church were transformed by the Renaissance, the Protestant Reformation, the Catholic Reformation, and the development of nationalistic ideals, a new way of thinking about religion, monarchy, and individual rights emerged. These new philosophies came to be known as the Age of Reason, or the Enlightenment, and they greatly transformed the course of history.

The Rise of Rationalist and Scientific Thought

In the seventeenth and eighteenth centuries, learning in science and mathematics was on the rise. Interest in the rational understanding of the universe that these disciplines could provide was growing. In place of faith in the mystery of God and his works, people sought measurable and quantifiable explanations for the world. Mathematicians and scientists such as Blaise Pascal and Isaac Newton could provide concrete, observable principles to explain the workings of the material world. The philosophy of these

Live It!

Use Your Head!

It may surprise you to learn that one important way we can know God is by reason—that is, by using the brains God gave us: "By natural reason man can know God with certainty, on the basis of his works" (*Catechism of the Catholic Church*, 50). Looking at the world around us (either informally, as we go from here to there, or more formally, as scientists do), we can learn about God. This is called natural revelation. However, historical conditions and the effects of Original Sin reduce our ability to know God through natural revelation alone. That is why God, in his wisdom and goodness, has freely chosen to make himself and his plan for humanity known to us. We call this Divine Revelation. He revealed his saving plan to us most fully by sending his own Divine Son, Jesus Christ. Both reason and Divine Revelation work together to bring us the truth about God. We never have to choose one or the other. We need both.

As you busily go about your days, rushing from classes to extracurricular activities to get-togethers with friends, take time to stop and notice the wonders of God's Creation, and to know him through the world he has made.

rationalism

A term that refers to a broad range of philosophical positions that maintain that human reason is the final determinant of truth.

deism

Belief that God exists and created the world but is not active in the universe or human life.

thinkers and others like them, which held that the universe was regulated completely by universal natural laws that could be explained by science, is called **rationalism**. In turn, the rationalists believed that these laws could be applied to human behavior. Accordingly, rationalists believed that people did not need the Bible or the Church as sources of truth and moral law. They believed that the human mind could govern human behavior without help from a divine authority. Even the rationalist philosophers who reasoned that God did exist rejected the idea of a personal God. They believed that although he had created the universe, God was not actively involved in it. This belief in a God who is distant and removed from the world and from the human experience is called **deism**. In effect, deism became the religion of the Enlightenment philosophers. However, deism was neither a formal religion nor a clearly defined one. Instead it was what might be called a natural religion, and it did not conform to God or his laws as defined in Sacred Scripture and through his Church.

Leading Enlightenment philosophers included Voltaire, Jean-Jacques Rousseau, and René Descartes. These philosophers wrote on a large spectrum of subjects, ranging from politics to art. A common theme their works address is the "natural rights" of man. They wrote for an educated audience, eager to read the newest Enlightenment works, and developed works in a range of artistic formats, from poetry to drama to political treatises. Some of the best-known works of the Enlightenment philosophers include Voltaire's *Candide*, a satire that unrelentingly pokes fun at religion and at the Church, especially those in monastic life. Rousseau's *On the Social Contract* was a modern political work making a strong case for democracy and individual empowerment. Rene Descartes' *Passions of the Soul* is a treatise on human emotions. Descartes is perhaps most commonly known for his philosophical statement "*Cogito ergo sum*" ("I think, therefore I am"), found in his *Principles of Philosophy*.

In his *Principles of Philosophy,* Descartes put forth the proposition that anyone who wants to know the truth should doubt everything as much as possible.

Empiricism and Science

Another movement and philosophy related to rationalism that also challenged religious faith was **empiricism**. Empiricists believed that all knowledge came through the senses and experience. In other words, what we know about the world we know by observing, hearing, tasting, touching, and smelling. Empiricists denigrated any belief based on faith. Faith in revelation and a loving and merciful God were chief among the "falsehoods" they disdained. Some empiricists, such as the British John Locke, tried to prove certain Christian beliefs as true because they could be proven by human experience. For example, Locke tried to show that the existence of God as Creator could be empirically known by observing the obvious order of the universe. Other philosophers sought to prove the opposite—that God could not exist. Empiricism had gained force in the 1700s because of the work of scientists such as Isaac Newton. Although Newton himself did not believe that science was at odds with

empiricism
The philosophical position that all human knowledge comes from experience—especially sensory experience.

Are Science and Religion Incompatible?

In the seventeenth century, the Italian astronomer Galileo Galilei (1564–1642), agreed with Copernicus's (1473–1543) theory that the earth rotated around the sun. At the time it was commonly believed that the earth was the center of the universe and that the sun revolved around the earth. This notion was held by ancient Greek philosophers and seemed to be supported by Sacred Scripture, in the Creation accounts in Genesis.

The Pope asked Galileo not to publish his findings, because they suggested that the Bible might be wrong. Galileo felt compelled to make his findings public, and published them. For this he was condemned and put under house arrest. During his papacy in 1992, Saint John Paul II expressed regret for this action and stated that there is no fundamental opposition between science and faith. Instead, as it did for Galileo, scientific knowledge can for all people contribute to the sense of wonder at God's Creation.

© Georgios Kollidas/Shutterstock.com

religion, some philosophers tried to use his scientific findings as evidence that the universe operated like a machine, guided by universal laws and not a divine being. Throughout Europe, and most dramatically in France, a new mood was setting in. This new atmosphere would greatly shape French history and bring about cataclysmic changes for the Church in France and lasting changes for all of Western society. ✝

Article 36 The French Revolution

The Age of Reason affected the way people thought about religion, science, and government. The longstanding belief that monarchs were endowed with a divine authority to rule was no longer accepted by the masses. Philosophers questioned the existence of God and taught about the natural rights of all people. In his *On the Social Contract*, French philosopher Rousseau stated that government, in order to be moral, must be built on the consent of the governed and must uphold individual political rights. In the eighteenth century, such ideas were revolutionary. For French society and for the Church, such ideas meant sweeping changes to the existing order.

The storming of the Bastille became a powerful symbol for the French Republican movement; the prison was a target because of its valuable stores of gunpowder.

© Chateau de Versailles, France / Giraudon / The Bridgeman Art Library

Revolution in France

In May 1789 King Louis XVI of France called the Estates General, the French Parliament, to Versailles to help resolve a financial crisis. Present at this general assembly were representatives of the three Estates: the First Estate, or the clergy; the Second Estate, or the nobility; and the Third Estate, or the commoners, most of whom were peasants. The Third Estate began a call for sweeping reforms to the autocratic rule of the monarchy and to economic policies that favored the First and Second Estates at their expense. On June 19, 1789, the First Estate voted to join the Third Estate in their calls for reform. In doing so they voluntarily gave up economic privileges, including tithes and exemption from taxes. Following this action the king ordered the Estates General to disperse, but his order was ignored. The king commissioned mercenary soldiers to defend his absolute power against the will of the people. This action enraged the masses, and on July 14, a mob of Parisians stormed the Bastille, a French prison that for the French was a symbol of the monarchy's oppression. This was the beginning of the French Revolution.

The anger of the crowd soon turned violent. Nearly one hundred Parisians died, and several prison guards were beheaded. In August 1789 the National Assembly, which had continued to meet and was growing more radical, passed the *Declaration of the Rights of Man and of the Citizen,* which defined the individual and collective rights of all the estates of France as universal, thereby declaring religious toleration.

The Church was now no longer protected by the monarchy and quickly became a target of the Revolution. On November 2, all Church property was nationalized. Religious men and women were forced out of their monasteries and convents. Church properties were seized and sold, with proceeds funding the Revolution. Laws were passed prohibiting the taking of religious vows and suppressing religious orders. Priests who refused to pledge support for the revolution were declared disloyal. Nearly forty thousand of them were forced into exile, and hundreds were killed. In January 1793 the king was beheaded, and the **Reign of Terror** began, resulting in the execution of thousands of nobles, priests, monks, and nuns.

Reign of Terror
A period of violence that occurred after the start of the French Revolution, marked by mass executions of "enemies of the revolution."

The Civil Constitution of the Clergy

The Civil Constitution of the Clergy (CCC) was a law passed on July 12, 1790, that subordinated the Church in France to the French government. As a result of the CCC, the number of dioceses in France was reduced by about 40 percent, from 135 to eighty three, with dioceses redrawn to match civil boundaries. Strict requirements were established regarding parish organization, with only one parish allowed for every six thousand citizens. Bishops and priests were to be elected and assigned by electors of civil leaders.

In November 1791 the National Assembly directed that all practicing clergy in France take an oath to uphold the Civil Constitution of the Clergy. Most bishops refused to do so. Among priests the response varied by region, but on the whole about half took the oath.

Pope Pius VI (1775–1799) condemned the CCC and the principles that had motivated the Revolution. He demanded that those who had taken the oath retract, and he prohibited bishops elected by civil electors from exercising their authority. There now existed two church structures in France—one loyal to the Pope and the other loyal to, and governed by, French civil authorities.

The French Revolution attempted to wipe out Christianity in France. At one point the leaders of the Revolution enthroned a stage dancer as the "goddess of reason" in the Cathedral of Notre Dame in Paris. They implemented a new calendar that wiped out all Christian holy days and replaced them with celebrations of reason and liberty. The Revolution declared a new religion, with one dogma—the immortality of the soul—and one moral principle—to do one's duty.

After the Revolution

Before long the bloodthirsty revolutionary leaders turned on one another and killed one another off. In 1795 a new government known as the Directory assumed control of the French state, and reversed some of the anti-Christian laws established by the Revolution. The Directory held power until 1799, when Napoleon Bonaparte assumed power in a military coup. Napoleon, recognizing the importance of the Catholic faith to the French people, restored many rights to the Church and protected the Catholic faith. However, Napoleon was motivated by personal gain and not by loyalty to the Church. In a concordat with Pope Pius VII (1800–1823), he allowed the Pope to name French bishops, but he required that the Pope not press for the return of Church properties confiscated during the Revolution. In 1808 Napoleon lay claim to the Papal States and imprisoned the Pope. In 1814 Napoleon was defeated by a combined force of other

Catholic Wisdom

Pope Pius VI Condemns the Principles of the Revolution

In a March 1791 letter known as *Quod aliquantum*, Pope Pius VI condemned the principles of the French Revolution. He described the "natural rights" promulgated by the Revolution contrary to God's Revelation and stated that they promoted individual freedoms at the expense of God's moral law. He wrote:

> [W]hat could be more senseless than to establish among men equality and this unbridled freedom which seems to quench reason. . . . What is more contrary to the rights of the creator God who limited human freedom by prohibiting evil, than "this liberty of thought and action which the National Assembly accords to man in a society as an inalienable right of nature"?

European nations. A limited form of French monarchy was briefly restored, and the Papal States were returned to the papacy. ✝

Article 37 Effects of the Enlightenment and the French Revolution

Given the terrible human cost and the losses to the Church resulting from the Enlightenment and the Revolution that the movement incited in France, the obvious conclusion may at first seem to be that these events were an affliction from which no good could come. However, the analysis is not that simple.

Fruits of the Enlightenment

One cultural historian called the Enlightenment "the last of the great European heresies" (Christopher Dawson, *Progress and Religion*, page 192). If, in fact, the Enlightenment can be likened to a heresy, then another parallel can be drawn: like the heresies of earlier times in the Church's history, which frequently resulted in clarifications and strengthening of the Church's teaching, this heresy also yielded some positive outcomes. In his reflections on politics and history in *Memory and Identity*, Pope Saint John Paul II had this to say about the Enlightenment:

> The European Enlightenment not only led to the carnage of the French Revolution but also bore positive fruits, such as the ideals of liberty, equality, and fraternity, values which are rooted in the Gospel. . . . [T]he French Enlightenment paved the way for a better understanding of human rights. (Page 107)

The preamble states the Constitution's purpose: "to form a more perfect Union, establish Justice, insure domestic Tranquility, provide for the common defence, promote the general Welfare and secure the Blessings of Liberty. . . ."

Among the positive effects of the Enlightenment and the French Revolution that Saint John Paul II names are the rights of nations to exist and to exercise political sovereignty and the abolition of feudal traditions. The latter outcome directly affects our own history, as the war for American independence and the ratification of the U.S. Constitution took place in the shadow of the Enlightenment. As Saint John Paul II also notes, the values of liberty, equality, and fraternity espoused by the Enlightenment were also critical to the enunciation of the values of social justice rooted in Jesus' teachings in the Gospels. (The principles of social justice will be the focus of a later article in this text.)

Saints of Post-Revolution France

Although the nineteenth century was a time of challenges for the Church in France, it was also a time of a reemergence of deep faith and zeal for God and his Church. Here are some saints who contributed to the renewal of the faith during this period:

Saint John Vianney (1786–1859), known as the Curé of Ars, was a gifted pastor who brought many back to the faith through his homilies and his spiritual counsel. He is known for his pastoral work in his parish, where he heard confession for many hours each day, and for the spiritual transformation he brought to his community and its surroundings.

Saint Catherine Labouré (1806–1876) was a sister of the Daughters of Charity, in Paris. In the 1830s she experienced visions of the Virgin Mary. In one apparition Mary showed Catherine the image that now appears on the medal known as the Miraculous Medal. Mary told Catherine to ask her spiritual director to  have the image reproduced on a medal, promising that all who wore it would receive great grace. After an investigation of Catherine's private revelation, the request was approved, resulting in a new devotion to Mary, the Immaculate Conception.

Saint Thérèse of Lisieux (1873–1897) entered the Carmelite Order at the young age of fifteen, with the permission of her bishop. Thérèse's wish was to serve God as a missionary. However, poor health prevented her from fulfilling this goal. She decided that she would instead serve God through her life of prayer and her "little way" to sainthood. Saint Thérèse wrote about her little way in *Story of a Soul*, emphasizing great love rather than great deeds. Her example and her writings have provided spiritual guidance for countless people seeking to grow in faith and in service to God.

Outcomes for the Church in France

Beginning in the early nineteenth century, a renewal of the Catholic faith emerged in France. Those who remained faithful to the Church or returned to the faith placed a renewed emphasis on piety and worship and the glorification of God through the Church's art, architecture, and music.

The nineteenth century also saw a rise in the number of religious orders and in the number of men and women joining the orders. In 1814 Pope Pius VII reestablished the Society of Jesus, which had been suppressed in 1773, and a surge of young men joined the order. In fact, during the papacy of Pius IX (1846–1878), the Jesuits doubled their membership.

Other new religious orders that began or were reestablished in France in the nineteenth century include the Marists, or Society of Mary, founded in 1816. The Sisters of Saint Joseph, an order originally founded in the seventeenth century but suppressed during the Revolution, was reestablished in 1807. In the 1830s members of this community were sent to Saint Louis, Missouri, and other U.S. cities, to care for the poor and to establish schools. The Congregation of Our Lady of Zion, founded in France in 1843, established missionary schools in the Holy Land and in other parts of the world. The religious orders that sprang up in France and in other regions of the world during this period were spurred by the reawakening of the Catholic faith that followed the Revolution, and in turn spurred the growth of the Church. ✝

Pray It!

The Miraculous Medal Prayer

The Miraculous Medal is a sacramental, a reminder of God's grace. On the front is an image of Our Lady, with this prayer written around the image: "O Mary, conceived without sin, pray for us who have recourse to thee."

On the back of the medal is a large *M*, for Mary, with a cross above it. Below the *M* are two hearts, one representing the Sacred Heart of Jesus, crowned with thorns, and the other the Immaculate Heart of Mary, pierced by a sword. These images are based in Sacred Scripture (see Mark 15:17 and Luke 2:34–35).

Pray the Miraculous Medal prayer in your times of need or simply to bring you closer to Mary and to her Son, Jesus Christ.

Part Review

1. Define *deism* and explain how its view of God is at odds with our own understanding of who God is.

2. Explain the principles of empiricism and tell why empirical methods are insufficient for attaining knowledge about God.

3. How did the position of the Church in France change after the French Revolution?

4. What were some of the negative consequences of the French Revolution for the Church in France?

5. Explain the Civil Constitution of the Clergy and tell why, for clergy, signing this oath is inconsistent with their call to serve the Church.

6. What were some positive outcomes for the Church in France after the Revolution?

Part 2

Pope Pius IX and Vatican I

As we have already learned, after the French Revolution, the Church experienced renewal with the birth of new religious orders and the growth of existing orders, such as the Jesuits, and a renewed emphasis on religious practices and piety. Still, during this period, modernist thought provided a persistent challenge for the Church as her beliefs, traditions, and practices were frequently at odds with the ideologies of the time.

During his papacy Pius IX worked to protect the Church from the assaults of modernism and to reaffirm her place in the modern world. His contributions include a strengthening of lay spirituality, a renewal of devotional practices, and his call for a new Ecumenical Council—Vatican Council I. At this Council two important constitutions were issued, one concerning papal infallibility and the other regarding the relationship between faith and reason.

The articles in this part address the following topics:

Article

38 Pope Pius IX and Religious Renewal

The nineteenth century was a time of dramatic religious, political, and social change. During this critical time for the Church, Pope Pius IX (1846–1878) clarified the role of the Church in the modern world, standing in firm opposition to modernism. This did not mean that the Church rejected everything modern in the world (that is, "modernity"); instead, it rejected the philosophy of modernism, which, as we shall see in article 46, Pope Pius condemned as erroneous. Pope Pius was a man of deep faith and holiness, devoted to the service of God and his Church. He was beatified in 2000. His pontificate lasted for thirty-two years, making him the longest reigning Pope in history.

Pius IX was Pope when the Church lost the Papal States (see article 17, "Charlemagne: Holy Roman Emperor"), including Rome, to the Italian revolutionaries in September 1870. Despite this temporal loss, during his reign Pope Pius IX greatly strengthened the spiritual authority of the Church.

© Bettmann/CORBIS

Pius IX was elected Pope two years before political upheaval marked a collapse of authority in 50 countries throughout Europe and parts of Latin America.

The Immaculate Conception

In 1854 Pope Pius declared the **dogma** of the Immaculate Conception. Mary, chosen by God to be the mother of his Son, was redeemed from the moment of her conception and born "full of grace," free from Original Sin. With the dogma of the Immaculate Conception, Pope Pius affirmed this truth in this way: "The most Blessed Virgin Mary was, from the first moment of her conception, by a singular grace and privilege of almighty God and by virtue of the merits of Jesus Christ, Savior of the human race, preserved immune from all stain of original sin"[1] (*CCC*, 491).

dogma
Teachings recognized as central to Church teaching, defined by the Magisterium and considered definitive and authoritative.

Syllabus of Errors

Concerned about the many philosophical and social movements that seemed to threaten the Church, Pius published the *Syllabus of Errors,* issued in 1864 as part of the encyclical

Our Lady of Lourdes

In 1858 the Blessed Mother appeared at Lourdes, France, to a young peasant girl named Bernadette Soubirous (1844–1879), who was later canonized. At age fourteen Bernadette reported the first of numerous apparitions in which she saw the Virgin Mary. Mary asked for a chapel to be built in her honor at Lourdes. Despite initial skepticism, a canonical investigation determined that Bernadette's claims were real. The shrine built at the site of Mary's apparitions to Bernadette became the most visited Catholic pilgrimage site in the world and is known for miraculous healings. In 2008 nearly fifty thousand people attended a Mass at the shrine commemorating the 150th jubilee of the first apparition. Each year Lourdes is visited by nearly five million pilgrims.

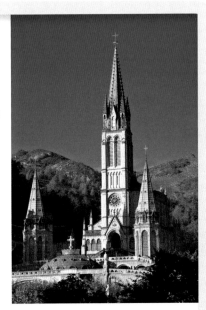

© Sylvain Sonnet/Corbis

fideism

A theological doctrine holding that religious truth is a matter of faith and cannot be established by reason.

pantheism

The belief that everything is God; in particular, the belief that God is identical to nature and everything in it, and that God therefore changes just as nature changes.

Quantra cura. The *Syllabus* was a scathing condemnation of eighty propositions held by liberals. These included **fideism, pantheism,** rationalism, socialism, modernism, liberal capitalism, and the authority of the state over the Church. Among the propositions condemned as errors were the following: "In this age of ours it is no longer useful that the Catholic religion should be considered the only religion of the state, to the exclusion of all other[s]" and "The Roman Pontiff can and should reconcile himself to progress, liberalism, and modern civilization."

Although Pope Pius's intent was to protect and defend the Church, these condemnations put him at odds with the movements of the time; further, to many, they made the Church appear as an enemy of individual rights and of progress. In the United States, for example, the *Syllabus* appeared to be attacking the freedoms established by the Bill of Rights. The Pope also appeared to be saying that the Catholic faith should be the religion of all people. This put him in conflict with the Protestant countries of Western Europe as well as the United States and all those who believed in the ideal of religious pluralism.

Religious Renewal

As we saw in article 37, "The Effects of the Enlighten-ment and the French Revolution," a number of religious orders were founded in France, as well as in other parts of the world, after the French Revolution. A number of these orders, such as the Salesians of Don Bosco, were established with the approval of Pope Pius IX. In addition, Pope Pius encouraged a renewal of the spiritual lives of Catholics by promoting frequent reception of the Sacraments and devo-tion to Mary. Pius also promoted devotion to the Sacred Heart of Jesus and in 1856 established a feast day honoring the Sacred Heart. Private devotion to the Sacred Heart dated back to the medieval Church, but this devotion became more popular in the seventeenth century, when Christ appeared to Saint Margaret Mary Alacoque (1647–1690) and revealed his physical heart as the representation of his divine love for humanity.

In 1868 Pope Pius convoked Vatican Council I, to address the rising influence of rationalism, materialism, and liberalism and to address the question of papal authority. The Council is the focus of article 39, "Vatican Council I." ✝

Live It!

Volunteer at Lourdes

For nearly sixty years, the U.S. National Rosary Pilgrimage has been sponsor-ing pilgrimages to Lourdes. This group asks young people to come and help with pushing wheelchairs, carrying flags in the daily processions, and just spending time with pilgrims, especially with those who have come burdened with illness. In addition, volunteers are given the opportunity to tour Lourdes and other significant places associated with the life of Saint Bernadette.

One participant wrote, "Lourdes gave me a different outlook on the world that surrounds us. . . . I learned that acceptance, solidarity, humility, and love are values of this new millennium and of the world that we owe to ourselves to improve."

If you cannot go to Lourdes, ask Our Lady to help you to find your own close-to-home way to help those who are sick or suffering.

Article 39 Vatican Council I

Pope Pius IX announced his desire to convoke a general council of the Church in 1864. He formally convoked the council in 1868. On December 8, 1869, 306 years after the Council of Trent, Vatican Council I—the twentieth Ecumenical Council of the Church—opened. More than seven hundred bishops, including forty-six from the United States, assembled at the Vatican Basilica for the council. In response to the needs of the time, the Council adopted two documents, *Dei Filius*, on faith and reason, and *Pastor Aeternus*, on papal infallibility.

© Bettmann/CORBIS

The First Vatican Council met in Saint Peter's Basilica, in Vatican City. Most papal ceremonies take place there, partly because of its enormous size, almost four acres.

Dei Filius

On April 24, 1870, the bishops of Vatican Council I unanimously adopted the dogmatic constitution on the Catholic faith, *Dei Filius*. In the face of the modern challenges of rationalism, fideism, and pantheism, the constitution affirmed the existence of a personal God who could be known by reason and through Revelation. The constitution further set forth the Church's teaching on the relationship between faith and reason and emphasized that there can be no conflict between the two.

Statements of *Dei Filius* include the following:

> If anyone says that the one true God, our Creator and Lord, cannot be known with certainty through his works in the natural light of human reason, let him be anathema.

> If anyone says that it is possible that the dogmas propounded by the church can, as a result of the progress of science, be given a meaning different from that which the church has understood and continues to understand, let him be anathema.

The Council, by approving this constitution, affirmed the validity of Revelation, the connection between faith and reason, and the Church's spiritual authority in matters related to the faith.

Pastor Aeternus

Although the question of papal infallibility had not been an intended focus of Vatican Council I, a majority of bishops called for an introduction of the discussion, and in March 1870 it was confirmed as a topic to be addressed by the Council. On July 18, 1870, the Council approved the constitution *Pastor Aeternus*. This constitution was an affirmation of papal primacy and infallibility: a fact of doctrine since the early Church, and one that became better understood over the centuries. Following is a statement from the document:

Catholic Wisdom

On the Infallibility of the Magisterium

The *Catechism of the Catholic Church* clarifies the doctrine of papal infallibility as follows:

> "The Roman Pontiff, head of the college of bishops, enjoys this infallibility in virtue of his office, when, as supreme pastor and teacher of all the faithful . . . he proclaims by a definitive act a doctrine pertaining to faith or morals. . . . The infallibility promised to the Church is also present in the body of bishops when, together with Peter's successor, they exercise the supreme Magisterium," above all in an Ecumenical Council.[2] (891)

ex cathedra

A Latin term literally meaning "from the chair," referring to pronouncements concerning faith or morals made by the Pope, acting with full Apostolic authority, as pastor and teacher of all Christians.

We . . . teach and define as a dogma divinely revealed: That the Roman Pontiff, when he speaks **ex cathedra** . . . , through the divine assistance promised him in blessed Peter, is endowed with that infallibility, with which the Divine Redeemer has willed that his Church—in defining doctrine concerning faith or morals—should be equipped. (In Henry Bettenson and Chris Maunder, editors, *Documents of the Christian Church*, page 277)

In other words, the Pope is infallible when, as the supreme pastor and teacher of the Church, he proclaims an authentic and definitive teaching about a question of doctrine. This infallibility does not apply to his private opinions as a theologian or to his specific ministry as the bishop of the See of Rome. Nor does papal infallibility mean that the Pope never makes a mistake and never commits a personal sin—the Pope is of course human, affected by Original Sin just as we are. Instead, papal infallibility extends as far as the deposit of Divine Revelation does, and it applies to any doctrinal proclamation that the Pope must make to preserve, explain, and observe the truths of the faith, including doctrinal questions concerning moral matters.

Pray It!

A Prayer for the Pope

During the Prayer of the Faithful at Mass, we pray for the Holy Father, that God may guide him as he leads the Church. Here is a prayer for the Holy Father that you can make part of your own prayers:

Lord, source of eternal life and truth, give to your shepherd, the Pope, a spirit of courage and right judgment, a spirit of knowledge and love.

By governing with fidelity those entrusted to his care may he, as successor to the Apostle Peter and Vicar of Christ, build your Church into a sacrament of unity, love, and peace for all the world.

We ask this through our Lord Jesus Christ, your Son, who lives and reigns with you and the Holy Spirit, one God, forever and ever. Amen.

(Roman Missal)

The Adjournment of the Council

When war broke out between France and Prussia, Napoleon III withdrew from Rome troops that had been protecting the Pope from Italian revolutionaries. As a result, the revolutionaries occupied Rome, leading Pope Pius IX to suspend the First Vatican Council just seven months after it opened, in late July 1870. The Council never reconvened. Thus the Council never took action on some issues the bishops had

Canon Law

Canon law is the set of laws (called canons), distinct from civil law, that provide for the governing of the Church and her members. Collections of Church laws began to appear in the fifth century. Such collections continued to be made through the Middle Ages. In 1139 Gratian, a Benedictine monk and jurist who taught at Bologna, completed a systematic compilation of canon law, the *Concordia discordantium canonum* (*Concord of Discordant Canons*) (later known simply as the *Decretum*). Gratian used scholastic methods to reconcile seemingly contradictory decretals, or canons, on ecclesial issues to compile this unified collection of all of the Church's canons.

Gratian's *Decretum* and other collections of decretals that supplemented it were compiled around 1500 to form the *Corpus Iuris Canonici* (*Body of Canon Law*). After receiving official approval in 1580, this collection formed the basis of Church law until 1917, when the first *Code of Canon Law* was promulgated to systemize the earlier *Corpus* and later legislation. The most recent *Code of Canon Law* for the Western Church was promulgated in 1983, to reflect the reforms of Vatican Council II.

intended to address. It was officially closed by Pope Saint John XXIII in 1960. ☩

Part Review

1. Explain the dogma of the Immaculate Conception.

2. In what ways did Pope Pius contribute to the renewal of the Church in the nineteenth century?

3. What was Pope Pius's intent in issuing the *Syllabus of Errors* and what were some of its effects?

4. What key points did the dogmatic constitution *Dei Filius*, issued at Vatican Council I, make about the relationship between faith and reason?

5. Explain the doctrine of papal infallibility.

6. Provide a brief time line of Vatican Council I.

Part 3

Catholics in America

Following the Protestant Reformation and the founding of the Anglican Church, Catholics in England began to face persecution, especially under Queen Elizabeth I. When a colony that promised freedom of worship to all was established in Maryland, a small group of Catholics came to America with the first colonial settlers. The seeds of an organized and lasting Church in America were sown. Under the guidance of the first American bishop, John Carroll, and through the contributions of other holy people, the Church in America began to take root and thrive. With the influx of European immigrants throughout the nineteenth century, the number of Catholics in America multiplied many times over. Sustained and enriched through the work of saints, missionaries, and countless other holy people (including bishops, priests, deacons, religious, and members of the laity), the Catholic Church in America thrived and made countless contributions to the nation.

The articles in this part address the following topics:

Article 40 The Church in America

In seventeenth-century England, after the Anglican Church had been founded, Catholics were subject to harsh treatment and discrimination under Queen Elizabeth I (1533–1603). When King James I (1566–1625) granted Lord Baltimore, a Catholic, land for an American settlement, the colony of Maryland, established in 1634, welcomed anyone who wanted to live there and extended freedom of worship to all. Many Catholics took refuge there. By 1704, however, non-Catholics in Maryland outnumbered Catholics, passing laws that discriminated against Catholics and deprived them of the right to have churches and to hold political office.

© Steven Wright/Shutterstock.com

The compass rose on this old map indicates that north is to the right; west is at the top. Find the falls on the Patowmeck River: the area below that is modern-day Washington, D.C. Baltimore Town is near the pink borderline.

From Discrimination to Freedom of Worship

Following the American Revolution, the U.S. Constitution and the Bill of Rights gave Catholics in America reason to be hopeful about their place in the new nation. The Constitution called for separation of church and state. Among other rights, the Bill of Rights gave all Americans freedom of worship. Although individual prejudices against Catholics did not vanish overnight, and in some states restrictions remained against Catholics, the climate in America had improved.

Despite the improved political climate, Catholics in America still faced practical challenges. At the end of the American Revolution, the thirty thousand or so Catholics in America were getting by with only a handful of priests available to minister to them. The Church was poor too, and finding funds to support priests and to build churches was difficult. In larger towns Catholic laypeople organized small parishes and tried to obtain at least the occasional services of a priest. A Maryland priest, the Jesuit John Carroll, took important steps to address the needs of the Church in America, and dramatically altered the outlook for Catholics.

A First Bishop for the Church in America

If it was to flourish, the Church in the United States needed a leader—a bishop. However, U.S. Catholics did not want a foreign bishop for the United States. After having won acceptance in the new country, they feared that having a foreign bishop appointed by the Pope might lead to suspicion about their loyalty to the new republic.

On March 12, 1788, a petition on behalf of the American priests was sent to Pope Pius VI (1775–1799) asking that at least in this first instance, the choice of bishop should be left to them. In July Pope Pius granted this request. The Pope also left to the priests the choice of the city in which the diocese would be located and authorized them to elect a bishop. They were then to present their choice to the Holy See for confirmation.

On May 18, 1789, the priests gathered, and after celebrating Mass, cast their votes. By a vote of twenty-four to two, John Carroll was elected as bishop of Baltimore. The Vatican approved his appointment, and in November 1789 he was named the first bishop of Baltimore.

Bishop Carroll worked hard to establish order in U.S. Catholic parishes. Many priestless parishes had been running their own affairs and expected to continue to do so. Many U.S. Catholics, fired up with the spirit of the new national democracy, wanted the Church to be run democratically too, with the voice of the people being the voice of God. Bishop Carroll's task was to maintain the support of American Catholics while also taking firm control of Church governance.

Other challenges Carroll faced included the need for priests who could speak the languages of non-English speaking newcomers to America. Some of the French missionaries who worked on the frontier still could not speak English either.

Despite the challenges, Carroll succeeded in planting in America the seeds of a Church that could grow and thrive. He did so by adopting a thoroughly American style, with a commitment to the principles of democracy and to separation of church and state, while also remaining fully loyal to the Pope. The Catholic Church in America had grown from a population of around thirty thousand at the end of the Revolution to a population of nearly 200,000 at the time of Carroll's death in 1815. And the growing Catholic population had established communities in new locales, away from the traditional Catholic strongholds of Philadelphia and Baltimore.

Although the shortage of priests remained a persistent problem, the number of priests in America had increased almost sixfold, thanks in part to three newly established seminaries. Women's religious orders also saw dramatic growth, and by 1815, European as well as native orders had established convents in all parts of the country, and religious sisters were running schools, orphanages, and hospitals. Finally, nearly thirty years after Carroll had proposed plans for Georgetown Academy, three Catholic colleges for men and several academies for women had been established. ✟

Catholic Wisdom

Building Up the Church in America

A century after Bishop Carroll's death, Cardinal Gibbons of Baltimore wrote this about his work in building up the Church in America:

> Bishop Carroll did not wish to see the Church vegetate as a delicate exotic plant. He wished it to become a sturdy tree, deep-rooted in the soil, to grow with the growth and bloom with the development of the country, inured to its climate, braving its storms. . . . His aim was that the clergy and people should be thoroughly identified with the land in which their lot is cast; that they should . . . be in harmony with its spirit. From this mutual accord of Church and State there could but follow beneficient effects for both. (Annabelle Melville, *John Carroll of Baltimore*, page 287)

Building the Church through Education

True to his Jesuit background, John Carroll placed a high value on education, which he believed to be essential to securing the continuation of the Church's ministry and the adaptation of Catholicism to American ideals. A national clergy and a way to educate them were central to his plans for the Church in America. So was education for laypersons.

By 1786 Father Carroll had published formal plans for an academy at Georgetown, along the Potomac in Maryland. In 1791 Carroll saw his dream of a national college fulfilled, when Georgetown Academy opened its doors to its first students. That same year the Sulpicians, an order of priests dedicated to the education of clergy, arrived in Baltimore. In what had been a local tavern, a group of four priests and five seminarians established Saint Mary's Seminary, the first in the country.

Just as in the Middle Ages when the Catholic Church spurred the growth of the university system in Europe, in America too the Catholic Church has made a great contribution to higher education. Since the opening of Georgetown in 1791, more than 240 Catholic colleges and universities have been established in America—making up nearly 20 percent of Catholic institutions of higher education in the world. Over time access to higher education also helped American Catholics to join the middle and upper social classes.

Article 41 An Immigrant Church

© Minnesota Historical Society/CORBIS

Around the mid-1800s, immigrants began to flood into the United States, seeking refuge from poverty in their homelands. These immigrants came with the hope of building a better life in America.

Waves of Migration

From 1830 to 1860, Catholic immigrants to America were predominantly from Ireland. In fact, Irish immigration was the main cause for the jump in the Catholic population from about a half million in 1830 to more than three million in 1860. From about 1860 to 1890, German Catholics formed the second wave of Catholic immigrants, in numbers about equal to that of the Irish immigrants. The third wave, lasting from 1890 to the 1920s, consisted of immigrants from Italy and Eastern Europe. Most of the immigrants lived in neighborhoods—often slums—with others from their homeland.

Ethnic churches continued to thrive into the twentieth century. In this 1925 photo, parishioners celebrate the Feast of Saint Anthony at a church serving the needs of the Italian community in Saint Paul, Minnesota.

Anti-Catholicism on the Rise

Starting in the 1830s, widespread anti-Catholic bigotry became a fact of life for immigrants. As the number of immigrant Catholics in the United States increased, groups of Protestants who called themselves nativists protested against the influx of immigrants. In the 1850s anti-Catholic sentiment developed into a political party nicknamed the Know-Nothings (so called because its members evaded questions about their organization by answering, "I don't know"). The Know-Nothings circulated rumors that the Vatican and Catholic immigrants were conspiring to take over the United States. They incited riots in cities such as New York and Louisville, Kentucky; fixed elections in Baltimore and other places; and harassed convents in places such as Boston and Providence, Rhode Island.

Prejudices Wane

By the late 1800s, anti-Catholic prejudice had declined, and the Know-Nothings ceased to be a powerful anti-Catholic force. During the Civil War, Catholics fought on both sides, with Union and Confederate Catholic soldiers making heroic sacrifices. This loyalty helped to ease doubt regarding Catholics' patriotism. Still Catholics continued to experience bigotry even into the twentieth century. Even in 1960 when John F. Kennedy, a Catholic, was campaigning for president, he had to defend his patriotism and quell the fears of those who thought he may be subject to the undue influence of the Pope.

Ethnic Parishes

Catholic immigrants who came to the United States in the second half of the nineteenth century and the early twentieth century wanted to practice their faith just as they had learned it and in their native language. Germans, for example, often resented the English-speaking priests—many of them Irish, because of the large numbers of Irish Catholic immigrants that preceded the Germans—and established their own parishes with German pastors.

Live It!

An Immigrant Story

The United States of America is often called a nation of immigrants, and every immigrant—those who arrived generations ago or and those who arrived just last week—has a story to tell. How can you tell your own "immigrant story," the story of your family, or the story of a friend or neighbor? Here are a few ideas:

- Interview family members about their experience. Write out the interviews or capture them digitally.
- Gather scrapbooks, pictures, and other artifacts from family or personal history.
- Did the person or family bring anything precious with them to remind them of their family history? Take a photo of that object for your display.
- In interviews, photos, and heirlooms you gather, be sure to ask about and include details related to the immigrant's faith. What religious objects did the person (or family) bring along? What prayers sustained them during the uncertainty of immigrating to a new land?

Nurturing the Immigrant Church through Education

In the nineteenth century, and even into the twentieth, public schools were dominated by Protestant practices and perspectives. Even though separation of church and state was the law of the land, the reality did not always reflect that separation as we understand it today. All public school students were required to read the Protestant version of the Bible and to recite Protestant prayers.

Catholics became intensely committed to Catholic schools as a means of passing on the faith and supporting their children in an often hostile society. Immigrants, mostly poor, supported the building of parish, or parochial, schools with their hard-earned dollars. Many Catholic men and women religious dedicated their lives to teaching the children.

Over time Catholicism became respected by non-Catholics for its successful system of education. In 1884 the Council of Baltimore (a U.S. bishops' council) ruled that within two years every parish had to have a parish school. The bishops also commissioned a catechism for all Catholics in the United States. The resulting text, the *Baltimore Catechism*, became the standard religion text for Catholic children from then through the 1950s.

The decisions of the Council of Baltimore had an enormous impact on the Church in the United States. Today not all parishes, or even most, have a parish school, but the Catholic school system is recognized for educational excellence and for its contribution in passing on the faith. In urban settings, in particular, Catholic schools provide a high quality education and a nurturing and faith-filled environment not only for Catholic students but for children of many faiths.

Ethnic parishes continued to form in the United States for many years, in some places continuing even into the present. Along with providing an opportunity for worship in a familiar language, ethnic parishes also served as a center of social life for immigrants. Most major cities had German, Polish, Italian, and Irish parishes, among others. Within a block or two in a city, several different ethnic parishes might be located. The parishes provided a sense of community and continuity from the old country.

The Eastern Catholic Churches

In the latter part of the nineteenth century, patterns of immigration shifted yet again. Immigrants from Eastern Europe (Czech Republic, Romania, Slovakia, Ukraine, and other countries) began to arrive. As did immigrants before them, they brought their faith to their new land. Many belonged to one of the Eastern Catholic Churches—those churches that either had not participated in the break from the Catholic Church in 1054 or had reunited at a later time. These churches have always celebrated their own liturgical customs and had their own eparchies, or dioceses, within the United States, with their own bishops. They also follow their own particular canon law, the *Code of Canons of the Oriental Churches*, codified in 1990. ✝

Eastern Catholics

Members of Eastern Catholic Churches are Catholic, but they are not Roman Catholic. The word *Roman* designates a particular Catholic Church distinct from the twenty-one Eastern Catholic Churches. The non-Roman Churches are called Eastern because they reflect the culture of Eastern Europe and the Middle East, and because some of their liturgical customs and practices are rooted in the Byzantine culture and liturgical rites. These Churches refer to the Roman Catholic Church as the Latin Church. Like Roman Catholics, Eastern Catholics acknowledge the Pope as the head of the universal Church.

Not all Eastern Christians are Catholic. The vast majority belong to the Greek Orthodox Church, which has been separated from the Catholic Church since the eleventh century (see article 19, "The Eastern Schism," in section 2). Though important differences remain, leaders of the Orthodox Church and the Catholic Church have been working to restore unity through dialogue.

Article 42 American Missionaries and Saints

September 14, 1975, was a milestone day for Catholics in America, one marked with prayer and celebration in churches and Catholic schools across the country. On that day the first native-born American was canonized. Although distinguished for being the first American-born saint, Elizabeth Ann Seton is one of many holy people who contributed to building up the Church in America.

© Gene Plaisted

Saint Elizabeth Ann Seton established the first free Catholic school in the United States.

Elizabeth Ann Seton and the Sisters of Charity

Elizabeth Ann Seton was born into a well-to-do Episcopalian family in New York City. At age twenty she married a wealthy shipping merchant, and together they had five children. Sadly Elizabeth was widowed before the age of thirty. She opened an academy for young girls in New York to support herself and her children. Moved by the Catholic faith of friends of her late husband, Elizabeth studied the teachings of the Catholic Church and became Catholic.

In 1809, at the invitation of Bishop Carroll, Elizabeth moved to Baltimore to start a Catholic school in that city—Saint Joseph's Academy and Free School, dedicated to the education of Catholic girls. Later that year Elizabeth founded a religious community called the Sisters of Charity—the first religious order to originate in the United States. The newly established religious order made provisions for Elizabeth to continue raising her children. The Sisters of Charity started schools in a number of states and in the frontier territory. These schools set the pattern for the parochial school system in the United States.

Saints in Service of the New Nation

Just as Saint Elizabeth Ann Seton and the Sisters of Charity made a great contribution to the Church in America and worked tirelessly in the service of those in need in the young country, many other holy people also dedicated their lives to the care of those in need in America. We will take a look at a few of them.

Saint Rose Philippine Duchesne (1769–1852)

Born in France, Rose Duschesne founded the first convent of the Religious of the Sacred Heart in America. She came to America as a missionary to the Louisiana Territory in 1818. She established a mission in Missouri and opened a school for Native Americans, dedicating her life to their service.

Augustus Tolton

© Quincy University

Black Catholics have been in America from early colonial days, some coming aboard slave ships, and many more converting later through the evangelization work of missionaries. In the nineteenth century, black religious orders, such as the Oblate Sisters of Providence and the Holy Family Sisters, were founded, and black parishes were established.

Although in 1839 the Vatican had condemned the slave trade, some U.S. Catholics felt that this did not apply to the holding of slaves already in the United States, leading to a lack of a unified position on slavery in the United States. Thus within the Catholic Church in America, blacks faced discrimination. Augustus Tolton (1854–1897), the first black priest ordained for ministry in the United States, had been refused admission to any American seminary. He had to go to Rome for his training and his ordination.

Upon returning to America, Tolton ministered in Quincy, Illinois. His attempt to organize a black parish there met with resistance from white Catholics and Protestants. After reassignment to Chicago, Tolton led the development and administration of the black "national parish" of Saint Monica's. The church quickly grew to six hundred parishioners. Good Father Gus, as he was called by many, came to be known for his eloquent sermons and his beautiful singing voice.

Saint Frances Cabrini (1850–1917)

Mother Cabrini was an Italian immigrant who came to America in 1889. Under the direction of her bishop in Italy, she had founded the Missionary Sisters of the Sacred Heart to care for the poor by running schools and hospitals. At the urging of Pope Leo XIII (1878–1903), she came to New York City with six sisters from her community in 1889 to work among the Italian immigrants. The group worked tirelessly, establishing orphanages, schools, and hospitals in many American cities, including Chicago, Philadelphia, New Orleans, and others.

Saint Theodora Guerin (1798–1856)

Born in France, Theodora Guerin settled in Indiana in 1841, arriving with a group of missionary Sisters of Providence. She established the Academy of Saint Mary-of-the-Woods—the first women's liberal arts college in the United States. She dedicated her life to serving God's people, especially through education. She later established schools throughout Indiana and in Illinois.

Pray It!

Praying with Father Tolton

After Father Tolton's father escaped slavery to fight in the Union Army during the Civil War (later dying in Saint Louis), Father Tolton's mother, Martha, rowed across the Mississippi River with their three children and walked into freedom in Quincy, Illinois. She then said to the children, "Never forget the goodness of the Lord!"

Let this be our prayer now:

Leader: In thanksgiving for the life of Father Tolton and his good influence on the Church in America, we pray:

All: Never forget the goodness of the Lord!

Leader: That, whatever our racial or ethnic background, we may accept one another in love as brothers and sisters in Christ, we pray:

All: Never forget the goodness of the Lord!

Leader: That we may ever seek, with God's help, to escape the chains that bind us, be they economic, social, or spiritual, we pray:

All: Never forget the goodness of the Lord! Amen!

Saint John Nepomucene Neumann (1811–1860)

John Neumann was a native of Bohemia (in Czechoslovakia). He was a Redemptorist missionary who became the fourth bishop of Philadelphia. Neumann was the first U.S. bishop to organize a diocesan Catholic school system. He worked among German immigrants and with other immigrant communities, work aided by his facility for languages. John Neumann was the first American bishop to be canonized.

Saint Katharine Drexel (1858–1955)

Katharine Drexel was born into a wealthy Philadelphia family. She established a religious order, the Sisters of the Blessed Sacrament. She dedicated her life and a large inheritance to the care of Native Americans and African Americans. She founded more than sixty missions around the United States, and founded Xavier University in Louisiana, a Catholic university with a particular mission to serving African American students. ✝

Part Review

1. Why did the Vatican grant permission for an election of the first American bishop by American priests?

2. What were Bishop Carroll's views on education, and what were some of his contributions?

3. Briefly summarize the prejudices nineteenth-century Catholic immigrants in America faced.

4. Tell how the parochial school system developed and how it contributed to the Church's successful growth in America.

5. Name two religious women saints who served Catholics in America in the nineteenth century, and provide a brief bio of each.

6. Name the first African American priest and describe some of the challenges he faced on the path to the priesthood and as a priest.

Part 4

Industrialization, Injustice, and the Church's Response

The mid- to late-nineteenth century was a period of extraordinary change for Europe and America. The Industrial Revolution, which began in Europe, brought major changes in manufacturing, agriculture, mining, and transportation, with social and cultural consequences. Almost every aspect of life was affected by the technological advances. Some of these changes were positive and brought innovations that eased the hardships of manual labor. Other changes, however, were a mixed blessing at best and catastrophic at worst. Industrialization brought about a range of economic and social problems, many of which seemed to appear overnight but took decades to correct.

The Church responded with new teachings to address social problems and the injustices wrought by industrialization and capitalism. The Church's first modern social encyclical was *On the Condition of Labor (Rerum Novarum),* promulgated by Pope Leo XIII. Over the next century, a series of other Church documents focusing on social justice followed.

The articles in this part address the following topics:

43 The Effects of Industrialization and Capitalism

The Industrial Revolution, which began in Europe in the mid- to late-nineteenth century, was driven by capitalist economic systems and affected almost every area of life—sometimes for the good and sometimes at a great social cost.

Capitalism and Social Darwinism

© Bettmann/CORBIS

The term sweatshop derives from the practices of subcontractors engaged by manufacturers. These middlemen would hire workers and "sweat" them for as much labor as they could get from them. These women are making cigars.

Western nations that developed industrial economies were motivated by **capitalism**—that is, by an economic system in which success and continued development depends on profit. In a capitalist economic system, profit is generated through control of the tools of production by the few who have the capital—the financial resources—to create the enterprise. Those who work for them receive wages. Increased profits for the enterprise do not translate into increased wealth for everyone. Instead they belong to the owners. The owners might in turn use those profits to create other enterprises or expand existing ones. Any profits not needed for running or expanding the enterprise belong to them.

In the nineteenth century, capitalists were motivated by a desire to grow their enterprises and increase their personal wealth—often at the expense of workers. A commonly accepted principle among industrialists of the time was Social Darwinism. The belief emerged in England and the United States in the 1870s, and sought to apply the principles of Darwin's theory of evolution and natural selection to sociology and economics. According to Social Darwinists, the concept of survival of the fittest applied in the economic sphere as well, meaning that "superior people" rise to the top—and grow wealthy—while the less capable can never attain more than the wages those at the top pay them.

Social Darwinism provided a theoretical rationalization for the harm done by unchecked capitalism. Unjust

capitalism
An economic system based upon the private ownership of goods and the free market system.

social doctrine

The Church's body of teaching on economic and social matters that includes moral judgments and demands for action in favor of those being harmed by unjust social and economic policies and conditions.

conditions and low wages were seen as necessary in the workplace in order for owners of industry to triumph over their competition.

Wealth for a Few, Suffering for Many

The Industrial Revolution arose from and generated technological advances that we continue to benefit from today. However, these advances came at a great cost to those who labored to keep the engines of industry and capitalism moving. These workers, often immigrant, poor, and uneducated,

A 1917–1919 Department of Labor survey shows that in families where children worked, their earnings contributed 23 percent of the total family income.

© Bettmann/CORBIS

Pray It!

A Prayer for Human Labor

Both the discipline and dignity of work contribute to our maturity and spiritual growth, and to the lives of others as well. This prayer asks that our work draw us closer together in unity and service:

God our Father,

by our labor you govern and guide to perfection

the work of creation.

Hear the prayers of your people

and give all men and women work that enhances their human dignity

and draws them closer to each other

in the service of their brothers and sisters.

We ask this through Christ our Lord. Amen.

(*Roman Missal*)

were frequently exploited. They endured many injustices, including working in sweatshops, where the conditions were deplorable and often dangerous, the hours long, and the wages so low that families remained in poverty. Workers did not receive pensions or sick leave. Children were exploited too. Children as young as four were employed in factories, in mines, and in cotton mills, earning 10 to 20 percent of an adult male's wages. ☩

Bishops Defend the Rights of Workers

Workers in the late 1800s were at the mercy of the capitalists who employed them. They suffered many indignities and had few, if any, protections. They were denied the right to form unions or mount strikes. Those who tried to unite to bargain for better wages would be fired when their union was discovered.

Bishops who spoke out on behalf of workers gave a voice to voiceless workers, who were often treated as cogs in the wheel of industry. In 1872 Cardinal Manning of Britain backed British farmers in a labor dispute. This was the first time a bishop had openly spoken out against management in support of laborers. In 1889 he sided with workers in the London Dock Strike.

In 1886 Cardinal Gibbons of Baltimore defended the Knights of Labor— a labor union that had grown to nearly 700,000 members, many of them Catholic—against condemnation by the Vatican. Not long after, in 1891, Pope Leo XIII wrote On the Condition of Labor (Rerum Novarum). (We will examine this encyclical more closely in article 44, "The Birth of the Social Doctrine of the Church".)

The Church's **social doctrine** places a strong emphasis on the just treatment of workers and defends the rights that workers should enjoy so that their dignity is respected and the value of their work is properly recognized. The first and most important right is the right to work itself, as a means to living with dignity. In addition, the Church defends the rights of workers to form labor unions and associations to advocate for their rights and to strike when it is necessary to protect their rights. However, striking becomes morally unacceptable when workers resort to violence or when their objectives are contrary to the common good.

44 The Birth of the Social Doctrine of the Church

© Bettmann/CORBIS

In countries affected by the Industrial Revolution, such as the United States and Great Britain, living conditions could be described as nothing short of miserable. In some countries many people were unemployed and starving, and those with jobs were paid such poor wages they had no hope of escaping poverty.

In response to the misery wrought upon so many by industrialization, Pope Leo XIII wrote the first of the modern **social encyclicals**, *On the Condition of Labor (Rerum Novarum)* in 1891. In the opening of the encyclical, he states the conditions that he felt obligated to address:

In this nineteenth-century engraving of a New York sweatshop, workers make garments in a tenement apartment, where they can keep an eye on their children.

In any case we clearly see, and on this there is general agreement, that some opportune remedy must be found quickly for the misery and wretchedness pressing so unjustly on the majority of the working class. . . . [T]he hiring of labor and the conduct of trade are concentrated in the hands of comparatively few; so that a small number of very rich men have been able to lay upon the teeming masses of the laboring poor a yoke little better than that of slavery itself. (3)

Live It!

Living the Common Good

What is the common good and how can we live it out in our lives? The common good can be defined as a "good" that benefits everyone, not just an individual or a small group of individuals. Most of the time the common good is a condition or a system. Examples include peace in the world, a clean environment, an affordable public health system, a system of public safety, a fair judicial system. We all depend on these common goods in order to live our individual lives.

How can you contribute to the common good? Consider these ways:

- Study history and civics. Prepare yourself to participate in government and politics. These systems are mandated to provide for the common good.
- Read world news. Subscribe to a weekly newsmagazine, either online or by mail. The common good is global.
- Put this saying into action: "My right ends where another's right begins." In the midst of a conflict, find ways to cooperate and compromise.

On the Condition of Labor was a groundbreaking document. It addressed the new social problems created by industrialization and made specific judgments about how to respond morally, based on Divine Law. It also identified and countered flaws in **Marxism**, which argues against private ownership of property. Here are some of the important points Pope Leo XIII makes in this social encyclical:

- Workers have a right to work with dignity and at a wage that can support families, reasonable work hours (including time off for Sundays and holidays), safe working conditions, with strict limits on child labor.

- Workers should be free to organize associations (unions) to negotiate working conditions.

- Governments must serve the common good and make the protection of basic human rights (of all people and classes) their first priority.

- The right to private ownership of property is enshrined in both natural law and Divine Law (including the Seventh Commandment). Private ownership of property is consistent with human nature. By promoting the dignity of work and enabling parents to provide for their families, private property provides for the "peace and tranquility of human existence" (*Rerum Novarum,* 11).

- The earth and all its goods belong to God, and he intends these goods to provide the things all human beings need to live with dignity. This principle of the universal destination of goods takes precedence even over the right to private property.

Catholic Social Doctrine Documents

Since *On the Condition of Labor,* numerous papal and Vatican documents have added to the Church's social doctrine. Letters of the U.S. bishops also address important social justice issues. Listed here are some of these documents, with a few key points from each.

The Reconstruction of the Social Order (Quadragesimo Anno)
Pope Pius XI, 1931
- criticizes capitalism and **socialism**

social encyclical
A teaching letter from the Pope to the members of the Church on topics of social justice, human rights, and peace.

Marxism
An economic, social, and political philosophy or system based on the theories of social scientist and philosopher Karl Marx (1818–1883). The system eschews the notion of private property and seeks to control wealth by taking the means of production away from the upper class for the benefit of the rest of society.

socialism
An economic system in which there is no private ownership of goods and the creation and distribution of goods and services is determined by the whole community or by the government.

- criticizes the growing gap between those who are rich and those who are poor
- introduces the concept of **subsidiarity**

Christianity and Social Progress (Mater et Magistra)
Pope Saint John XXIII, 1961

- expresses concern for workers and women
- criticizes the gap between rich nations and poor nations
- says that excessive spending on weapons threatens society

The Principle of Subsidiarity

On the Condition of Labor addresses the principle of subsidiarity, which opposes all forms of collectivism, or socialism, and requires that services are provided and laws are made at the lowest practical level of government. According to this principle, a higher civil authority should not take over the responsibility for regulations and services that a lower civil authority can do just as well. The principle of subsidiarity also requires that "neither the state nor any larger society should substitute itself for the initiative and responsibility of individuals" (*CCC*, 1894). Instead such entities should intervene only when there is a real need, and always with an eye to serving the common good. They should also help families to fulfill their responsibilities but should not interfere in family life. This principle arises out of the belief that God has given individuals personal freedom, and that just as he entrusts each of us with the freedom to make choices regarding how to live, so should civil bodies or organizations.

© Glenda M. Powers/Shutterstock.com

Peace on Earth (Pacem in Terris)

Pope Saint John XXIII, 1963

- warns against modern warfare, especially nuclear weapons
- says peace can be achieved through only a just social order
- gives a detailed list of the human rights necessary for a just social order

The Church in the Modern World (Gaudium et Spes)

Second Vatican Council, 1965

- says the Church must serve the world and work with other organizations in promoting the common good
- condemns the use of weapons of mass destruction
- maintains that peace is not just the absence of war but justice throughout society

The Development of Peoples (Popularum Progressio)

Pope Paul VI, 1967

- calls for true progress toward the economic, social, cultural, and spiritual fulfillment of human potential
- teaches that economic development of poor people and the moral development of those with material wealth are linked
- criticizes unrestrained capitalism where profit is the primary motive and where private ownership is an absolute right

A Call to Action (Octogesima Adveniens)

Pope Paul VI, 1971

- encourages Christians and all people of goodwill to continue their work for social justice
- urges awareness of important social needs and social injustices
- offers analysis of the most appropriate responses to those needs and injustices

On Human Work (Laborem Exercens)

Pope Saint John Paul II, 1981

- says work is at the center of social issues
- says all people who are able to work have both the right and the duty to work
- emphasizes that workers have rights and are more important than profits or the things they make

subsidiarity

The moral principle that large organizations and governments should not take over responsibilities and decisions that can be carried out by individuals and local organizations, and that large corporations and governments have the responsibility to support the good of human beings, families, and local communities, which are the center and purpose of social life.

The Hundredth Year (Centesimus Annus)
Pope Saint John Paul II, 1991

- says **communism** collapsed because it treated people as objects, not spiritual beings
- says capitalism is efficient, but it is flawed when it is not oriented toward the common good
- teaches that the right to private property does not take precedence over the just distribution of the world's resources

Charity in Truth (Caritas in Veritate)
Pope Benedict XVI, 2009

- says justice must be applied to every aspect of economic activity
- teaches that both the exclusion of religion from society and religious fundamentalism are obstacles to a just society
- says that technology should not drive our society but should serve the common good

The Challenge of Peace: God's Promise and Our Response
U.S. Conference of Catholic Bishops, 1983

- says peace based on **deterrence** may be acceptable as an interim measure but is not a genuine peace and is not an acceptable long-term solution to the threat of nuclear war

communism
A system of social organization in which all economic and social activity is controlled by a totalitarian government dominated by a single political party. Communism in the twentieth century became closely linked with atheism.

deterrence
The belief that war, especially nuclear war, can be prevented through the ability to respond to a military attack with a devastating counterattack.

Catholic Wisdom

Justice

It has always been part of the Church's mission to pass moral judgment in political and economic matters when human rights or the salvation of souls must be protected. The social justice issues addressed by popes and bishops might be said to have at their core the Seventh Commandment: Thou shalt not steal. Following this commandment requires charity and care of the earth's good and for all people. It requires justice. Here is how the *Catechism of the Catholic Church* defines this moral virtue:

> Justice . . . consists in the constant and firm will to give their due to God and neighbor. Justice toward God is called the "virtue of religion." Justice toward men disposes one to respect the rights of each and to establish in human relationships the harmony that promotes equity with regard to persons and to the common good. The just man, often mentioned in the Sacred Scriptures, is distinguished by habitual right thinking and the uprightness of his conduct toward his neighbor. (1807)

- says money spent on the nuclear arms race is money that cannot be used to help fight poverty and hunger
- teaches that the nuclear arms race must end, the stockpiles of existing nuclear weapons must be reduced and eventually eliminated, and the creation of new nuclear weapons must be stopped

Economic Justice for All: A Pastoral Letter on Catholic Social Teaching and the U.S. Economy
U.S. Conference of Catholic Bishops, 1986

- says economic decisions must be judged by how they protect or undermine human dignity
- says all members of society have an obligation to help those who are poor and vulnerable
- says the Church should be an example of economic justice in how it treats its employees, invests its savings, and serves people in need ✝

Part Review

1. Explain the principle of Social Darwinism and some of the injustices during the era of industrialization.

2. Briefly explain the basic principles of a capitalist economic system. What are some benefits to such an economic model? What are some challenges for society?

3. What were some positive effects of the Industrial Revolution? What negative impact did it have on society, either directly or indirectly?

4. Briefly explain the principle of subsidiarity? Why does the Church support this principle?

5. Name the first modern social encyclical and briefly explain its focus and message.

6. Name two of the Church's modern social doctrine documents and tell the key points of each.

The Church in the Post-Modern Era (Twentieth to Twenty-First Centuries)

Part 1

The Early Twentieth Century

War erupted early in the twentieth century. This war, World War I, lasted more than four years (1914–1918) and took the lives of more than fifteen million soldiers and civilians. Twenty million more were injured. A little more than twenty years after this conflict ended, the world was embroiled in another global conflict, this time involving nuclear weapons. In this part we will look at the various ways the Church dealt with the events and developments of the first half of the twentieth century. This will include looking at the popes of the period and how they guided our journey through the joys and sorrows of their papacies. We will learn about Pope Pius X, his program of Church renewal, and his resistance to modernism. We will also explore a number of early twentieth century renewal movements. Then we will turn to Pope Benedict XV and the turmoil of World War I. Finally, we will learn about Pope Pius XII and World War II and consider the Church's response in the post-war era.

The articles in this part address the following topics:

Article 45 To Restore All Things in Christ

Gregorian chant
A monophonic, unaccompanied style of liturgical singing that takes its name from Pope Gregory the Great (540–604).

Born to a poor family near Venice in 1835, Pope Pius X (1903–1914; born Giuseppe Sarto) lived to see the first shots fired in World War I, on July 28, 1914, about a month before his death on August 20, 1914.

Before becoming Pope, while he was Patriarch of Venice, Cardinal Sarto had improved the education of seminarians, promoted **Gregorian chant** in worship, and championed aid to workers and those who were poor. When he became Pope, he expanded these reforms to the entire Church. His motto as Pope was "To restore all things in Christ" (Ephesians 1:10).

To improve the education of seminarians, he advised the consolidation of individual diocesan seminaries into larger regional ones, where possible. This was especially important in Italy, where dioceses and thus seminaries tended to be smaller.

Concerned about obstacles preventing the frequent reception of Holy Communion, he dispensed the sick from the obligation of fasting. He recommended that children should be prepared to receive First Communion soon after they reached the age of reason (seven years of age), rather than at age twelve. He promoted the reception of daily Communion for all Catholics. Regarding catechetical matters, he considered the catechetical instruction of adults as well as children to be a necessity, and decreed that suitable religious instruction be provided in every parish for children attending public schools. This was the beginning of CCD (Confraternity of Christian Doctrine), a name still used in some places for the parish religious education program.

© Bill Wittman/www.wpwittman.com

Pope Pius X wrote that daily reception of the Eucharist helps the faithful to lead holier and more perfect lives.

As a priest and cardinal, Giuseppe Sarto had sought to revive and implement the singing of Gregorian chant in the churches, and, as Pope, he ordered that authentic Gregorian chant, along with appropriate modern compositions, be used at Mass. His concern for Church renewal extended to biblical studies, so he founded the Biblical Institute at Rome and entrusted it to the care of the Society of Jesus, or the Jesuit Order of religious priests and brothers.

Pope Pius X continued his concern for those who are poor. He began what was called **Catholic Action**, and established guidelines for lay Catholic participation in social justice programs. His concern was that these programs be truly Catholic, under the guidance of the bishops, and that the clergy would take an advisory, not an administrative, role.

Pope Pius's concern for efficiency and justice extended to the inner workings of the Church as well, and during his pontificate he commissioned the revision and codification of canon law. The work was completed in 1917, under Pius's successor. For the first time, the laws of the Church were collected in one volume.

Catholic Action
A lay apostolic group encouraged by Pope Pius X; eventually this term became an umbrella term for any apostolic action initiated and carried out by laypeople.

The Question of Modernism

During the pontificate of Pope Pius X, the question of modernism and its possible effect on the Church came to a crisis point. What is modernism? This question does not have an easy answer because modernism was not a well-developed system of thought; rather, it was a diverse collection of ideas, some of which opposed the Church's teaching. In the late nineteenth and early twentieth centuries, the social sciences—history, sociology, psychology—were emerging, and the application of these sciences to Church issues or affairs was considered modernism. Initially in theology, modernism was a well-intentioned attempt to develop a deeper understanding of the Revelation with the aid of advances in

Live It!

Catholic Action Today

Where do you see the need for Catholic Action today? What groups in your parish are concerned for those who are in need in any way? You might want to make a survey of these groups in your parish to find out what they do and how they do it. Then choose one and ask how you can help! Or, if you see an unmet need, form your own group, under the guidance of your pastor or teachers, and implement Catholic Action with your friends and classmates.

The Saint Vincent de Paul Society is one group of laypeople that has been helping those in need since its founding in France by Blessed Frederic Ozanam (a layman, husband, and father) in 1833. The first group in America was established in Saint Louis in 1845. Having been established before the time of Pope Pius X, it is one of the oldest organized forms of Catholic Action still active today.

social sciences and historical method. Significant problems arose when aspects of the Revelation were tested against these advances, on the assumption that only that which can be verified by science and historical method is true. At the time of Pope Saint Pius X, modernism in its most radical form espoused several erroneous ideas. Here are a few examples:

- Religion is a psychological experience, unrelated to objective truth.
- Church doctrines and structures are relative and thus always subject to change.
- The Bible is a compilation of religious experiences rather than a source of Divine Revelation.

These and similar ideas were noted by Pope Pius X in his 1907 decree "*Lamentabili*" (meaning "lamentable things"), which listed the errors of modernism in sixty-five propositions. A number of priests who taught modernist ideas were excommunicated, and, in 1910, the Pope required that all priests take an oath against modernism. The scholarship of Catholic and non-Catholic scholars followed different paths for decades after this, until it became clear that the uses of social sciences in scholarship did not necessarily lead to the errors of modernism.

This crisis and the subsequent suppression of modernism helps to shed light on the value of balance between authority and learned inquiry. If the Magisterium only kept repeating the answers of a previous age, never attempting to communicate the teachings of the Church in a contemporary context, how would people hear and understand these teachings? Pope Pius X came down squarely on the side of authority rather than inquiry. Yet just some fifty years later (a very short time, historically speaking), another pope, Saint John XXIII (1958–1963), convened Vatican Council II and announced that it would bring the Church back to her roots and would encourage dialogue with the modern world. In this dialogue a clear distinction would always be made between what is fundamental and unchanging in Church doctrine and practice and what can be adapted to a new age.

What can we learn from history in this instance? As the bishops of the United States remark in their *Doctrinal Elements of a Curriculum Framework for the Development of*

Catechetical Materials for Young People of High School Age, a balance of truths must be maintained. Some truths are more important than others. As the bishops note, sometimes Catholics "overemphasize some aspects of truth at the expense of other aspects. Serious, respectful, and loving pursuit of the whole truth can help us recapture the needed balance" (page 53). It is the role of the Pope and the bishops, as the primary teachers in the Church, to guide the Church in seeking the whole truth and maintaining a balance of truths. ✝

A Pope and a Saint

© Hulton-Deutsch Collection/CORBIS

What made Pope Pius X a saint? Perhaps part of the answer is that he became, in short, a parish priest for the world. He gave a sermon at Saint Peter's every Sunday, taught weekly catechism lessons to local children in a Vatican courtyard, and opened the Apostolic Palace (his home as Pope) to refugees from an earthquake.

Saints are people who imitate Christ to a heroic degree and share his love to the best of their ability. Pope Pius X, in his focus on simplicity and poverty, imitated Christ even amidst the grandeur of his office. Thus he rejected customs that in the past had put the Pope on a lonely pedestal and made the papal quarters like a "royal household." For example, he rejected the custom of the Pope dining alone; Pope Pius X invited friends to dine with him whenever possible. He also refused to give special titles or favors to his relatives. When it was suggested that he make his two sisters "papal countesses," he replied, "I have made them sisters of the Pope; what more can I do for them?" (in Steven M. Avella and Jeffrey Zalar, "Sanctity in the Era of Catholic Action: The Case of St. Pius X," in *U.S. Catholic Historian,* volume 15).

Pope Pius X was canonized in 1954. He is popularly known as "the Pope of the Eucharist."

Article 46 Rivulets of Renewal

Before looking at the Church's role during the two devastating world wars of the twentieth century (World War I and World War II), we will keep our focus, in this article, on the Church herself in the first half of the twentieth century. Despite the condemnation of modernism, the quiet bubbling of rivulets of renewal could be heard: Renewal in liturgy, theology, catechetics, Scripture studies, and lay participation in the Church's social justice work, was enriching the life of the Church, and those riches were shared with the world. These renewal movements were in fact remote preparation for the renewal initiated by the Second Vatican Council many years later. Let us take three of these aspects in turn: the liturgical movement, advances in Scripture studies, and the catechetical movement.

The Liturgical Movement

You will recall that Pope Pius X was instrumental in reintroducing the use of Gregorian chant in the liturgy. This reform recaptured the simplicity and grandeur of worship in the Middle Ages and presented it anew. Yet, with the discovery of other, older texts describing even earlier liturgies, liturgical scholars were encouraged to broaden their understanding of what liturgy, with full participation by the people, could be.

In the early twentieth century, the liturgy of the Roman Catholic Church was still celebrated in Latin. However, as early as 1909, at a liturgical conference convened by Pope Pius X, liturgists began to consider whether liturgy in the vernacular, or local language, would promote more understanding and participation by the people. The vernacular would underscore the growing understanding that liturgy involves the active participation of all the faithful in God's work. It is not an action of the priest alone. (The liturgy had gradually moved from the Greek language to Latin as the Roman Empire became more dominant, and Latin itself had at one time been a "common tongue.") Various efforts to encourage participation of the laity were begun, but the most practical efforts in this direction would not be made until after World War II.

The Reforms of Pope Pius XII

Pope Pius XII continued the liturgical reforms begun by Pope Saint Pius X. Some of the liturgical customs we observe today owe their existence to Pope Pius XII:

- **The Easter Vigil** Previously the Easter Vigil was celebrated on the Saturday morning before Easter. Pope Pius XII restored the Easter Vigil to its original time, in the evening. The renewal of baptismal promises was also introduced into the Vigil, in the vernacular.

- **The vernacular** Pope Pius XII approved the use of the vernacular for the Sacraments and for other rites outside of the Mass. The use of the vernacular was particularly helpful in mission countries.

© Bettmann/CORBIS

These and other changes helped Catholics to participate more fully in the liturgy, whether for the great Solemnity of Easter or for a weekday Mass. The reforms also helped to pave the way for the general re-evaluation of liturgical practices mandated by Vatican Council II.

Advances in Scripture Studies

Pope Pius XII's (1939–1958) diplomatic and scholarly background prepared him well for his work during and after World War II (1939–1945). In 1943, during the darkest days of that war, most appropriately on the Feast of Saint Jerome (who translated the Scripture from the original languages of Greek and Hebrew into Latin, a translation now called the Vulgate), Pope Pius XII issued the encyclical *Divino Afflante Spiritu.* The Latin title is taken from the first words of the document, "Inspired by the Holy Spirit." This encyclical is a landmark for Catholic biblical scholars because it allowed

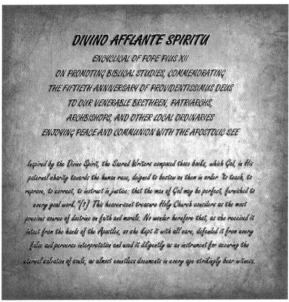

© Molodec/Shutterstock.com

for historical research and literary criticism of biblical texts as a tool for Scripture scholars to uncover the truth God reveals to us in Sacred Scripture.

Think back to our discussion of modernism. For many years fear of modernism creeping into biblical studies resulted in a negative reaction to the use of history and literary analysis in scholarship concerning the Bible. Even well-known Catholic scholars like Joseph-Marie Lagrange, a Dominican priest who founded the academic establishment École Biblique in Jerusalem in 1890 and the scholarly journal *Revue Biblique* in 1892, came under suspicion.

In such an atmosphere, *Divino Afflante Spiritu* offered welcome clarification. It gave guidelines for the study of biblical texts, advocating that determining the literal meaning of the words and the intention of the sacred writer under the guidance of the Holy Spirit be a focus of **biblical exegesis**:

Pray It!

Praying with Scripture

Pope Pius XII directed that those who study and teach Scripture be prepared for this task through the study of ancient languages and the use of textual criticism. He noted that such studies open to us the real meaning of these "letters of God," which have come down to us through his Providence (see *Divino Afflante Spiritu*, 15–19). The Scripture scholar must also seek out the spiritual sense of the Scripture, "provided it is clearly intended by God" (26).

As we read, study, and pray with Sacred Scripture, we open ourselves to truth. The more we learn of the truth by reading the Bible and praying with the sacred text, the more we know of God and his presence and action in the world.

Being thoroughly prepared by the knowledge of the ancient languages and by the aids afforded by the art of criticism, let the Catholic exegete undertake the task, of all those imposed on him the greatest, that namely of discovering and expounding the genuine meaning of the Sacred Books. In the performance of this task let the interpreters bear in mind that their foremost and greatest endeavor should be to discern and define clearly that sense of the biblical words which is called literal. Aided by the context and by comparison with similar passages, let them therefore by means of their knowledge of languages search out with all diligence the literal meaning of the words . . . so that the mind of the author may be made abundantly clear. (*Divino Afflante Spiritu*, 23)

To facilitate this study, the encyclical points out, exegetes should use biblical texts in the language in which they were written, rather than the Latin translation of Saint Jerome.

This encyclical also encouraged exegetes to use critical-historical methods in discerning the message God intended to communicate to his people. Exegetes were told to investigate the life and times of the Scripture writers, their written or oral sources, and the particular forms of expression a writer used. These directives paved the way to a new era in biblical scholarship and to a sharing of biblical riches with the entire Church that still continues today.

biblical exegesis
The critical interpretation and explanation of Sacred Scripture.

catechists
Catechists are the ministers of catechesis, the process by which Christians of all ages are taught the essentials of Christian doctrine and are formed as disciples of Christ.

The Catechetical Movement

You may recall that Pope Pius X directed that children be prepared for First Holy Communion as near to the age of reason (age seven) as possible. He mandated that children in public schools receive religious instruction from the parish, and he was also concerned about adult education. These priorities resulted in a need for the training of **catechists** who would give religious instruction at the parish level.

Pope Saint Pius X was instrumental in formulating a question-and-answer catechism that became a popular tool for religious instruction in many European dioceses. (In the United States, the bishops had approved *The Baltimore Catechism* in 1885.) However, even in the years before World War I, German priests and catechists began to adapt their catechetical methods to the methods of teaching that had begun to surface in the work of educational psychologists.

After the war Josef Jungmann (1889–1975) took catecheti-cal renewal beyond advances in methodology by advocating for a renewed focus on the *kerygma,* the proclamation of the Good News, with a call for conversion. The kerygmatic movement was closely allied with the liturgical movement described earlier. Both movements aimed for a renewed focus on Christ as the center of the Church's life.

Advances Interrupted

So much progress in these three areas—liturgy, Scripture study, and catechetics—had been made. But progress was interrupted by the two world wars. Through these diffi-cult years, life moved on, and religious education certainly continued in parishes all over the world, but the kinds of international meetings and correspondence required for deep thinking and dialogue became impossible. As the world recovered from these devastating wars, the Church could turn her attention once again to these important issues. ✝

Article 47 The Church and World War I

The looming world war had horrified and saddened Pope Pius X. It is said that because of this, he died of a broken heart. The immediate cause of the war in the summer of 1914 was the assassination of Archduke Ferdinand of Austria, the heir to the throne of Austria-Hungary. Due to previous alliances, the countries of the world were lined up against one another, centered either around the Central Powers (Germany and Austria-Hungary) or the Entente

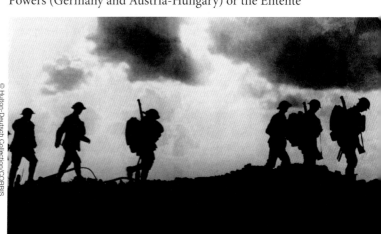

British soldiers in Belgium, which Ger-man troops invaded in order to reach France. Both sides dug long, narrow ditches protected by barbed wire and fired at each other over "no man's land" from the trenches.

© Hulton-Deutsch Collection/CORBIS

(Britain, France, and Russia). The United States entered the war in 1917 on the side of the Entente.

A New Kind of War

This war was a new kind of war. First of all, it involved the major powers of the world, not only in Europe but in the western hemisphere as well. Second, it was the first war to take place not only on land and sea, but in the air. Finally, it was the first war in which deadly weapons, such as poison gas, were used to kill people from a distance.

The newly elected Pope, Benedict XV (1914–1922), devoted his entire papacy to aiding the victims of World War I. Officially the Church remained neutral, and Catholics were fighting on both sides. In the midst of the war, the Pope organized army chaplains and helped to arrange prisoner exchanges. On August 1, 1917, he issued a seven-point peace plan and offered to mediate the conflict among nations. Unfortunately, these efforts were generally ignored.

Following the war, Pope Benedict advised the victorious powers that compromising with the losing side (Germany and Austria-Hungary) rather than punishing them would be the wisest avenue to peace. Ignoring this advice, France, Britain, and Russia used the Treaty of Versailles (1919) as an instrument of punishment. The political and economic consequences of this treaty, together with the effects of the Great Depression, played a part in sowing the seeds in Germany for the rise of Adolf Hitler. He, one of the most sinister leaders in history, was elected chancellor of Germany on a promise to renew German power and prestige.

The Church Between the Wars

In 1917 the Russian Revolution resulted in a Marxist state in Russia that ruthlessly suppressed Christianity and Christian Churches, both Catholic and Orthodox. Catholic bishops and priests were sent to work camps, along with other "enemies of the state." In the first eight years of the revolution, two hundred thousand Catholics, including every Catholic bishop, disappeared.

In the 1930s the Great Depression had a worldwide reach. The resulting poverty and disillusion resulted in a search for strong leadership to provide a remedy. The result

Pope Benedict XV's Peace Plan

In his peace plan, Pope Benedict proposed the following seven points to guide peace negotiations following the war:

1. The moral force of right should be substituted for the force of arms.
2. There must be a simultaneous mutual reduction in armaments.
3. A mechanism for international arbitration must be instituted.
4. True freedom of the seas should be established to enable prosperity for all.
5. There should be a renunciation of war indemnities.
6. Occupying forces should evacuate occupied territories.
7. There should be a fair and just evaluation of rival claims to territories and lands.

Although Pope Benedict XV was not involved in crafting the peace treaty that ended World War I, many of his proposals were adopted by President Woodrow Wilson in his own proposal of Fourteen Points, which did play a part in ending the war.

© Bettmann/CORBIS

was the spread of **fascism**, complete state control. In Russia, Italy, Spain, and Germany, dictatorships filled the leadership vacuum. In the pontificate of Pope Pius XI (1922–1939), the Church dealt carefully with these regimes, and through **concordats**, tried to preserve the rights of religion and religious groups to exist as independent entities.

These efforts failed completely in Russia. In Italy the Lateran Treaty (1929) was signed between the Italian dictator Benito Mussolini and the Church. In this treaty Italy agreed to pay the Vatican for the seizure of the Papal States in the nineteenth century and to recognize the Vatican as a sovereign and independent state. In addition, Mussolini made concessions to the Church, allowing the Pope (rather than the state) to appoint bishops and permitting Catholic Action lay groups to continue unimpeded. Just a few years later, however, in 1931, Mussolini began to violate this agreement. In response Pope Pius XI condemned fascism and insisted on the right of Catholics to organize. Mussolini, who needed Catholic support to stay in power, backed down.

When the Nazis in Germany began to persecute the clergy and disband Catholic groups, Pope Pius XI wrote an encyclical in 1937 to the bishops in Germany condemning Nazi crimes. Called *Mit Brennender Sorge* ("*With Burning Concern*") and smuggled into Germany, it was read aloud from the pulpit in every parish church in Germany. In response the Nazi persecution intensified, and both priests and lay Catholics were arrested. The Nazi response to the Pope's encyclical was a portent of the horror to come. ♱

fascism
A political ideology, movement, or regime that exalts nation and often race above the individual and that supports a centralized, highly autocratic government headed by a dictatorial leader, and forcibly suppresses opposition.

concordat
An agreement between the Holy See and a sovereign state on religious matters. Concordats do not give Church approval to dictators or corrupt governments; instead they are a way in which the Church seeks to be able to continue to provide the Sacraments to the faithful in nations hostile to the Church.

Article
48 The Church and World War II

Pope Pius XI died in February 1939. In only one day, Cardinal Eugenio Pacelli, who had been the Vatican secretary of state, and so already had had dealings with many of the countries preparing for war, was elected to replace him. He took the name Pius XII. As yet another world conflict loomed, Pope Pius XII (1939–1958) pleaded for peace. But on September 1, 1939, Hitler invaded Poland, and World War II began.

The Most Widespread War in History

At its end in 1945, World War II was judged the most widespread war in history, involving more than one hundred million military personnel. Between fifty and seventy million people died, including the mass deaths of civilians in the Holocaust in Germany and German-occupied territory and as a result of the atomic bombs dropped on the Japanese cities of Hiroshima and Nagasaki.

Nations focused all of their resources toward the war. For example, in the United States and elsewhere, automobile factories built planes and tanks; food was rationed so that necessary staples could be sent to the military; and fuel was rationed. Pots, pans, and other metals were collected regularly so that they could be recycled into bullets and other weapons for the war effort.

Throughout the war Pope Pius XII reminded the world that peace was both necessary and possible. He remained impartial because he felt he could not favor or oppose any of his children, yet his pronouncements on what would constitute the principles of a just peace were clear. Like Pope Benedict XV had done during World War I, Pope Pius XII called for the establishment of an international body of arbitration so that political and economic stability would be possible for all nations.

© Bettmann/CORBIS

Two nuclear attacks by the United States, one on Hiroshima, the other on Nagasaki, were followed by Japan's surrender on August 15, 1945. Historians estimate that over 200,000 people died in the combined attacks.

Pope Pius XII and the Jews

Throughout the war, especially in his Christmas messages, Pope Pius XII pleaded, year after year, for the preservation of human rights in the midst of this terrible conflict. In 1941 *The New York Times* commented on the Pope's Christmas message of that year in an editorial: "[T]he Pope put himself squarely against Hitlerism. . . . [H]e left no doubt that the Nazi aims are also irreconcilable with his own conception of a Christian peace" (December 25, 1941).

The Jewish people were a particular target of the Nazi regime. In his propaganda Hitler singled out the Jews as an easy scapegoat for Germany's troubles. He also saw a way to use them as a source of labor for his war machine.

In Germany and in German-occupied territory, Jews were systematically rounded up, packed into boxcars, and taken to work camps—which became known as death camps because so many eventually died there. By the war's end, a total of six million Jews had been executed, their bodies thrown into burning ovens or mass graves. Hitler also targeted the Roma, or gypsies, the disabled, and homosexuals for eradication from Germany. The most notorious Nazi death camp was in Auschwitz, Poland. It is preserved today as a memorial to those innocent victims of hatred.

Through his diplomatic contacts, Pope Pius XII knew what was happening, and, though officially impartial, he shared information with the allied headquarters in London. Believing that speaking out against Nazism (as his predecessor Pope Pius XI had done) would result in even more atrocities, the Pope and the Vatican worked behind the scenes to save as many Jews as possible. In addition to Jews saved through diplomacy, many more were hidden in Roman monasteries and convents and were issued false baptismal certificates to protect them in case they were discovered. An Israeli diplomat estimated that, through the work of Pope Pius XII, possibly 860,000 Jews were able to escape Hitler's persecution. Prominent Jews and Jewish leaders, such as the chief rabbi of Rome, Rabbi Israel Zolli, Albert Einstein, and Israeli Prime Minister Golda Meir, publicly acknowledged Pope Pius XII's work on behalf of Jews and expressed their gratitude, praising him as a "righteous gentile." In recent years Pope Pius XII has been the subject of controversy and

Catholic Wisdom

Pope Pius XII on the Moral Use of Power

In his first encyclical, *On the Unity of Human Society* (*Summi Pontificatus*), issued in October 1939, shortly after the start of World War II, Pope Pius XII offered this insight about the moral use of power:

> Once the bitterness and the cruel strifes of the present have ceased, the new order of the world, of national and international life, must rest no longer on the quicksands of changeable and ephemeral standards. . . . [T]hey must rest on . . . the solid rock of natural law and of Divine Revelation. There the human legislator must attain to that . . . keen sense of moral responsibility, without which it is easy to mistake the boundary between the legitimate use and the abuse of power. (82)

criticism for what some have called his inaction on behalf of Jews during World War II. However, the historical record provides testimony to his heroic, behind-the-scenes actions on behalf of Jews. In an atmosphere where public condemnation may have provoked violent retaliation, against both Jews and Catholics, Pius XII chose carefully when to speak out and when to effect more good by remaining silent.

Post-War Catholicism

For many of the combatants, this war was a war of Christian against Christian. Germany was a Christian nation (the Christians being divided between Catholics and Lutherans). Italy was largely Catholic too, as was France. The United States and Britain were largely Christian as well, both Protestant and Catholic. After the war a movement called *Pax Christi* ("Peace of Christ") was established in Europe. Its first goal was to reconcile European Christians who had supported opposite sides during the war. It still exists today, having spread to over fifty countries and five continents, and is a voice of prayer and action for peace and reconciliation all over the world.

The rise of atheistic communism, with its roots in Russia's Marxist regime, also concerned the Church, as well as the attendant arms race between the Soviet Union and the United States, which involved the stockpiling of more and more weaponry, including nuclear weapons. The animosity and competition between these two powers, not only in arms but in other areas as well, which developed immediately following World War II, became known as the cold war. This cold war, however, had its offshoot in the American war against Vietnam (1955–1975), which was fought to limit the influence of Chinese communism in the Far East. This effort, with its extremely high cost in human lives, failed with the fall of Saigon (now Ho Chi Minh City) to the communists in 1975. Similarly, the Korean War (1950–1953) was also a conflict between military powers on opposing sides in the cold war, and was also an effort to stem the spread of communism. Although an armistice brought the war to an official end in 1953, minor outbreaks of fighting continue to the present, and North Korea remains a communist country today.

Light in the Darkness

During his papacy Pope Pius XII wrote forty-one encyclicals, many of them on the subject of war and peace. Others, however, were on topics of special interest to Catholics and these too helped to hold up the spirits of Catholics, both in wartime and in the somewhat anxious peace that followed.

The year 1950, proclaimed a Holy Year by Pope Pius XII, was a highlight of this papacy, and, on November 1 of that year, the Pope defined the doctrine of the Assumption of the Blessed Virgin Mary and established that it be celebrated as a feast of the highest rank, a solemnity (on August 15). Through his writings Pope Pius XII brought a scholarly mind and a sensitive heart to not only the concerns of the Church but also the concerns of the entire world.

© Pascal Deloche/Godong/Corbis

At its inception, communism appealed to idealists because it preached a slogan that seemed to lead to justice and peace: "From each according to his ability; to each according to his need." In one sense this reminds us of the communal life of the early Christians. Yet their life was voluntary and it was based on the Gospel of love. Soviet communism was forced by the government, which saw itself as the supreme ruler of all, and had no room for God and indeed persecuted the Church and believers. In 1991, when the Soviet Union collapsed, the cold war was officially over, and Russia (the former Soviet Union) began its long climb toward democracy.

Nuclear weapons have proliferated since World War II and remain a threat to the world. The bishops of the United States have spoken on the immorality of nuclear war. In

2010 Cardinal Francis George, president of the United States Conference of Catholic Bishops, wrote to President Barack Obama, in the name of all the U.S. bishops, in favor of the ratification of the Strategic Arms Reduction Treaty (START) between the United States and the Russian Federation: "The horribly destructive capacity of nuclear arms makes them disproportionate and indiscriminate weapons that endanger human life and dignity like no other armaments. Their use as a weapon of war is rejected in Church teaching based on just war norms. . . . We can point with moral clarity to a destination that moves beyond deterrence to a world free of the nuclear threat." ✝

Part Review

1. How did Pope Pius X influence the liturgy?

2. What is modernism and why was it condemned by Pope Pius X?

3. Choose one focus of renewal (the liturgical movement, Scripture study, or the catechetical movement) and explain its advances in the early twentieth century.

4. What did Pope Benedict XV do to alleviate the effects of World War I?

5. What is fascism and how did the Church combat it in Italy and in Germany?

6. Why did Pope Pius XII choose to work behind the scenes to help the Jews during World War II?

Part 2

Vatican Council II: A Pastoral Approach to the World

From a few months after his election as pope until his death, Saint John XXIII's primary focus was the success of the Second Vatican Council (1962–1965). Unlike previous Councils, called in times of theological confusion or other conflicts, this Council would be pastoral in its tone. It would declare no new doctrines and would issue no *anathemas* (literally, curses) against error. It would focus on the situation of the modern world and respond to contemporary needs rather than focus on matters internal to the Church. In assessing what is good about the modern world and adapting the Church to contemporary needs, the Council would help both the world and the Church to face the present and the future with thoughtfulness and hope.

Pope John's vision for the Council was *ecumenical*, meaning "worldwide." In addition to the bishop-delegates in attendance, Protestant and Orthodox leaders, as fellow followers of Christ, as well as Catholic lay theologians would be invited to observe Council sessions.

In this part we will take a closer look at the beginnings of the Council under the papacy of Saint John XXIII, its continuation and conclusion under the papacy of Paul VI, and the content of its documents, which still influence the Church today.

The articles in this part address the following topics:

49 Pope Saint John XXIII: Winds of Change

The death of Pope Pius XII in October of 1958 marked the end of the post-war era. Pope Pius XII had worked tirelessly through the horrendous events of World War II and the recovery of a devastated Europe in the years after. The Vatican had been a significant hub for relief efforts both during and after the war, and the Pope never hesitated to ask the bishops of wealthier and more stable countries to contribute funds to help European refugees, displaced persons, and other victims of the war in Europe. He died a beloved father to his people.

The election of Cardinal Angelo Giuseppe Roncalli as Pope John XXIII (1958–1963) seemed to symbolize the winds of change that would soon be blowing through the Church. In personality and in appearance, no man could have been more different from Pope Pius XII. Where the previous Pope was tall, reserved, and ascetic looking, Saint John XXIII was short, fat, and could even be called jolly. A Church administrator his entire priestly life, he understood and enjoyed his interactions with people. With a gift for the apropos remark, he enjoyed telling a good joke, especially if it poked fun at himself. Yet he was a serious student of history, and his familiarity with the issues of the past helped him to see the current reality of the Church and the world with clarity. He realized that the Church needed a new Pentecost, a new approach to the people of the world that she was called to serve. The idea of a council came as a surprise to many, including the cardinals who elected him Pope. They thought, because of his age, he would take a caretaker approach rather than a proactive approach to the papacy.

Pope Saint John XXIII in 1963, the year he was named *Time* magazine's Person of the Year.

© Bettmann/CORBIS

During his papacy, Saint John Paul II (1978–2005), who was himself present at the Second Vatican Council, beatified Pope Saint John XXIII in the year 2000 and at that time summarized him and his life's work in this way:

> Everyone remembers the image of Pope John's smiling face and two outstretched arms embracing the whole world. . . . The breath of newness he brought certainly did not concern doctrine, but rather the way to explain it; his style of speaking and acting was new, as was his friendly approach to ordinary people and to the powerful of the world. It was in this spirit that he called the Second Vatican Ecumenical Council, thereby turning a new page in the Church's history: Christians heard themselves called to proclaim the Gospel with renewed courage and greater attentiveness to the "signs" of the times. ("Homily of His Holiness John Paul II," September 3, 2000)

While pope, Saint John Paul II beatified Pope Pius IX on the same day as Pope Saint John XXIII, suggesting the continuity between Vatican I and Vatican II in matters of faith. The feast day of Saint John XXIII is celebrated on October 11, the anniversary of the opening of the Second Vatican Council.

Preparation for the Council

While pope, Saint John XXIII announced his plans for a Council on January 25, 1959—a scant three months into his papacy. A planning committee was appointed, with instructions to have the Council open in 1962. The opening date was set for October 11 of that year, the Feast of the Motherhood of Mary.

During the period of preparation, the delegates themselves (bishops and abbots of both the Roman Catholic and Eastern Catholic Churches) prepared items to be debated. These were funneled into preparatory commissions and further refined by the Central Commission, which made the rules by which the items were to be discussed. The debate on the floor of the Council would be supervised by ten "presidents" (later expanded to twelve) appointed by Pope John. The Pope had the right to intervene in any debate and to veto any conciliar decree.

The voting delegates would be a large group of 2,450 bishops and abbots from all over the world. In addition, the bishops were invited to bring theologians and experts (called *periti*) with them to advise them on various topics. Protestant and Orthodox Church leaders were invited as observers, as were some lay theologians, including women. Serious Catholics all over the world prayed for the success of this Council. What, they wondered, would the Holy Spirit say to the Church? ✝

Some Sayings of Pope Saint John XXIII

As pope, Saint John XXIII was known for his insightful sayings. Here are a few.

"Listen to everything, forget much, correct little." (Henri Fesquet and Salvator Attanasio, collector and translator, *Wit and Wisdom of Good Pope John*, page 85)

"Don't remain motionless like statues in a museum." (Page 161)

"Obedience and peace." Of this motto on his episcopal coat of arms, he said: "There lies the secret of my success." (Page 85)

"Unity in necessary things, freedom in doubtful things, charity in all things." (Page 86)

"Give all, but without expectation or hope of recompense." (Page 86)

"If God created the shadows it was in order to better emphasize the light." (Page 98)

© Bettmann/CORBIS

Article 50 Vatican Council II: A New Pentecost

On the eve of the opening of the Second Vatican Council, nearly half a million people poured into Saint Peter's Square. Their torches and candles lit up the darkness as Pope Saint John XXIII looked out from his balcony. He warmly thanked the people and assured them that the Council would lead the Church on the path God willed for her.

pastoral
From the Latin *pastor*, meaning "shepherd" or "herdsman"; refers to the spiritual care or guidance of others.

© Bettmann/CORBIS

Vatican II was truly a worldwide council, with 489 bishops from South America, 404 from North America, 374 from Asia, 84 from Central America, and 75 from Oceania, in addition to more than 1,000 from Europe.

The Opening of Vatican Council II

The Pope's opening speech to the delegates of the Council expressed his **pastoral** vision for the work of the Council. Speaking of the doctrine of the Church, the Pope said the following:

> Our duty is not only to guard this precious treasure, as if we were concerned only with antiquity, but to dedicate ourselves with an earnest will and without fear to that work which our era demands of us, pursuing thus the path which the Church has followed for twenty centuries. . . . The substance of the ancient doctrine of the deposit of faith is one thing, and the way in which it is presented is another. And it is the latter that must be taken into consideration with patience if necessary, everything being measured in the forms and proportions of a magisterium which is predominately pastoral in character. (Walter M. Abbott, general editor "Pope John's Opening Speech to the Council," in *The Documents of Vatican II*, page 715)

This, in more formal language, is what Pope Saint John XXIII meant when he spoke of *aggiornamento* (an "updating" or "adaptation"): the message of the Gospel, carried by the Church into a new age and communicated in a new and pastoral way. The root of the word *pastoral* is *pastor,* Latin for "shepherd." Saint John XXIII wanted the work of the Council and all its documents to concentrate on the needs of the people of the world, with the Church as shepherd and guide. The Council would fulfill the Pope's desire to throw open the Church's windows.

Teens Encounter Christ

A retreat movement for teens, emphasizing a personal meeting with Christ and a personal participation in his Paschal Mystery (his life, Passion, death, Resurrection, and Ascension), began in the years following Vatican II. The first retreat weekend was held in 1965 and the movement, called Teens Encounter Christ, or TEC, continues today, sponsoring weekend retreats specifically intended for older adolescents and young adults.

The weekend is intended to reach Catholic youth, who, although they may have received the Sacraments of Baptism, Confirmation, and the Eucharist, may never really have thought about the meaning of their faith. They may have known *about* Christ but did not really *know* Christ.

TEC seeks to help teens to encounter Christ by respecting and using contemporary culture to help them to know Christ's love and to awaken the gifts of faith, hope, and love in their hearts.

The First Session (October–December, 1962)

On the very first day of the first session, the Council adjourned after only a few minutes! Cardinal Lienart of France had offered a motion to expand the representation on the various Council commissions. This was a signal that the Council wanted the fullest and widest participation from its delegates with thoughtful consideration of all proposals made by Vatican officials.

When the Council convened again three days later, the slate of commission members, now expanded, was approved. The Council also rejected all but one of the original preparatory documents, called *schemata*, and the commissions began working on new ones. Though nothing was officially presented or decided at the first session of the Council, it was an important and significant beginning to the great work ahead.

The Death of Pope Saint John XXIII

The first session of Vatican II was adjourned on December 8, 1962, and preparation for the second session began. However, before that session could begin, Pope Saint John XXIII, often called Good Pope John, died, on June 3, 1963. When a pope dies, any Council that may have been meeting is automatically dissolved. It remained for the newly elected Pope Paul VI (1963–1978) to announce whether the Council would continue. On September 29, 1963, the Council reopened for its second session.

Pope Paul VI

When he was elected Pope, the former Cardinal Giovanni Montini chose the name of the Apostle Paul in order to

Catholic Wisdom

A Rallying Cry for Peace

In a speech to the United Nations in New York City (October, 1965), Pope Paul VI cried out: "No more war! Never again war! . . . If you wish to be brothers, drop your weapons." This was the same Pope who, in his New Year's message for the Day of Peace on January 1, 1972, wrote: "If you want Peace, work for Justice." This was the origin of the popular phrase: "No justice, no peace."

emphasize the worldwide mission of the Church and her mandate to spread the message of Christ. Like Pope Pius XII, he had a background in diplomacy. As a cardinal he traveled widely—to Africa, Brazil, and the United States.

Certainly one of Pope Paul's greatest achievement as Pope was the guidance of the Second Vatican Council to its completion. The Council's next three sessions (September 29, 1963, to December 4, 1963; September 14, 1964, to November 21, l964; and September 14, 1965, to December 8, 1965) produced several significant documents that would guide the Church throughout the coming years. We will discuss these documents, and other events related to the Second Vatican Council, in article 51, "An Overview of Vatican Council II." ✝

Although an Ecumenical Council is a meeting of the Church's bishops, hundreds of non-voting guests also attended the Second Vatican Council: among them were advisers, experts, translators, and observers.

Article

51 An Overview of Vatican Council II

The work of Vatican II was not limited to the actual months when it was in session. Between, and in addition to, the formal sessions, the work of the commissions continued. When the drafts, or *schematas*, were presented to the bishops at the Council, they were then subject to further commentary and revision. Only then was a document put to a vote.

Documents were of three varieties: constitutions, decrees, and declarations. They can be described as follows:

© David Lees/CORBIS

- Constitutions were concerned with doctrine and dogma. The constitutions restated dogma in contemporary language so that people of the modern world could better understand it.

- Decrees were concerned with renewal of some aspect of Church life. They required further action and implementation and were the foundation of that future work.

- Declarations gave instruction on subjects important to the Church and to the world. It would be up to each bishop, diocese by diocese, to teach and implement the content of these declarations as appropriate to his local area.

The Declaration on Religious Liberty

Today most Americans take for granted the principle of the separation of church and state. However, for centuries in Europe, the accepted maxim was "*Fides rex, fides populorum*,"—that is, "The faith of the king is the faith of the people."

The difficult question for the Council fathers was this: Should people be free to make an erroneous choice—that is, a choice against the Catholic Church, in whom subsists the fullness of truth? The principle of religious liberty—that is, the freedom to choose one's religion—was seen by some to contribute to error and thus could not be tolerated *in principle* by the Church. It took persuasive argument, and draft after draft of the document, much of it under the direction of American Jesuit Fr. John Courtney Murray (1904–1967), to influence the thinking of the Council fathers. Finally, it was accepted that each individual person should, in principle and as a matter of human dignity, be free to make a decision of conscience, even if in error, about his or her practice of religion.

© Bettmann/CORBIS

Key Documents of Vatican II

Vatican Council II approved and promulgated four constitutions, nine decrees, and three declarations. The constitutions are the foundation on which the decrees and declarations are built. The Council documents touched on nearly all areas of the Church's life. The following are some of the key documents.

Constitution on the Sacred Liturgy
(*Sacrosanctum Concilium,* December 4, 1963)

This constitution defines the liturgy as the source and summit of the Christian life, encouraged fuller participation in the liturgy, and called for the revision of liturgical texts used for Mass and other Sacraments. It also sets down new norms for the celebration of the Liturgy of the Hours, as well as for music and architecture.

Dogmatic Constitution on the Church
(*Lumen Gentium,* November 21, 1964)

This constitution defines the Church in language inspired by Scripture, most significantly, as the People of God. It also emphasizes that all are called to holiness and that the Church helps us to live lives that will lead us to God, now and forever.

Dogmatic Constitution on Divine Revelation
(*Dei Verbum,* November 18, 1965)

This document stresses the meaning of Divine Revelation as God's communication of himself and his will so that we might share in the divine life. It also discusses the origin and interpretation of Scripture and clarifies the relationship of Sacred Scripture to Sacred Tradition and the role of the Magisterium as the authentic interpreter of both. It encourages Scripture study and the wide availability of Sacred Scripture to the members of the Church.

Live It!

Unity through Compassion

"The joys and hopes, the grief and anguish of the people of our time, especially of those who are poor or afflicted, are the joys and hopes, the grief and anguish of the followers of Christ as well. Nothing that is genuinely human fails to find an echo in their hearts" (*The Church in the Modern World,* 1).

Sharing joys, hopes, grief, and anguish with others is a profoundly human and profoundly Christian thing to do. Take opportunities during your day to share significant experiences with friends, classmates, and family members. Often you do not need to go out of your way to find someone who needs a listening ear or a helping hand.

You may also have the chance to share with others through a service project. Take this as an opportunity rather than just a duty. As you share with others, you yourself will become more genuinely human and more genuinely Christian.

Pastoral Constitution on the Church in the Modern World (*Gaudium et Spes,* December 7, 1965)

Beginning with its first words "The joys and hopes" (1), this document emphasizes a pastoral concern for the people of the modern era, declaring that their joys, hopes, grief, and anguish must be the Church's as well. While analyzing modern problems, it reiterates the dignity of man and woman and the need for social justice in a world of political and economic inequality. It encourages Christians to serve the people of the world with generosity and effectiveness.

Decree on the Mass Media (*Inter Mirifica,* December 4, 1963)

This document stresses the responsibility of journalists, producers, and others involved in mass media to lead humankind, through their influence, on a good path rather than an evil one. The decree notes that those who participate in commercial media must take particular care to resist sordid influences and encourage the good.

Decree on Ecumenism (*Unitatis Redintegratio,* November 21, 1964)

Catholics are called to engage in ecumenical dialogue, to appreciate Christian values in other faiths, and to renew their own expression of Catholicism.

Decree on the Up-to-Date Renewal of Religious Life (*Perfectae Caritatis,* October 28, 1965)

Religious men and women are called to take the Gospel as their supreme rule and to adapt their practices to the needs of modern life.

Decree on the Apostolate of the Laity (*Apostolicam Actuositatem,* November 18, 1965)

Laypeople are encouraged to renew the world by their own lives and to see themselves as ambassadors for Christ at all times.

Declaration on the Relation of the Church to Non-Christian Religions (*Nostra Aetate,* October 28, 1965)

The Church expresses her high regard for non-Christian religions (mentioning Hinduism, Islam, and Judaism) and advises, "Let Christians, while witnessing to their own faith and way of life, acknowledge, preserve and encourage the spiritual and moral truths found among non-Christians" (2).

Declaration on Religious Freedom (*Dignitatis Humanae,* December 7, 1965)

Each individual person should, as a matter of human dignity, be free to make a decision of conscience about his or her practice of religion. ✝

Article 52 Images of the Church

The *Dogmatic Constitution on the Church*, or *Lumen Gentium*, is, as noted in article 51, "An Overview of Vatican

Council II," one of the most important documents to come from the work of Vatican Council II. One reason is that its articulation of the nature of the Church highlights many helpful biblical images that the majority of Church members were previously unaware of. So, before moving on to the post-Vatican world in the next part, let us pause, step back, learn from this great document on the Church, and ask the question anew: What is the Church?

© Bill Wittman/www.wpwittman.com

What Is the Church?

First of all, the Church is a sacrament—a sacrament of the Holy Trinity's communion with us. Christ, the Son of the Father, pours the Holy Spirit upon his Church to build, enliven, and make holy the Church that is his Body, together with all her members. The Church is a sacrament because in and through the Church, we encounter God.

The word *Church* means "convocation"—a calling together. Who calls? God calls. He calls us to form his people, and then nourishes us with the Body of Christ. If we receive in faith, we become what we receive. We ourselves become the mystical Body of Christ, the Church, in the world.

You may remember from other religion courses that God has a plan for us, and the Church is both the goal and the means of that plan. The goal is life forever with God in Heaven, in the perfect assembly, the perfect convocation, the perfect Church. The means to that goal is the Church herself—the Church begun with God's call in the Old Testament, prepared for by the Old Covenant, founded by the words and actions of Jesus Christ in the New Covenant, fulfilled by his cross and Resurrection, and brought to the world as the "mystery" (or sign) of salvation by the outpouring of the Holy Spirit.

As we noted in the introduction, the Church is both visible and spiritual, a hierarchical society (headed by the Pope with the bishops in communion with him and led by ordained ministers who are helped by designated laypeople in various roles) and also the Mystical Body of Christ, in which all are one. The Church is one but is made up of two elements, one human and one divine. This is a mystery. We can see and study the human aspect of the Church, but we cannot always see or study the divine aspect. The divine aspect is built on the visible reality, but only faith can accept it.

In summary, the Church is, in this world, "the sacrament of salvation, the sign and the instrument of the communion of God" (*Catechism of the Catholic Church [CCC]*, 780) with us. Through the Church we encounter God.

The Church Is the People of God

The *Dogmatic Constitution on the Church* states: "All women and men are called to belong to the new people of God. This people therefore, whilst remaining one and unique, is to be spread throughout the whole world and to all ages in order that the design of God's will may be fulfilled: he made human nature one in the beginning and has decreed that all his children who were scattered should be finally gathered together as one (see John 11:52)" (13). God's goal is that the human race may be one family and one People of God.

The Church Is the Body of Christ

Through the action of the Holy Spirit, especially in the Sacraments and most especially in the Eucharist, Christ (who

© SUCHETA DAS/Reuters/Corbis

Members of the Missionaries of Charity, a religious congregation founded by Saint Mother Teresa of Calcutta in 1950, take a vow to serve the poorest of the poor.

died once and for all and now is risen) forms the community of believers into his own Body. This **Body of Christ** is one in unity but diverse in her members and in the functions of those members in building up the body. All are linked to one another in Christ, especially to those who are poor, suffering, or persecuted in any way. Christ is the Head of this Body which is his Church, who lives "from him, in him, and for him; he lives with her and in her" (*CCC*, 807).

The Church Is the Bride of Christ

The symbol of the bride as an image of the People of God has a long history in Sacred Scripture and in the writings of the Fathers of the Church. The Church is the Bride of Christ because he loves her and gave himself up for her. He has purified her by his own blood and made her the fruitful mother of all the children of God.

The Church Is the Temple of the Holy Spirit

If we see the Church as the Body of Christ, we can also see the Holy Spirit as the soul of the Mystical Body. The Holy Spirit is "the source of its life, of its unity in diversity, and of the riches of its gifts and charisms" (*CCC*, 809). The Holy Spirit is the Church's principle of life, renewing her always from within, and strengthening her to reach out to the world in love and compassion.

The Spirit and the Bride

Dogmatic Constitution on the Church very beautifully summarizes the meaning of the work of the Holy Spirit in forming God's People: "By the power of the Gospel he rejuvenates the church, constantly renewing it and leading it to perfect union with its spouse. For the Spirit and the Bride both say to Jesus, the Lord, Come! (see Apoc 22:17). Hence the universal church is seen to be, [quoting Saint Cyprian] 'a people made one by the unity of the Father, the Son and the holy Spirit'" (4).

The Marks of the Church

The **Marks of the Church** are that she is One, Holy, Catholic, and Apostolic.

One

The Church is *One* because Christ is her source. In Saint Paul's Letter to the Ephesians, he asks that the Church remain "one body and one Spirit, as you were also called to the one hope of your call; one Lord, one faith, one baptism" (4:3–5).

Holy

The Church is *Holy,* because she was authored by the Most Holy God. Christ gave himself up to make her holy, as Bridegroom to his Bride; the Spirit of Holiness animates her very life. Although made up of sinners, she remains sinless and holy. The failures of her members during her history—for example, during the Crusades, the Inquisition, the persecution of the Jews and the Galileo case—are lamentable. On various occasions during his papacy, Saint John Paul II apologized for the sins that were committed in the midst of events such as the Inquisition and the Crusades. (It is helpful to keep in mind that people in earlier times used different means to address problems and that in many spheres of life policies and punishments that would be considered wrong and even shocking today were officially and socially sanctioned.) Despite the sins of her members, including the ordained, the Church is entrusted with the truth of the Gospel and the means of salvation. In Mary, the Mother of God, she is already all holy, and her holiness also shines through the lives of the saints, who validate the truth and power of the Church's Sacraments and teaching. Throughout her history, many members of the Church have made sacrifices, some to the point of martyrdom, that demonstrate heroic holiness.

Catholic

The Church is *Catholic,* meaning "universal." She proclaims the fullness of the faith everywhere and for everyone. In herself, for all times and all places, she is the total means of

Body of Christ

A term that when capitalized designates Jesus' Body in the Eucharist, or the entire Church, which is also referred to as the Mystical Body of Christ.

Marks of the Church

The four essential features or characteristics of the Church: One, Holy, Catholic (universal), and Apostolic.

salvation and offers this great gift to all. By her very nature, she is "missionary," that is, sent on mission to call all people to God through her.

You might wonder, why, if the Church has the fullness of truth, other churches have broken away. The problems that led to divisions among Christians arose from sin on the part of all members of Christ's Church, all of whom suffer the effects of Original Sin and are in need of ongoing conversion. Not all members of the Church live her fullness of the truth. Over time this has taken the form of disagreements about expressions of belief, the desire to change forms of worship, and impatience on the part of those who call for reform. In some cases, political or personal reasons contributed to a break. The Catholic Church works continuously to try to restore the unity that Christ called for (see John 17:21) without compromising the truth of the faith.

Apostolic

The Church is *Apostolic* because she is founded on the Apostles, the witnesses chosen by Christ himself; with the

Pray It!

A Litany of Prayer for Christian Unity

Vatican Council II was also concerned with Christian unity. Join in this prayer for unity and peace:

Leader: When we read the Bible together in our diversity of language and content,
All: Revealing One who makes us one, make our unity visible and bring healing to the world.
L: When we establish relations of friendships among Jews, Christians, and Muslims, when we tear down the wall of indifference and hatred,
A: Merciful One . . . (as above)
L: When we work for justice and solidarity, when we move from fear to confidence,
A: Strengthening One . . . (as above)
L: Whenever there is suffering through war and violence, injustice and inequality, disease and prejudice, poverty and hopelessness, drawing us near to the cross of Christ and to each other,
A: Wounded One . . . (as above)
A: The Lord's Prayer (in each one's own language)
(Pontifical Council for Promoting Christian Unity, "Resources for The Week of Prayer for Christian Unity and Throughout the Year 2001")

help of the Holy Spirit, she keeps hold of the teaching of the Apostles, and she is guided by the Apostles through their successors. She is the possessor of infallible truth, and Christ himself governs her through Peter and the other Apostles, now present in their successors, the Pope and the college of bishops. This line of Apostolic Succession is unbroken.

In summary, then, the Church of Christ "subsists in the Catholic Church, which is governed by the successor of Peter and by the bishops in communion with him. Nevertheless, many elements of sanctification and of truth are found outside its visible confines. Since these are gifts belonging to the church of Christ, they are forces impelling towards catholic unity" (*Dogmatic Constitution on the Church*, 8). ✝

Part Review

1. Describe the personality and demeanor of Pope Saint John XXIII. How do you think his background as a historian influenced his decision to call an Ecumenical Council?

2. What were the aims of the Second Vatican Council?

3. What does it mean to say that the Second Vatican Council was a pastoral council?

4. Why was the first session of Vatican Council II especially significant?

5. Name the four Constitutions promulgated by Vatican II and describe the content of one of them.

6. Choose one image of the Church and explain its meaning.

Part 3

Developments after the Second Vatican Council

The end of Vatican Council II in 1965 marked the beginning of many years of implementation in the midst of turmoil, both within the Church and within the world.

The Pope leading the Church through these years of change was Pope Paul VI (1963–1978). It fell to this Pope to not only expedite the completion of the Council but also to oversee its implementation for the remainder of his papacy. The papal visits of Pope Paul VI merit special mention, not only for the historical precedent they set but also for the vibrant message of the Gospel of peace this Pope announced to the world.

In 1985, the twentieth anniversary of the closing of Vatican Council II, Pope Saint John Paul II (1978–2005) called the bishops of the Church to an Extraordinary Synod to celebrate and evaluate the Second Vatican Council. This evaluation is discussed in the concluding article in this part.

The articles in this part address the following topics:

- Article 53: The Papacy of Pope Paul VI (page 241)

- Article 54: The Pilgrim Pope (page 246)

- Article 55: The Mass, Then and Now (page 249)

- Article 56: Vatican II: A Gift of God to the Church (page 253)

Article
53 The Papacy of Pope Paul VI

The Second Vatican Council officially closed on December 8, 1965. It had been a great achievement, both for the Church as a whole and for Pope Paul VI in particular. His organizational gifts and diplomatic skill helped him to steer the Council to its ultimate conclusion with the promulgation of sixteen significant texts, each of which had an important influence on the life of the Church. Yet while the work of the Council itself was at an end, the implementation of the Council's decrees was only beginning. The responsibility to implement the work of the Council fell to the bishops of the world, under the leadership of Pope Paul VI.

© Wally McNamee/CORBIS

In the fall of 1969, hundreds of thousands of protesters took part in anti-war demonstrations in the nation's capital.

From One Crisis to Another

The fifteen years of Pope Paul VI's reign as Pope were years of change and uncertainty for the entire world. Student revolts protesting the war in Vietnam were common in both the United States and Europe. Pope Paul VI himself protested this war, particularly at his speech at the United Nations in October, 1965. (See the sidebar "A Rallying Cry for Peace," in article 50.)

Other problems included the ever-widening gap between the rich and the poor in the world, and the "sexual revolution," which saw a decline in marriage and an upswing in abortions after the Supreme Court declared abortion to be legal in the United States in January of 1973.

The years after the Council also saw a shift in the life of the clergy and religious. Many clergy and religious asked to be dispensed from their commitments. It should be affirmed that, in recent years, vocations to both the priesthood and the consecrated life are increasing in a number of places in the United States and new communities of both men and women religious are emerging. Nevertheless, following Vatican II, the losses of sisters, brothers, and priests who had been "full time workers" committed to the Church was significant.

Humanae Vitae

The encyclical *Humanae Vitae* regarding openness to new life proved controversial. Even though a commission of doctors and laypeople had been set up during the papacy of Saint John XXIII to study this issue, Pope Paul VI found that, "within the commission itself, there was not complete agreement concerning the moral norms to be proposed, and especially because certain approaches and criteria for a solution to this question had emerged which were at variance with the moral doctrine on marriage constantly taught by the magisterium of the Church" (*Humanae Vitae*, 6). Therefore Pope Paul VI invoked the right and duty of the Church to set moral guidelines based not purely on human judgment but on the Law of God revealed in nature—that is, the natural law illuminated by Divine Revelation.

With this understanding of the Church's authority, *Humanae Vitae* stated that abortion, sterilization, and artificial contraception are contrary to the very nature of marriage: "The Church . . . in urging men [and women] to the observance of the precepts of the natural law, which it interprets by its constant doctrine, teaches that each and every marital act must of necessity retain its intrinsic relationship to the procreation of human life" (11).

Humanae Vitae is a beautiful statement about married love. But because it affirmed the Church's long-standing teachings against contraception and abortion, at a time of widespread social change, this encyclical met with severe criticism and dissent. Some even erroneously questioned the Pope's authority, seeking to undermine the Church's responsibility to teach on matters of sexual morality. Yet today *Humanae Vitae* remains a testament to the moral courage of a sensitive Pope and persistent teacher who met the challenge of guiding the Church through great social and cultural change.

Amid these problematic situations, Pope Paul VI continued, throughout his papacy, to be open to dialogue with other Christians, adherents of non-Christian religions, and even atheists. He also continued to monitor the renewal of the Church mandated by Vatican Council II as the Church stepped forward to meet the challenges of the modern world.

Three Key Encyclicals of Pope Paul VI

Pope Paul VI is also remembered for being a courageous teacher of faith and morals. His last three encyclicals—perhaps his best known—tackled major and pervasive problems, both in the world and in the Church. *Populorum Progressio* (*On the Progression of Peoples,* 1967) urged developed countries to provide aid to countries struggling with poverty; *Sacerdotalis Caelibatus* (*On Priestly Celibacy,* 1967) reaffirmed the reasons for priestly celibacy; and *Humanae Vitae* (*On the Regulation of Birth,* 1968) affirmed that every conjugal act must be open to new life, and that both abortion and any act deliberately rendering procreation impossible (such as sterilization or contraception) are illicit (see sidebar *"Humanae Vitae"*). These teachings set the course for the Church's understanding of the issues these three encyclicals addressed (the relationship of development to world peace, priestly celibacy, and regulation of birth by artificial means) up to the current day.

Effects of Vatican Council II

The Council had made possible many important changes to the Church's life and to the lives of her members. Here we explore a few of these changes: (1) renewal of Scripture study, (2) emphasis on religious freedom, (3) focus on social justice, (4) expanded role of the laity in the Church and in the world, (5) principle of collegiality between the college of bishops and the Pope, and (6) renewal of Eastern Catholic Churches. We will look at each of these in turn.

Renewal of Scripture Study

The work and study by Scripture scholars (and by liturgical experts in the realm of liturgy) preceding Vatican II greatly prepared the Church to make the renewal of the liturgy and the emphasis on Scripture study a reality and mandate at Vatican Council II (see article 55, "The Mass, Then and

collegiality
The principle that the bishops, in union with the Pope and under his leadership, form a single college that has authority over the universal Church.

Now," for more on the changes in liturgy). In addition to encouraging serious Scripture study among scholars, the Council Fathers encouraged all members of the Church to read and study Scripture, and they mandated that the riches of the Bible be made available to the laity. The entire Mass, along with its Scripture readings, was now in the vernacular, enhancing the participants' ability to understand the readings. Following Vatican II many more parishes began to offer Bible study groups and Scripture prayer groups, thus increasing biblical literacy among laypeople.

Emphasis on Religious Freedom

The *Decree on Religious Liberty* affirmed the rights of each person to believe in God and to worship according to his or her conscience.

Focus on Social Justice

Through the *Pastoral Constitution on the Church in the Modern World* (*Gaudium et Spes,* 1965), Vatican Council II emphasized the responsibility of the members of the Church to concern themselves with economic and social issues that affect people in every part of the world who are poor and in need.

Expanded Role of the Laity

The Second Vatican Council envisaged an active laity in the Church, from liturgical ministry (lay readers and lay Extraordinary Ministers of Holy Communion, for example) to catechetical work (lay catechists and teachers) to lay employees, especially in the areas of education and social justice. In fact, many laypeople, already encouraged by the Church's support of Catholic Action (begun under Pope Pius X), were leaders in these important areas. In addition, parish life was enhanced by pastoral councils elected by parishioners and formed to advise and assist pastors in their work. Lay Catholics were also urged to work with their "separated brethren" (non-Catholic Christians) in ecumenical work, fostering unity through mutual prayer and service.

Principle of Collegiality

The term **collegiality** means that all the bishops together with the Pope are united in a single college that has authority over the universal Church. The Pope's role as head of the college mirrors Peter's role as head of the Apostles. The college of bishops has authority only when united with its head, the Pope, and it exercises power over the Church at Ecumenical Councils.

One way Pope Paul VI encouraged a collegial spirit among bishops was by calling for periodic meetings in synods. Bishops also work together in national or regional conferences. In the United States, the national conference of bishops is known as the United States Conference of Catholic Bishops (USCCB).

Renewal of Eastern Catholic Churches

Vatican Council II's *Decree on the Catholic Churches of the Eastern Rite* (*Orientalium Ecclesiarum,* November 21, 1964) emphasized the equality of rites and the restoration of the heritage of each Eastern Catholic Church. The decree also stressed the special role of Eastern Catholics in promoting the unity of all Christians, especially with the Eastern Orthodox Church, "by prayer above all, by their example, by their scrupulous fidelity to the ancient traditions of the east, by better knowledge of each other, by working together, and by an understanding attitude towards persons an things" (24). The Second Vatican Council's special focus on the needs and traditions of the Eastern Catholic Churches resulted in a revitalization and spiritual renewal of the Churches, with

Live It!

How Are You Living Vatican Council II?

Now may be a good time to consciously choose to expand your understanding of the Council by taking a personal look at some aspects discussed in this part. How are you doing in the following areas?

- **Scripture studies** Do you look for opportunities to learn more about Sacred Scripture or to pray with Scripture?
- **Social justice** Opportunities abound to give service in this area, where there is always such need. Offer your time and talents!
- **Involvement as a lay Catholic** How are you involved in your Church? Do you serve during the liturgy? Do you participate in parish or diocesan events, especially those for youth? Be there and be counted!
- **Principle of collegiality** Are you attentive to the Church's teaching and to the messages of the American bishops and your own bishop, especially on matters related to how you live your life?

growth in the numbers of various Eastern Rite Churches. The actions and decrees of the council brought about a renewed commitment to Christian unity. ✝

Article 54 The Pilgrim Pope

In choosing the name Paul, Pope Paul VI set himself the task of renewed evangelization, of bringing the Gospel to the world, as the Apostle Paul had done in his time. Pope Paul VI was the first Pope to visit the Western Hemisphere, Africa, and Asia during his papacy. Because of his frequent travels throughout the world, he became known as the pilgrim Pope.

His first papal visit (the first time a pope had left Italy since 1809 and the first time a reigning pope had traveled on an airplane) was a pilgrimage to the Holy Land in January 1964. At the Mount of Olives near Jerusalem, a very significant meeting took place between Pope Paul VI and Patriarch Athenagoras I of Constantinople, the patriarch of the Greek Orthodox Church. This meeting eventually led to the dissolving, in 1965 at Vatican II, of the mutual excommunications that began the Eastern Schism between the Roman Catholic Church and the Eastern Orthodox Churches in 1054 (see article 19, "The Eastern Schism").

Pope Paul VI was the first reigning Pope to visit the United States.

© AP/Corbis

In December of 1964, the Pope traveled to Lebanon and then India to celebrate the Thirty-eighth International Eucharistic Congress in Bombay. The next year he visited the United States. In New York City, he met with President Lyndon Johnson, addressed the United Nations General Assembly (see the sidebar "A Rallying Cry for Peace" in article 50), celebrated Mass at Yankee Stadium, and visited the World's Fair in Queens, New York, to which the Vatican had contributed an exhibit of Vatican treasures.

Further travels in the following years included Portugal (to visit the Shrine of Our Lady of Fátima), Turkey (where he had a second meeting with Patriarch Athenagoras), Colombia (for the Thirty-ninth International Eucharistic Congress in Bogotá), Switzerland, Uganda, Iran, East Pakistan (now Bangladesh), the Philippines, American Samoa, Samoa, Australia, Indonesia, Hong Kong, and Ceylon. In Manila, Philippines, he was the intended victim of a failed assassination attempt at Manila International Airport (November 27, 1970).

What is the reason for all this travel? It would seem that Pope Paul VI, with his background in diplomacy, understood that he himself, as the Vicar of Christ, must show himself open to meeting the world's people and the world's leaders in person. Through his travels he truly became a second Apostle Paul for the Church.

Pope Paul VI's concern for the spread of the Good News throughout the world was further communicated to the Church through his apostolic exhortation *On Evangelization in the Modern World (Evangelii Nuntiandi)*, issued on December 8, 1975. In this document Pope Paul invited all the members of the Church to engage "in their mission as evangelizers, in order that, in this time of uncertainty and confusion, they may accomplish this task with ever increasing love, zeal and joy" (1). Pope Paul also emphasized the importance of the link between evangelization (proclaiming the Good News of Christ) and the development and advancement of peoples, especially directed to those who do not know Christ. However, he noted that the faith of those who are already believers must be deepened and nourished, especially in the face of secularism, "through a catechesis full of Gospel vitality and in a language suited to people and circumstances" (54). The Pope noted that laypeople, families, and young people can bring the Gospel of Christ to others in their own unique ways, always with gentleness and respect. ✞

Pope Paul VI at Yankee Stadium

On October 4, 1965, Pope Paul VI celebrated Mass at Yankee Stadium in New York. This was during the Vietnam War. During his homily the Pope spoke words of joy and peace:

> This is the day which the Lord has made; let us rejoice and be glad today! This is the day which We have desired for centuries! The day which, for the first time, sees the Pope setting foot on this young and glorious continent! An historic day, for it recalls and crowns the long years of evangelization of America, and the magnificent development of the Church in the United States!

After warning Americans of the dangers "which prosperity itself can entail, and which the materialism of our day can make even more menacing," Pope Paul VI went on to speak to the people of three things:

> First of all, you must love peace. . . . Second thought: You must serve the cause of peace. . . . Peace must be built; it must be built up every day by works of peace. These works of peace are, first of all, social order; then, aid to the poor, who still make up an immense multitude of the world population, aid to the needy, the weak, the sick, the ignorant. . . . Third thought: Peace must be based on moral and religious principles, which will make it sincere and stable. Politics do not suffice to sustain a durable peace. . . . Peace must have its roots anchored in wisdom, and this wisdom must draw nourishment from the true concept of life, that is the Christian concept. ("Homily of the Holy Father Paul VI," Yankee Stadium, New York, October 4, 1965)

Article 55 The Mass, Then and Now

Scene: A parish church, built in the gothic style, sometime in the 1950s. It is Sunday morning. The bells in the church tower have just stopped ringing, and suddenly a loud "Clang!" is heard from a bell hanging near the sacristy door. The Mass is about to begin! All the people stand. The choir, which will sing all the music of this Mass, begins singing a Latin Introit (Entrance Chant). Some people begin to follow this chant and other words of the Mass in their thick black Latin–English missals.

The priest, preceded by two altar boys, enters from the side door and stands, facing the altar, which is set against the back wall of the sanctuary. The altar boys take their places on either side of him, also facing the altar. They genuflect and bow, all making the Sign of the Cross as the priest begins: "*In nómine + Patris et Filii et Spíritus Sancti.*" The altar boys respond: *Amen.* The priest then begins the Prayers Before the Altar: "*Introíbo ad altáre Dei,*" the priest prays in

Pray It!

Prayer to Saint Michael the Archangel

It may surprise you to learn that, after Mass on a pre–Vatican II Sunday, the priest knelt before the altar of Our Lady and led the assembly in praying three Hail Marys for the conversion of Russia (as requested by Our Lady of Fátima in 1917) and the prayer to Saint Michael the Archangel:

> Saint Michael the Archangel,
> defend us in battle.
> Be our protection against the malice and snares of the devil.
> May God rebuke him, we humbly pray;
> and do thou, O Prince of the Heavenly Host,
> by the divine Power of God,
> cast into Hell Satan and all the evil spirits
> who roam through the world seeking the ruin of souls.
> Amen.

Although this prayer is no longer said at the end of Mass, Pope Saint John Paul II asked that we pray it in private to obtain Saint Michael's help in fighting evil. Saint Michael the Archangel is the special patron of police forces and others responsible for public safety.

a low voice. ("I will go into the altar of God.") *"Ad Deum, qui laetíficat juventútum meam,"* respond the altar boys. ("To God, who gives joy to my youth.") (Missal Commission of St. Andrew's Abbey, *Saint Andrew Bible Missal*, page 929).

Let us now return to the present. What differs between the Mass of the 1950s and the Mass we celebrate today? Here are a few examples of differences between then and now:

1. *Then:* The church was built in the gothic style, with a cruciform layout. The tabernacle was placed behind the altar, in the center of the sanctuary. An altar rail separated the assembly from the altar. *Now:* The church itself may look very different today, and may no longer be in the cruciform style of gothic architecture. It may be built "in the round," a style intended to emphasize community. The tabernacle may be placed in a side altar.

2. *Then:* The priest and servers entered the sanctuary directly from the sacristy. *Now:* Sunday Masses today begin with an entrance procession. The entrance procession includes the servers (boys, girls, men, or women), readers (both laypeople; on Sunday there are usually two readings other than the Gospel, and it is recommended that a separate reader read each one), and the priest. Before the renewal of Vatican II, there were no lay readers. The priest read all three readings in Latin. The Latin–English missal was a very necessary item to bring to church in order to follow the readings.

3. *Then:* The choir sang the Introit, or Entrance Chant, in Latin. *Now:* We all sing the Entrance Chant in the vernacular. Usually this Entrance Chant is a hymn, but in some places, the tradition of singing the Entrance Chant from the *Roman Missal* in the style of Gregorian chant (in the vernacular) has been retained. In any case we are invited to sing this Entrance Chant together, with or without a choir, as a sign of our unity and of our readiness to participate in the liturgy.

4. *Then:* The altar boys gave the responses, in Latin, not only at the beginning of the Mass but for the entire Mass. It was a great privilege but also a great responsibility to give these responses in the name of the people. If you were a new altar boy, you were

allowed to use a card to help you to remember the Latin words. But it was understood that before too long, and with some practice on your own, you would know the Latin responses by heart. *Now:* The people, as well as the altar servers, respond to the prayers of the priest. In this way we take our rightful place as full participants in the action of the liturgy.

5.   *Then:* People knelt behind the altar rail to receive the Eucharist. *Now:* Members of the assembly stand to receive the Eucharist, which may be distributed by an Extraordinary Minister of Holy Communion as well as a priest.

Reasons for Change

We have already seen some reasons for needed change in the liturgy. From the examples just discussed, we can see that the participation of the people is much more outwardly evident today than it was when everyone prayed along silently with the priest and the altar boys. Our Mass today more closely resembles the practices of the early Christians than did the Mass of the 1950s. And that was the aim of Vatican II: to bring the Church back to the participative roots of the liturgy and to remove from it various "accretions" or additions (like the Prayers Before the Altar), which had crept in over the centuries. These accretions, though good and even beautiful, interrupted the primary action of the Eucharistic celebration.

However, there were good things about the pre–Vatican II era of liturgical worship too. Some people find that praying in Latin (which was at one time the vernacular for everyone) makes the experience of the Mass more reverent. Using Latin demands thoughtful attention in order to follow the words in the missal. For those who understood and appreciated the beauty of the Mass when celebrated in Latin, with

© Bettmann/CORBIS

Kneeling and standing to receive Communion are both signs of respect. Kneeling has a centuries-long history in the Church; standing brings to mind the modern-day practice of rising to show respect for an important person.

its accompanying Gregorian chant, it was wrenching to have it replaced by Mass vernacular. Although the pre–Vatican II Mass, called the Tridentine Mass, continued to be celebrated in a small number of churches, with special permission from the Vatican, it was not an option readily available to most people. Pope Benedict XVI extended permission for every priest, who is willing, to celebrate the Tridentine Mass on appropriate occasions.

Today Latin is used more frequently in the Mass, and gradually some of the beautiful Latin chants are finding their way back into the liturgy, even in Masses that are predominantly English.

The Language of World Youth Day

At World Youth Day, young people from all around the world come together to celebrate their belief in Jesus Christ and their Catholic faith. Because each country now celebrates the liturgy in its own language, it was discovered that it was helpful to use Latin, the official language of the Church's liturgy, as a common liturgical and prayerful language during the World Youth Day gatherings. Therefore the praying of the Lord's Prayer, Hail Mary, and Glory to the Father can be heard in Latin during World Youth Days. Similarly the chants from the ecumenical Monastery of Taizé in France, written in Latin, are also popular for their unifying appeal. It is perhaps a sign of the presence of the Holy Spirit that a language thought "dead" would be reclaimed by the youth in the Church!

Interior Renewal of the Liturgy

In *The Final Report* (see article 56, "Vatican II: A Gift of God to the Church"), the bishops of the Church evaluated the conciliar renewal of the liturgy as follows: "The liturgical renewal is the most visible fruit of the whole conciliar effort" (II.B.2.a). They further reminded the Church that "the active participation, so happily increased after the council, does not consist only in external activity but, above all, in interior and spiritual participation, in living and fruitful participation in the paschal mystery of Jesus Christ" (II.B.2.a). In other words the bishops ask that we not only do the liturgy well but that we also insert our entire lives into the great mystery of the dying and rising of Christ and reflect his sacrificial love to the world. ✝

Article 56 Vatican II: A Gift of God to the Church

Twenty years after the close of Vatican Council II, in 1985, Pope Saint John Paul II called together the bishops of the world for an Extraordinary Synod. Its purpose was to consider and evaluate the aims and results of the Second Vatican Council. Gathered in Rome, the bishops issued *The Final Report* and thus shared with the Church and the world their evaluation.

Throughout history the Church has faced the challenge of engaging the world while remaining true to its own identity, to be "in the world," but not "of the world."

© Stevan Kordic/Shutterstock.com

The aim of the Extraordinary Synod was "the celebration, verification, and promotion of Vatican Council II" (*The Final Report*, I.2). This significant paragraph appears early in the document: "Unanimously we have celebrated the Second Vatican Council as a grace of God and a gift of the Holy Spirit, from which have come forth many spiritual fruits for the universal Church and the particular Churches, as well as for the men [and women] of our time. Unanimously and joyfully, we also verify that the council is a legitimate and valid expression and interpretation of the deposit of faith as it is found in sacred Scripture and in the living tradition of the Church" (I.2).

Yet even after twenty years, the bishops asserted that the work of the Council was not yet finished: "Therefore, we are determined to progress further along the path indicated to us by the council. There has been full consensus among us regarding the need to further promote the knowledge and application of the council, both in its letter and in its spirit. In this way, new progress will be achieved in the reception of the council, that is, in its spiritual interiorization and practical application" (*The Final Report*, I.2).

Reception of the Council by the People

The bishops noted that most of the members of the Church accepted the Council wholeheartedly. Some, however, did have reservations about some of its recommendations. History tells us that this is not unusual; after the Council of

The Council's Moving Forward

The Final Report was issued almost thirty years ago. Yet the report still has relevance today, both in noting what has been accomplished in the past thirty years in regard to the implementation of Vatican II as well as in what has yet to be accomplished.

To further the aims of the Council, the bishops made several suggestions. Some have been implemented in the last thirty years. One suggestion called for a new catechism or compendium of doctrine to be presented in both biblical and liturgical terms and "suited to the present life of Christians" (*The Final Report*, II.B.1.d). That suggestion ultimately resulted, under Pope Saint John Paul II's direction, in the *Catechism of the Catholic Church*, released in 1992. The *Catechism* has played an important role in the formation of the spiritual lives of the faithful. Most religion textbooks for Catholic elementary and high schools and for parish religious education programs in the United States are based on this catechism.

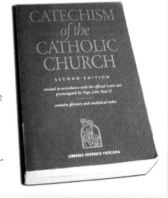

The work of Vatican Council II has shaped the Church and the lives of Catholics in the last fifty years and will continue to shape our lives in the years to come.

Nicaea, which affirmed the full divinity of Christ, riots broke out between factions of the Church—some agreeing with the Council's decision and some not. In *The Final Report,* the bishops point out that, in some places, understanding and application of the Council's directives has been incomplete.

Difficulties in Accepting the Church

In *The Final Report,* the bishops also note that in some places in the world, particularly in the more affluent areas, people have become estranged from the Church. The bishops suggest that some of the reasons for this are "pride in technical advances and a certain immanentism [the belief that God is an abstract spirit that pervades the world] that leads to the idolatry of material goods (so called consumerism). From this can follow a certain blindness to spiritual realties and values" (I.4).

The bishops also note that because of concentration on changes mandated by Vatican Council II, the Church itself may have been concentrating too much on her identity as an institution and too little on the Mystery of God to which she bears witness. In addition, the document clarifies that the Council never intended openness to the secular world to mean taking on the secular world's mentality and order of values; rather, it intended for the Church's members to engage the world and to be leaven in the world.

A Deeper Reception of the Council

The bishops affirmed that a deeper reception of the Council, through knowledge and understanding, was needed within the Church, as well as continued practical implementation of the Council's ideas and decrees. The bishops thus suggested

Catholic Wisdom

The Role of Young People

The Extraordinary Synod of 1985 also concerned itself with young people. The bishops noted: "This extraordinary Synod addressed young people with special love and great confidence and expects great things from their generous dedication. It exhorts them that they might embrace and dynamically continue the heritage of the council, assuming their role in the mission of the Church" (*The Final Report,* II.C.6).

that, in every diocese, pastoral programs of education be established so that the Council documents can be studied and understood by all members of the Church in the midst of contemporary issues, including a widespread secular view of life along with the emergence of sects and cults, the need for the Church to preach Christ, the Church's importance as connected to Christ, and a renewal of the universal call to holiness proclaimed by the Council. ✝

Part Review

1. For what three topics of teaching (promulgated in encyclicals) is Pope Paul VI particularly remembered?

2. Name six effects of Vatican Council II and explain one of them.

3. Why did Pope Paul VI choose Paul for his papal name?

4. What was one of the main purposes for the liturgical changes made in the liturgy during and after Vatican Council II?

5. In addition to necessary changes in externals, what else is needed in liturgical renewal?

6. What did the bishops verify about Vatican Council II in their evaluation during the Extraordinary Synod of 1985?

7. What need in the Church did the bishops identify during this Extraordinary Synod, and how did they propose that this need be met?

Part 4

The Church in the New Millennium

The events described in this part may actually be within your memory, or at least you will not find them totally unfamiliar. You have no doubt heard of Pope Saint John Paul II. Because of his unique contribution to the life of the Church and the world, he is the focus of two articles in this part. You will also recognize Saint John Paul II's successor, Pope Benedict XVI, and our current Holy Father, Pope Francis. The last two articles present two important facets of the Church in the United States today in relation to the modern world: abounding in hope, yet aware of challenges and choices to be made. As you read these articles, consider how you can help the Church as a whole to realize these hopes and take up these challenges. What will be your impact on the history of the Church?

The articles in this part address the following topics:

Article 57 The Life and Times of Pope Saint John Paul II

After the death of Pope Paul VI on August 6, 1978, the cardinals of the Church gathered in Rome to elect his successor. They chose the patriarch of Venice, Cardinal Albino Luciani, who took the names of his two immediate predecessors and became Pope John Paul I. This double name, the first in history for a pope, signaled that he intended to carry the Church in the direction indicated by the papacies of both Saint John XXIII and Paul VI. Known for his good humor, Pope John Paul I quickly acquired the nickname the smiling Pope. His sudden death in his sleep from a heart attack on September 28, a little more than a month after his election, plunged the Church and the world once more into mourning. The new Pope had reigned only thirty-three days.

A Pope from Poland

Once more the cardinals gathered for a papal election. On October 16, 1978, they chose a relatively young man as Pope—Cardinal Karol Wojtyla (voy-TEE-wah) of Krakow, Poland, who was fifty-eight. He was the first non-Italian Pope to be elected since Pope Adrian VI, who was Dutch, in 1522. He is the only Polish Pope in the Church's history. In deference to his predecessors and also in honor of the Pope who had so suddenly died, Cardinal Wojtyla took the name John Paul II. With his election the year 1978 came to be called "The Year of the Three Popes."

The Making of a Modern Pope

The forces that shaped the life and character of Karol (the Polish form of Charles and pronounced "Karl") Wojtyla were not only familial but historical and political. Karol was born on May 18, 1920, in Wadowice, Poland, the youngest of three children. (His sister Olga had died before he was born.) When Karol's mother died when Karol was nine, he clung to his father and his elder brother Edmund for comfort. Then, when Karol was thirteen, he again faced the loss of a member of his family with the death of his brother. Sadly, just a few years later, in 1941, his father died. By age twenty Karol had lost every member of his family and found himself alone in the world.

The Nazis required every able-bodied Pole over the age of fourteen to work ten hours a day, six days a week. Those suspected of not working were shipped to labor camps in Germany.

© CORBIS

In 1939, shortly after Karol had entered a local university, as well as a school for drama, World War II began with the Nazi invasion of Poland. Karol's university was closed. For four years he did hard manual labor in a stone quarry and then worked in a chemical factory. This experience no doubt shaped Karol's views on workers' rights in his later years as priest, bishop, and Pope.

Live It!

Live Your Faith

Through Baptism we are called to put our faith into action. How can we do this? Let us take a few cues from the life of Pope Saint John Paul II.

1. Pray. There is no substitute for prayer, which is talking to God and also listening to him. Prayers do not have to be long or involved. They can be brief messages just to let God know how you are doing, to thank him, and to ask for his guidance and the strength to do his will.

2. Be willing to be inconvenienced. As a seminarian Karol Wojtyla risked his life to study for the priesthood. Such heroism is not asked of us, but we can go out of our way to get to Mass, to stop in a church to pray, or to help someone out.

3. Stretch your world. How wide is your circle of awareness? Hopefully, it extends beyond yourself to others—even to local problems and world issues.

Pope Saint John Paul II and Communism

Shortly after the Nazis invaded Poland in 1939, the Soviet Russians also invaded. After the war, when the Nazis were defeated, the Soviets remained in Poland. Polish resistors met with arrest and deportation by the hundreds of thousands. Communism had taken over Poland. By the time Karol Wojtyla became archbishop of Krakow in 1963, he had had a lot of practice preaching about Christian humanism, dignity, and freedom without directly criticizing the communist government. In 1979, the year after he was elected Pope, he made a pilgrimage to Poland. He had warned the Polish government, behind the scenes, that the whole world would be watching. In Poland he saw the usual banners flying the communist party slogan, "The Party Is for the People," but with a line added by citizens empowered by the Pope's visit: "But the People Are for the Pope." Inspired by the Pope's visit, an electrician named Lech Walesa formed a union called Solidarity. This was the first trade union not controlled by the communist party in a Soviet-controlled country. Eventually Solidarity developed into a broad anti-communist movement, one built on the principles of nonviolence, and grew to become a political force in Poland.

In 1990 Lech Walesa became Poland's first non-Communist president since World War II. Many historians credit Saint John Paul II and his support for Solidarity for the beginning of the end of communism, not only in Poland but in the entire western world as well. Later, when questioned about his role in the fall of communism, Saint John Paul II said: "I did not cause this to happen. The tree was already rotten. I just gave it a good shake" (In Michael Satchell, "The End of Communism," in *U.S. News and World Report* online, April 2, 2005).

Gradually Karol began to realize that he might be called to the priesthood. But the Nazis had closed the seminary. One night Karol knocked on the door of the archbishop's house in Krakow. He was taken in and enrolled in night classes in the archbishop's underground seminary. When World War II ended, he finished his studies at the reopened major seminary of Krakow. He was ordained a priest on November 1, 1946.

Father Karol Wojtyla eventually earned two doctorates. He also ministered in parishes and to university students. A lover of the natural world, he sponsored and participated in mountain hiking, skiing, and kayaking trips with the students, often saying Mass outdoors. His love of young people was very much evident in his years as Pope, and the now annual World Youth Day began at his suggestion and under his direction. Today, World Youth Day draws over a million young people, gathered for worship and spiritual renewal.

The Impact of World War II and the Holocaust

The impact of Pope Saint John Paul II's experience during World War II can be witnessed in his papacy. When the Nazis took over Poland early in the war, they brought with them their systematic scheme for eliminating the Jewish people. As in Germany the majority population looked on in horror as their Jewish neighbors were rounded up and taken away to "labor camps," which eventually became death camps. (Karol joined a resistance movement giving aid to escaping Jews.) By the end of the war, over three million Polish Jews had been killed, among them some of Karol's friends and former classmates. Throughout his papacy Saint John Paul II condemned anti-Semitism. In two history-making events, he visited Rome's chief synagogue and prayed at the Western Wall of the Jewish Temple in Jerusalem. Saint John Paul II's concern for human rights and dignity was undoubtedly shaped by his own witnessing of the horrors of the Holocaust and living under a communist regime. ✝

Article 58 Pope Saint John Paul II: Evangelist and Pastor, Teacher and Writer

Many books have been written, and more will continue to be written, about the papacy of Saint John Paul II. Because his was the second-longest papal reign in history (twenty-six years and 168 days), there are many achievements to record. Only Pope Pius IX served as Pope longer (thirty-one years). This and the next article highlight only a portion of the achievements of one of the most active and influential Popes in history.

Evangelist to the World

As pope, Saint John Paul II was an evangelist, a proclaimer of the Good News of the Gospel, in both simple and profound ways. In all, he made 104 papal visits—to every continent except Antarctica. When meeting people he kissed and blessed babies and wore every kind of cultural hat given to him. In setting a course for the Church and the world through his writings, he proclaimed the Gospel through his thorough and profound theological and pastoral writings.

Spiritual leaders representing the Anglican Church, the Eastern Orthodox Church, and Buddhism pray for world peace with Pope Saint John Paul II.

© Reuters/CORBIS

He did not limit his efforts at evangelization to members of the Catholic Church but saw the Church as the leader of what he called "the dialogue of salvation" with other religions. In this dialogue, undertaken by ordinary people and theologians alike, every human being sees himself or herself as one with all humanity, as part of the human family. With that respectful acknowledgment of self and others, a true dialogue on religious topics can begin. As a symbol of this dialogue, Pope Saint John Paul II asked that all leaders of world religions join him in a World Day of Prayer for Peace in Assisi, Italy, in 1986 and again, after the terrorist attacks against the United States, in 2001. Pope Benedict XVI held a similar

meeting in October 2011, to celebrate the twenty-fifth anniversary of the first World Day of Prayer in Assisi in 1986.

Pastor

As pope, Saint John Paul II was pastor to the world, but especially to his "family of the faith," (Galatians 6:10), the Church. We have already briefly mentioned his role in the development of the *Catechism of the Catholic Church* (see the sidebar "The Council's Moving Forward" on page 254). In 1986, in response to the recommendation of the bishops in attendance at the Extraordinary Synod of 1985, Pope Saint John Paul II appointed a commission of cardinals and bishops to oversee the preparation of a new universal catechism. A French-language edition was published in 1992. In 1993, a new commission, headed by Cardinal Joseph Ratzinger (later Pope Benedict XVI) was mandated to bring together a definitive edition. This edition was published in 1994. In a special way, this catechism can be seen as a fruit of Vatican II, which reminded us that true catechesis requires both content (that is, the truths of the Catholic faith) and formation (education in ways to live these truths in our own lives).

As chief pastor of the Catholic Church, Saint John Paul II never forgot that singular title of the Pope—Servant of the Servants of God—a title that Pope Gregory the Great instituted in the late sixth century. Every Holy Thursday, a day made holy by Jesus' Last Supper, his institution of the Eucharist, and of the priesthood, Saint John Paul II wrote a pastoral letter to bishops and priests. In these letters he touched upon themes important to those in the ordained ministry, thus making an invaluable contribution to priestly formation. There is no doubt that these letters will be treasured and studied by seminarians, priests, and bishops for years to come.

Finally, Saint John Paul II was the preeminent youth minister to Catholic young people. He never ceased to reach out to youth, particularly through World Youth Days held all over the globe and made all the more exciting by his presence. The Pope's presence at the World Youth Day celebration held in Denver, Colorado, in 1993 is noteworthy for invigorating youth ministry in the Church in the United States. At the end of Saint John Paul II's life, thousands of people, including many young people, came to Saint Peter's

Square. The Pope, now weak and dying, could hear them singing. He said, "I have searched for you, and now you have come to me, and I thank you" ("Final Days, Last Words of Pope John Paul II").

Teacher and Writer

It is expected that a Pope would teach, preach, and issue encyclicals to guide the Church in unfolding the meaning of the Gospel in contemporary times. In the almost twenty-seven years of his papacy, Saint John Paul II produced a tremendous volume of work (encyclicals, documents, homilies, and other writings).

Pope Saint John Paul II was a linguist by training; when he traveled, he often addressed the faithful in their own language. Here he delivers his first speech from the balcony of Saint Peter's, in fluent Italian.

© Vittoriano Rastelli/CORBIS

Themes of Hope and Encouragement

Before examining some of Saint John Paul II's writings, however, we will focus on some of the main themes of his teaching, themes that he repeated often in his preaching and that also found their way into his various writings.

Be Not Afraid

From the beginning of his pontificate, Saint John Paul II urged the world to "be not afraid" of welcoming Christ. On the day he was installed as the successor of Saint Peter and the Bishop of Rome, Saint John Paul II said: "Brothers and sisters, do not be afraid to welcome Christ and to accept his power. Help the Pope and all those who wish to serve Christ and with Christ's power to serve the human person and the whole of mankind. Do not be afraid. Open wide the doors for Christ" ("Homily of His Holiness John Paul II for the Inauguration of His Pontificate," October 22, 1978, 5). This day of installation is now celebrated by the entire Church as the feast day of Pope Saint John Paul II, who was beatified on May 1, 2011, by Pope Benedict XVI and canonized by Pope Francis on April 27, 2014.

Mary, *Totus Tuus* (All Yours)

As a seminarian the future Pope Saint John Paul II read a prayer in the book *True Devotion to Mary*, by Saint Louis de Montfort. The prayer in Latin is: *Totus tuus ego sum, et omnia mea tua sunt* ("I am all yours, and all that I have is yours"). He took it as his motto as bishop, cardinal, and then as Pope. In his book *Crossing the Threshold of Hope*, Saint John Paul II explains that devotion to Mary is ultimately rooted in the mystery of the Holy Trinity, as Mary was chosen by the Father to be the mother of his Son through the power of the Holy Spirit.

Human Dignity

The dignity of each human person, from the child newly conceived but yet unborn to the elderly person close to death, is a consistent theme of the teachings of Pope Saint John Paul II. In his writings, he particularly notes the dignity of the worker (*On Human Work*, 1981) and the protection and promotion of human life for all (*The Gospel of Life*, 1995). From this foundation of human dignity, it follows that actions against human life and dignity are forbidden. These include abortion, euthanasia, genocide, torture, the

new evangelization
A renewed effort, called forth by Pope Saint John Paul II, to bring the Gospel of Christ to individual believers, especially to those who, though baptized, have never fully heard or accepted the Christian message.

intentional targeting of non-combatants in war, and murder. Similarly, capital punishment is to be avoided and, as Saint John Paul II noted in *The Gospel of Life*, should be rare to nonexistent.

The Theology of the Body

As pope, Saint John Paul II was particularly concerned with fostering human dignity through relationships, particularly through the relationships of men and women in marriage. In several years of Wednesday audiences, beginning with the Book of Genesis, the Pope unfolded the meaning not only of human sexuality and marriage but also of God's plan for human life and the integrity of the human person. These reflections became known as the *Theology of the Body,* and have been published in book form and are available to the general public.

The New Evangelization

During his papacy, in his encyclical *Mission of Christ the Redeemer* (*Redemptoris Missio*), Saint John Paul II spoke of a particular situation of the Church in some places, where people have lost a sense of living faith, no longer consider themselves members of the Church, and "live a life far removed from Christ and his Gospel. In this case what is needed is a '**new evangelization**' or a 're-evangelization'" (33). The Pope went on to assert that there is an interdependence between the mission to non-Christians peoples and countries and the mission to non-Christians or lapsed Christians at home. Both are needed, and the Pope urged each member of the Church to give some time to missionary activity.

Three Major Encyclicals

Of Pope Saint John Paul II's many encyclicals, three stand out for their teaching and insight into the truths of faith and their relationship to the issues of today. These encyclicals are *Splendor of Truth (Veritatis Splendor), Gospel of Life (Evangelium Vitae),* and *Faith and Reason (Fides et Ratio).* In *Splendor of Truth*, the Pope emphasizes that all moral theology must be based on the truth. In the *Gospel of Life*, he stresses that all human life, from conception to natural death, must be protected. In *Faith and Reason*, the Pope clarifies the relationship between theology and philosophy as a creative one, describing faith and reason as "two wings on which the human spirit rises to the contemplation of truth" and stating that it is only in knowing God that we can come to truly know ourselves. Consider reading these encyclicals for yourself, to catch and share the vision of this Pope who was not only an expert theologian and philosopher but also a gifted writer. ✝

Article 59 The Papacy of Pope Benedict XVI

Pope Saint John Paul II died on April 2, 2005. Outside his window thousands had been keeping vigil with him, day and night, in Saint Peter's Square. His last words were, in Polish, "Let me go to the house of the Father" (in Associated Press report). And some hours later, one of the greatest leaders of the Church, and of the twentieth century, went home to God.

Despite his concerns about the values of modern culture, Pope Benedict XVI appreciated the reach of social media. He launched a YouTube channel, released a Facebook app, and opened a papal Twitter account.

© MAX ROSSI/Reuters/Corbis

The subsequent election of Cardinal Joseph Ratzinger to the papacy was no great surprise, as he had been entrusted during the papacy of Saint John Paul II with a great deal of responsibility. Cardinal Ratzinger was the dean (leader) of the college of cardinals, and had held several important offices in the Vatican, among them the prefect of the Congregation for the Doctrine of Faith and president of the Preparatory Commission for the *Catechism of the Catholic Church*.

Cardinal Ratzinger, from Germany, chose the name Benedict, recalling Pope Benedict XV, who was Pope during the turbulent years of World War I, and Saint Benedict of Nursia, whose Benedictine Order was so influential in the Christianization of Europe.

The Writings of Pope Benedict XVI

Pope Benedict XVI was trained as a theologian and was one of the expert theologians present at the Second Vatican Council. His first encyclical stressed God's love and our response: *God Is Love (Deus Caritas Est)*. He later wrote *Saved by Hope (Spe Salvi)* and *Charity in Truth (Caritas in Veritate)*. In addition, his apostolic exhortation on the Eucharist, *Sacrament of Love (Sacramentum Caritatis)*, summarizes the Church's teaching on the Eucharist as the source and summit of the Church's life and mission. It is also an instruction on the celebration of the Eucharist, and a reminder that reception of the Eucharist should not be taken for granted but should be an occasion approached with reverence and with an appropriate examination of our lives as Christians.

Culture and Faith

Both Pope Benedict XVI's official teachings and his more popular meditations reflect his concern that the culture of our day lacks the permeating influence of faith. Our modern culture today—how we live, our attitudes toward life and people, our work, our leisure activities, and our moral choices—reflects our faith or our lack thereof. We shape our culture by our choices, and these choices are important, because our culture, in turn, shapes (but does not ultimately define) us. In the Gospel of John, Jesus prays for his Apostles and for all who would later follow him, "Holy Father . . . I do not ask that you take them out of the world but that you keep them from the evil one" (John 17:11,15). This has been the challenge for the Church and for every follower of Christ, to the present day.

In March 2011 a group of young people gathered in Paris, in the square in front of Notre Dame Cathedral. Both believers and unbelievers, they met to dialogue about God, religion, and other profound questions. Pope Benedict addressed them by video, saying: "The question of God is not a menace to society, it does not threaten a truly human life! The question of God must not be absent from the other great questions of our time. . . . Striving for truth is not easy. But each of us is called to make a courageous decision to seek the truth." ("Benedict XVI's Message to Courtyard of Gentiles")

Ecumenism

We have already discussed briefly the prayerful meeting of religious leaders of all faiths who gathered at Pope Benedict's invitation at Assisi in 2011 (see article 58, "Pope Saint John Paul II: Evangelist and Pastor, Teacher and Writer"). In calling this meeting, Pope Benedict intended to commemorate the first meeting of world leaders of religious faith called during the papacy of Saint John Paul II in 1986. The theme of this meeting, "Pilgrims of truth, pilgrims of peace," reflected Pope Benedict's concern that the Catholic Church prayerfully join with others of goodwill to promote peace and justice throughout the world.

Pope Benedict's outreach to Anglicans in England resulted in the establishment, in 2009, of the Ordinariate of Our Lady of Walsingham. Anglicans (members of the Church of England) who felt called to be Catholic, yet who wished to keep some traditions of Anglican prayer and liturgy, were received as a large group and are allowed to form Ordinariate parishes. These parishes retain some episcopal autonomy and Anglican practices, but profess the faith of the Church and maintain fidelity to the Pope. This particular privilege may pave the way for more Anglicans to request membership in the Catholic Church.

Throughout his papacy Pope Benedict encouraged the Eastern Churches to preserve their Eastern identity and traditions, calling them a treasure for the whole Church. In addition, Pope Benedict noted that these Eastern Churches, in their canonical disciplines and traditions, share these same disciplines and traditions with the Eastern Orthodox Churches, which have been separated from the Roman Catholic Church since the Eastern Schism of 1054. Thus, in keeping to these traditions, the Eastern Catholic Churches can, hopefully, pave the way for a reunion with the Eastern Orthodox Churches. (It should be noted that differences on points of doctrine still remain a major stumbling block to this reunion.)

Resignation and Retirement

On February 11, 2013, Pope Benedict XVI surprised the Church and the world by announcing his resignation, to take effect on February 28. In his announcement, Pope Benedict (now Bishop Emeritus of Rome) declared that, after much thought and prayer, he believed that he could no longer exercise his ministry with the needed strength of mind and body. He declared that he was making this decision freely and

The Popular Writings of Pope Benedict XVI

Pope Benedict XVI was also a popular writer and teacher, as evidenced by the success of his books about Jesus Christ: *Jesus of Nazareth: From the Baptism in the Jordan to the Transfiguration* (San Francisco: Ignatius Press, 2008), *Jesus of Nazareth: Holy Week: From the Entrance into Jerusalem to the Resurrection* (San Francisco: Ignatius Press, 2011), and *Jesus of Nazareth: The Infancy Narratives* (also from Ignatius Press, 2012). All have been praised by scholars and by ordinary Christians for their insights into the meaning of Jesus Christ for each of us. Another book, about the Church, titled *Light of the World* (San Francisco: Ignatius Press, 2010), has also found a wide and eager audience.

With Pope Benedict's permission, books for children featuring him as a main character have been written (by author Jeanne Perego) and published: *Joseph and Chico: The Life of Pope Benedict XVI as Told by a Cat* (San Francisco: Ignatius Press, 2008) and *Max and Benedict: A Bird's Eye View of the Pope's Daily Life* (San Francisco: Ignatius Press, 2009), about a bird who, from his vantage point in the Vatican Gardens, reports on the doings of the Pope. These popular books have helped to make connections with all members of the Church, even the very youngest.

© Maurizio Gambarini/dpa/Corbis

would continue to support the Church through a quiet life of prayer and study.

Pope Benedict's decision was seen as an honest and courageous one. After all, no Pope has resigned in the past six hundred years! In the final days of his papacy, Pope Benedict was the recipient of an outpouring of love, support, and gratitude from people throughout the world. Now that he is no longer Pope, his official title is Pope Emeritus Benedict XVI. ☦

Article 60 — Pope Francis: Servant of the Servants of God

The ancient title "Servant of the Servants of God" has been traditionally and exclusively used by the popes of the Church to describe the ministry of the successor of Saint Peter. The ministry of the Pope is primarily a ministry of service. The theme of service quickly became one of the major themes of the papacy of Pope Francis (formerly Cardinal Jorge Mario Bergoglio), who, on March 13, 2013, was chosen to be the leader on earth of the Church.

Serving as Jesus Served

From the evening of his election, Pope Francis, through his words and actions, made clear that, like Christ, he "did not come to be served but to serve" (Matthew 20:28). In the homily of his Inauguration Mass, the Pope said, "Let us never forget that authentic power is service, and that the Pope too, when exercising power, must enter ever more fully into that service which has its radiant culmination on the Cross."

Pope Francis giving a homily during a Mass at the Vatican's parish church of Saint Anna, prior to leading his first Angelus at noon in Saint Peter's Square.

Protection of the Poor

In his life as Archbishop of Buenos Aires, Cardinal Bergoglio (now Pope Francis) tried to live as simply as possible. He often took public transportation rather than his own car to work at his office. He cooked his own meals rather than employing a cook. He regularly visited the poorest areas of the city. He seemed to take seriously the well-known slogan, "Live simply so that others may simply live."

In the homily of his Inauguration Mass on the Feast of Saint Joseph (March 19, 2013), Pope Francis outlined the role of Saint Joseph as protector of Mary and Jesus, and noted that all of us are called to be "protectors." What does this mean? The Pope explained, "It means protecting people, showing loving concern for each and every person, especially children, the elderly, those in need, who are often the last we think about."

Protection of the Environment

The Pope also called on all people to be protectors of the environment. We must do this, the Pope noted, not only because we are Christian but because we are human. Being a "protector" means "protecting all creation, the beauty of the created world. . . . It means respecting each of God's creatures and respecting the environment in which we live."

Building Bridges

In greeting ambassadors from around the world, Pope Francis spoke of the need for peace and friendship among nations. In explaining that the word *pontiff* means "builder of bridges," he said, "My wish is that the dialogue between us should help to build bridges connecting all people, in such a way that everyone can see in the other not an enemy, not a rival, but a brother or sister to be welcomed and embraced" (*New York Times*, March 22, 2013).

Many Firsts

The election of Pope Francis was unique in many ways. He is the first Pope to take the name Francis. He is the first Pope to come from the Americas, from "the New World"—that is, not from Europe. Born in Argentina of Italian immigrant

Can a Pope Resign?

Pope Benedict XVI's decision to resign his official ministry as Pope took the Church and the world by surprise. Many wondered: "Could the Pope really do this? Isn't he expected to remain in office for the rest of his life?"

Such a reaction is understandable. After all, a papal resignation is indeed a rare event. In the long history of the Church, there have been popes who were forced from office by persecution, political authorities, or by necessary Church reforms. Only one Pope, Celestine V, voluntarily renounced his office, in 1294. After a reign of less than one year, Celestine abdicated, with the goal of returning to his life as a hermit.

Pope Benedict XVI's decision to resign because of declining health was seen as honest and courageous, and from it the Church and the world learned much. Pope Benedict explained his decision in these words: "In order to govern the barque of Saint Peter and proclaim the Gospel, both strength of mind and body are necessary, strength which in the last few months has deteriorated in me to the extent that I have had to recognize my incapacity to adequately fulfill the ministry entrusted to me" ("Declaratio").

Shortly after his election, just two weeks after Pope Benedict's resignation, Pope Francis asked the vast crowd gathered in Saint Peter's Square for prayers for his predecessor, now Bishop Emeritus of Rome (also called Pope

© L'Osservatore Romano/Corbis

Emeritus) Benedict XVI. Within the first two weeks of his papacy, Pope Francis visited the former Pope. This was an unprecedented and unique historical event, for it was perhaps the first time that a current Pope had met with a former Pope. After spending time in prayer, kneeling side by side, Pope Francis and Pope Emeritus Benedict XVI spent time in conversation and had lunch together. Many saw this visit as a sign of the unity and harmony that should mark all of our relationships with one another.

parents, he has an understanding of those who are uprooted and must make their way in a new culture. He is the first Pope to be a member of the Society of Jesus (the Jesuits). He is the first modern Pope to speak Spanish as his native language. (Because of his Italian parentage, he also has a native language of Italian.) Pope Francis is also the first Pope to meet his predecessor, Pope Emeritus Benedict XVI.

The Papal Shield

Used with permission of the Catholic News Service

The papal shield reflects the unique background of each Pope. Pope Francis's papal shield contains the same symbols he had on his episcopal coat of arms, with some modifications in their design. On the top is the monogram of the Society of Jesus (the letters IHS, standing for the first three letters of the name of Jesus in Greek, with a red cross rising out of the H, set in a blazing yellow sun). Below that at left is an eight-pointed star to represent Mary, and at right is a plant called a spikenard, a symbol of Saint Joseph. The shield is surrounded by the papal insignia—a miter and crossed gold and silver keys. The motto is "Miserando atque eligendo," which means "lowly but chosen." This motto is one the Pope had already chosen as Bishop. It alludes to an eighth-century homily about Saint Matthew the Evangelist, whom Jesus chose to be his Apostle, despite his lowly status as a tax collector. Pope Francis's message is that God is a God of mercy and love. ✝

Article 61 The Church in the United States: Abounding in Hope

When Bishop John Carroll was appointed the first bishop of the United States, his diocese, the Diocese of Baltimore (established in 1789 as the first in the United States) encompassed the original thirteen states. In 1808 the Dioceses of Boston, New York, Philadelphia, and Bardstown (later moved to Louisville) were formed.

Today the dioceses of the Catholic Church in the United States stretch, like the country itself, from sea to sea: from Baltimore to Los Angeles, from Fairbanks, Alaska, to Honolulu, Hawaii. According to the Pew Research Council, around 25 percent of Americans identified themselves as Catholic in 2007.

However, these numbers reflect only one measure of success. Growth in holiness is certainly the greater achievement. And though the holiness of the Catholic Church in the United States cannot be measured in earthly terms, we can look to some areas of growth and achievement in the twentieth and twenty-first centuries that reflect true Catholic values in our world today.

© Bonnie Schupp/iStockphoto.com

The Baltimore Basilica was the first cathedral to be built in the United States. Today the American Catholic Church can boast almost two hundred cathedrals, each serving as the principle church of a bishop.

Reasons for Hope

As we have seen (in article 57, "The Life and Times of Pope Saint John Paul II"; article 58, "Pope Saint John Paul II: Evangelist and Pastor, Teacher and Writer"), the papacy of Saint John Paul II has had a tremendous impact on the Church in the entire world, including the Church in the United States. Pope Saint John Paul made five visits to the United States (not including two stopovers in Anchorage and Fairbanks, Alaska), with stops in twenty cities, including Boston, New York, Philadelphia, Chicago, San Antonio, Phoenix, Los Angeles, Baltimore, and Saint Louis. Saint John Paul's interest in the people of the United States, and his genuine concern for the issues facing the Church in the United States, cannot be doubted.

Perhaps Pope Saint John Paul II's visits also contributed to a revitalization of the Church in the United States. More candidates for the priesthood began to enroll in seminary programs. New religious orders of both men and women began to emerge. Two examples are the Franciscan Friars of the Renewal (founded in 1987 in New York City and particularly dedicated to evangelization) and the Sisters of Life (founded in 1991, also in New York, dedicated to protecting the lives of the most vulnerable by helping pregnant women).

In addition, religious education at all levels, particularly from high school to preschool, began to be greatly influenced by the *Catechism of the Catholic Church*. The bishops of the United States have established the Subcommittee on the Catechism, which reviews religion textbooks to ensure they meet the theological guidelines established for the topic of that book and reflect the Church's teachings as presented in the *Catechism*. The goal is to ensure that religion textbooks are complete and correct in their presentation of doctrine.

Lay leadership in the Church has also come of age, with members of the laity serving in many capacities—for example, as parish finance managers, pastoral council leaders, and directors of religious education. Lay leaders have taken opportunities to further their knowledge of the faith in formal ways, through enrollment in religious education programs in colleges and universities, as well as in weekend retreats and days of recollection offered by parish and diocesan groups.

More and varied programs and activities for young adults and teens have also emerged. In addition to religious education, teens and young adults have opportunities for retreats, service trips, and pilgrimages, here and around the world. Participation in a World Youth Day has, in many dioceses and parishes, become a goal for youth.

Another reason for hope is the new influx of immigrants from Latin America. The United States has long been known as "a nation of immigrants," as most of our citizens settled here from another part of the globe, except, of course, for Native Americans, and even they may have migrated from parts of Asia. Because many Latin American immigrants are Catholics with young families, their presence has given "a shot in the arm" to many older parishes and have revitalized the Church in many parts of the country. Finally, although the Church encountered challenges following Vatican

Catholic Wisdom

Hope in God

Fr. Pedro Arrupe, SJ (1907–1991), a former superior general of the Society of Jesus, wrote the following about hope:

> I am quite happy to be called an optimist, but my optimism is not of the utopian variety. It is based on hope. What is an optimist? I can answer for myself in a very simple fashion: He or she is a person who has the conviction that God knows, can do, and will do what is best for mankind. (In James Martin, *My Life with the Saints*, page 103)

Council II, she was also strengthened by holy people, such as Pope Saint John XXIII, Pope Saint John Paul II, and Saint Mother Teresa, whose lives were a witness to the Gospel and to God's presence in the Church and the world. ✝

Saint Kateri Tekakwitha

Kateri, born in present-day Auriesville, New York, to a Christian Algonquin mother and a Mohawk chief who was not Christian, was the first Native American to be beatified. When she was four, smallpox killed her parents and younger brother and left her disfigured and partially blind. She met Christian missionaries in later childhood, and through their influence was baptized in 1676. Her new way of life made it difficult to remain in her village, so she walked two hundred miles to live in a Christian village near Montreal. Having made a vow not to marry, she led a life of prayer, fasting, teaching, and service until her death at the age of twenty-four.

Kateri surely exhibited remarkable trust in God. She once said:

> I am not my own; I have given myself to Jesus. He must be my only love. The state of helpless poverty that may befall me if I do not marry does not frighten me. . . . With the work of my hands I shall always earn what is necessary and what is left over I'll give to my relatives and to the poor. If I should become sick and unable to work, then I shall be like the Lord on the cross. He will have mercy on me and help me, I am sure.

Kateri was canonized in October 2012. Her feast day is July 14.

Article 62. The Church in the United States: Choices and Challenges

In the Gospel of Matthew, we find a very strong promise from Jesus to Peter concerning the Church: "Upon this rock [Peter] I will build my church, and the gates of the netherworld shall not prevail against it" (Matthew 16:18). Jesus is promising that the Church will prevail against the power of evil. This promise does not mean that the Church will not face challenges. To the contrary it seems to forewarn that she will indeed be tested and will encounter opposition and resistance. This is certainly true in the world today.

© Bill Wittman/www.wpwittman.com

The Culture of Death

During his papacy, Saint John Paul II described the culture surrounding us as "the culture of death" (*Gospel of Life*, 21). The Church must somehow engage with this culture yet not be trapped in it. The Church must not be trapped in a culture that tolerates or promotes abortion, human cloning, contraception, euthanasia, capital punishment, poverty, hunger, and unjust war. The Church must advance "the culture of life" (21) in every way possible. The Church must point to the true values of love, charity, marriage, parenthood, and consecrated life. This is our choice and our challenge today.

This does not mean that everything in our culture leads to death. But as the Church, all members of the Body of Christ must do their part to choose life: in our decisions, in forming our conscience, in our music, in our employment, in our choice of friends, in our reading of books, and in using the Internet.

Abortion, Contraception, and Challenges to Family Life

Let us look a little more closely at the challenges we face as a Church and as a society as well. Abortion, or the deliberate termination of a pregnancy by killing the unborn child, was legalized in the United States in 1973. Abortion is a grave sin and a crime against human life. Following the legalization of abortion in the United States, a wide-scale response among Catholics quickly took root as the pro-life movement, and the National Right to Life Committee (NRLC) was established. The NRLC also organized non-Catholics to join the movement, and today continues to be an important voice in defending the unborn.

Another sin against human life in its early stages of development is embryonic stem-cell research, in which stem cells from aborted fetuses are harvested for scientific research. It can be hoped that society as a whole will come to see that using human embryos to harvest replacement cells for medical research or treatments is immoral and is a violation of human dignity and the Fifth Commandment. A breakthrough in adult stem-cell research has shown that adult stem cells are equally useful in such research and in medical therapy. This offers a positive and moral alternative to embryonic stem-cell research.

Another issue related to the dignity of life affecting the Church and the modern world is the wide acceptance of contraception as a method of birth control. *Humanae Vitae* teaches that artificial contraception violates natural law and harms the relationship between a husband and wife. For example, the availability of contraception can make it easier for a spouse to be unfaithful to his or her marriage, with less risk of consequences. Using contraception can also lead each spouse to consider the other "a mere instrument for the satisfaction" (17) of selfish desires. As both examples indicate, contraception can make it difficult to make and keep a firm commitment of mutual love and fidelity.

Ignoring *Humanae Vitae* may well have repercussions in the sphere of society and family, as Pope Paul VI warned. By 1968, when he wrote *Humanae Vitae*, the growing acceptance and availability of contraception was coinciding with increased demand for "no-fault" divorce legislation, which makes it easier for either spouse to obtain a divorce. Indeed,

secularism
A focus or emphasis on matters of this world, and a separation from, or rejection of, religion and religious values and beliefs.

it is no secret that 50 percent of marriages (including Catholic marriages) today end in divorce. Calls for the legalization of gay marriage also challenge the stability of family life and its place in society.

A society is only as strong as its family life, and family life in the United States can be said to be stressed and threatened. There may be good reasons for this: Many families live far apart from grandparents and other relatives, so these family members are not available to help when a family needs respite for one reason or another; economic realities often compel both parents to work full time outside the home, allowing less time for shared family time; the proliferation of formal activities for young children means that a family's leisure time is spent driving children from one event or lesson to another rather than talking at the dinner table.

Secularization

We live in a society that has become more and more secular; that is, it has become more acceptable to push God and the acknowledgement of him to the margins of our lives. This attitude is called **secularism**. We still, as a society, give lip service to God ("So help me, God," is still part of our legal oath, and "In God We Trust" is written on our money), but it seems that our society is less and less concerned with discerning and following God's will. According to the Center for Applied Research in the Apostolate, Church attendance, including Sunday Mass attendance, has declined since the 1950s (from a peak of 62 percent to about 31 percent now).

This has repercussions, as Pope Saint John Paul II explained:

> Those who allow themselves to be influenced by this climate easily fall into a sad vicious circle: when the sense of God is lost, there is also a tendency to lose the sense of man, of his dignity and his life; in turn, the systematic violation of the moral law, especially in the serious matter of respect for human life and its dignity, produces a kind of progressive darkening of the capacity to discern God's living and saving presence. (*Gospel of Life*, 21)

Even many of those who claim to be "religious" or "churchgoers" have very low religious literacy, and, again, this includes Catholics. In 2010 a survey conducted by the Pew Forum on Religion and Public Life found Catholics to be among the lowest-scoring groups, with even atheists and gnostics scoring notably better. Of course, factual knowledge is not everything. It is not as important as loving God and neighbor. However, this survey does give a snapshot of general Catholic involvement in religion and understanding of religious belief.

The Sex Abuse Crisis

Catholics were justifiably horrified when the details of the sex abuse crisis began to emerge in the mid-1980s. They were horrified by the crimes themselves, severely disappointed to learn of this breach of trust in regard to vulnerable children, and ashamed at the slow response of some bishops and other Church representatives in dealing with perpetrators. Even though such heinous acts were the result of the actions of a small minority of priests, all priests, and to some extent all Catholics, bore and still bear, fairly or not, the burden of justifiable anger on the part of the victims, the victims' families, and the general public. In response to the crisis, many dioceses have put guidelines in place, reflecting

Pray It!

O Sun of Justice!

The image of Jesus Christ as the light of the world and sun of justice has roots in Scripture, for the Prophet Isaiah wrote:

The people who walked in darkness
have seen a great light.
(Isaiah 9:1)

In the Gospel of John, Jesus himself declares, "I am the light of the world" (8:12). Every Advent, during the darkest time of the year, the Church sings the O Antiphons at Evening Prayer. This O Antiphon, sung on December 21, sums up the longing of our Church and our world for its Sun, its Savior, its Light:

O Radiant Dawn,
splendor of eternal light, sun of justice:
come, shine on those who dwell in darkness and the shadow of death.
(Lectionary for Mass)

May this be our prayer for the Church, and may we faithfully follow where the Light leads.

a no-tolerance policy on any kind of abuse by anyone, and by a firm directive that abuse should be reported not only to local Church authorities but to civil authorities as well. Yet the confidence of some Catholics in the Church, represented by priests and religious who had been given respect and admiration as a matter of course, is admittedly shaken.

Changes in Vocations

Although the sex abuse crisis in itself may not have escalated the "vocation crisis" carried forward from the 1960s, it certainly did not help. (However, it did prompt a closer examination of candidates to the priesthood in terms of psychological stability.) In addition to this development, a number of sociological factors have also contributed to a decline in numbers of men and women entering religious life. In the 1940s and 1950s, consecrated religious and priests taught in parish schools, where they were visible to a fairly large percentage of the Catholic population. After Vatican II the number of religious declined, and Catholic schools were increasingly staffed by laypeople. With the religious life now less known to children, fewer young adults were aware of a calling to religious life as a possible vocation for them.

In addition, because opportunities have expanded for women in many areas of life, some young women have come to see the religious life as "too confining." (What they may not realize, of course, is that many religious communities engage in a variety of work, not just teaching and nursing as in the past, and usually match apostolic work to the interests and talents of the sisters.)

Nonetheless, after a period of decline, there is good news: Vocations to both the priesthood and consecrated life are once again on the rise, and new seminaries have been established and religious communities founded. Statistics in the 2010 *Annuario Pontificio* (the Pontifical Yearbook) revealed slight increases in the numbers of priests and candidates for priesthood, especially in parts of Africa, Asia, and the Americas, including the United States. And a 2010 survey of vocations directors in the United States reported a four-year increase in the number of inquiries from people who are discerning a call to priesthood and consecrated life. These inquirers are expressing nearly equal interest in active ministry and contemplative life.

A Divine Mystery

In speaking of the identity of the Church, Pope Saint John Paul II stated that the Church's memory "reveals itself gradually in history, starting from the Acts of the Apostles, but it cannot be totally identified with history" (*Memory and*

The Church in an Age of Violence

Throughout the modern era, the Church and the world have lived in an age of violence, from the threat of nuclear war to worldwide terrorism. At times the Church, as a voice for peace in the world, has been the target of violence.

In 1980 the Four Churchwomen of El Salvador (three religious sisters and one lay associate) were killed in the midst of a civil war. Sent to El Salvador to help the poor and to evangelize, they were seen as a threat to the government.

In 1989 another group, now known as the Jesuit Martyrs of El Salvador, consisting of six Jesuits, all professors at the University of Central America, with two women (the wife of a university caretaker and her daughter) were killed. They were targeted by the government because they were suspected of aiding the guerillas.

In 1996 in Algeria, seven monks of the Cistercian Order of the Strict Observance (often called Trappists) were kidnapped from their monastery, held for two months, and then killed. The monks were natives of France. A group called the Armed Islamic Group (GIA) claimed responsibility for their deaths.

Even in the face of violence and persecution, the Church steadfastly remains in this world "the sign and the instrument of the communion of God" (*CCC*, 780), cooperating with God's plan to lead all his people to eternal union with him.

Identity, page 149). Indeed, the Church's identity is far more than its human history reveals. When we study the human history of the Church, we have the opportunity to witness enduring greatness accomplished through the work of the Holy Spirit, and at times, failings of the Church's human members. Yet the Church remains a divine mystery, through which God wills that his work of salvation be fulfilled. As members of the Church, we are each called to be witnesses to the faith, hope, and charity with which God sustains his Church, that we might cooperate with his plan of bringing all people into communion with him in Heaven. ✝

Part Review

1. What factors in Saint John Paul II's early life prepared him to be a good priest and a good Pope?

2. As Pope what was Saint John Paul II's role in the formation of the *Catechism of the Catholic Church*?

3. What was Saint John Paul II's attitude toward youth throughout his papacy?

4. Name four consistent themes in Pope Saint John Paul II's teachings. Explain one of them.

5. How did Pope Benedict XVI see the relationship between faith and culture in the modern world? What do you think might be a remedy for this?

6. Name three themes that Pope Francis identified as central to his ministry as the Bishop of Rome and successor to Peter. Explain one of them.

7. Name five reasons the Church looks forward to the future with hope.

8. Name four challenges the Church faces at this time in history. Choose one challenge and explain how you could contribute to a solution.

Glossary

A

abbot, abbess The superior and spiritual leader of a monastery (masculine: abbot; feminine: abbess). *(page 69)*

antipope A person claiming to be Pope in opposition to the Pope chosen in accordance with Church law. *(page 79)*

apocrypha Writings about Jesus or the Christian message not accepted as part of the canon of Sacred Scripture. *(page 136)*

apologist One who speaks or writes in defense of someone or something. *(page 43)*

Apostle The general term *apostle* means "one who is sent" and can be used in reference to any missionary of the Church during the New Testament period. In reference to the twelve companions chosen by Jesus, also known as "the Twelve," the term refers to those special witnesses of Jesus on whose ministry the early Church was built and whose successors are the bishops. *(page 13)*

Apostolic Succession The uninterrupted passing on of apostolic preaching and authority from the Apostles directly to all bishops. It is accomplished through the laying on of hands when a bishop is ordained in the Sacrament of Holy Orders as instituted by Christ. The office of bishop is permanent, because at ordination a bishop is marked with an indelible, sacred character. *(page 18)*

Arianism A heresy developed in the late third century that denied Christ's full divinity, stating that Christ was a created being who was superior to human beings but inferior to God. *(page 55)*

B

biblical exegesis The critical interpretation and explanation of Sacred Scripture. *(page 212)*

Body of Christ A term that when capitalized designates Jesus' Body in the Eucharist, or the entire Church, which is also referred to as the Mystical Body of Christ. *(page 236)*

C

capitalism An economic system based upon the private ownership of goods and the free market system. *(page 195)*

catechists Catechists are the ministers of catechesis, the process by which Christians of all ages are taught the essentials of Christian doctrine and are formed as disciples of Christ. *(page 213)*

Catholic Action A lay apostolic group encouraged by Pope Pius X; eventually this term became an umbrella term for any apostolic action initiated and carried out by laypeople. *(page 207)*

chancel The part of a cathedral that contains the high altar. *(page 106)*

charism A special gift or grace of the Holy Spirit given to an individual Christian or community, commonly for the benefit and building up of the entire Church. *(page 16)*

Christendom The Church's sphere of power and authority, both politically and spiritually, during the Middle Ages. *(page 77)*

college of bishops The assembly of bishops, headed by the Pope, that holds the teaching authority and responsibility in the Church. *(page 47)*

college of cardinals A Church body made up of all the cardinals whose function is to advise the Pope about Church matters and to elect a successor following the death of a Pope. *(page 123)*

collegiality The principle that the bishops, in union with the Pope and under his leadership, form a single college that has authority over the universal Church. *(page 244)*

communism A system of social organization in which all economic and social activity is controlled by a totalitarian government dominated by a single political party. Communism in the twentieth century became closely linked with atheism. *(page 202)*

Conciliar movement A reform movement that emerged in the Church in the fourteenth century that held that final authority in spiritual matters rested with church councils, not with the Pope. Conciliarism emerged in response to the Avignon Papacy. *(page 96)*

concordat An agreement between the Holy See and a sovereign state on religious matters. Concordats do not give Church approval to dictators or corrupt governments; instead they are a way in which the Church seeks to be able to continue to provide the Sacraments to the faithful in nations hostile to the Church. *(page 217)*

Congregation for the Propagation of the Faith A Vatican office created in 1622 by Pope Gregory XV to coordinate and oversee foreign missionary activity. *(page 151)*

conquistadors Spanish for "conquerors," the name for the Spanish soldiers and explorers who brought much of the Americas under Spanish rule in the fifteenth and sixteenth centuries. *(page 145)*

consubstantial Having the same nature or essence. *(page 60)*

covenant A personal, solemn promise of faithful love that involves mutual commitments and creates a sacred relationship. *(page 10)*

D

deism Belief that God exists and created the world but is not active in the universe or human life. *(page 162)*

Deposit of Faith The heritage of faith contained in Sacred Scripture and Sacred Tradition. It has been passed on from the time of the Apostles. The Magisterium takes from it all that it teaches as revealed truth. *(page 33)*

deterrence The belief that war, especially nuclear war, can be prevented through the ability to respond to a military attack with a devastating counterattack. *(page 202)*

deuterocanonical Books of the Old Testament that do not appear in the Hebrew Scriptures but are accepted by the Church as part of the canon of Scripture. *(page 136)*

Divine Office Also known as the Liturgy of the Hours, the official public, daily prayer of the Catholic Church. The Divine Office provides standard prayers, Scripture readings, and reflections at regular hours throughout the day. *(page 106)*

Doctor of the Church A title officially bestowed by the Church on those saints who are highly esteemed for their theological writings, as well as their personal holiness. *(page 55)*

dogma Teachings recognized as central to Church teaching, defined by the Magisterium and considered definitive and authoritative. *(page 173)*

E

Ecumenical Council A gathering of the Church's bishops from around the world convened by the Pope or approved by him to address pressing issues in the Church. *(page 59)*

Edict of Milan A decree signed by emperors Constantine and Licinius in AD 313 proclaiming religious toleration in the Roman Empire, thereby ending the persecution of Christians. *(page 53)*

empiricism The philosophical position that all human knowledge comes from experience—especially sensory experience. *(page 163)*

enculturation The process of learning the requirements of a new or adopted culture and acquiring values and behaviors appropriate or necessary to live within that culture. *(page 149)*

ex cathedra A Latin term literally meaning "from the chair," referring to pronouncements concerning faith or morals made by the Pope, acting with full Apostolic authority, as pastor and teacher of all Christians. *(page 178)*

F

fascism A political ideology, movement, or regime that exalts nation and often race above the individual and that supports a centralized, highly autocratic government headed by a dictatorial leader, and forcibly suppresses opposition. *(page 217)*

Fathers of the Church (Church Fathers) During the early centuries of the Church, those teachers whose writings extended the Tradition of the Apostles and who continue to be important for the Church's teachings. *(page 55)*

feudalism A system that evolved in Western Europe in the eighth and ninth centuries in which society was ordered around relationships derived from the holding of land in exchange for service and protection. *(page 76)*

fideism A theological doctrine holding that religious truth is a matter of faith and cannot be established by reason. *(page 174)*

filioque Latin for "and from the Son," this phrase was added to the Nicene Creed in the Roman Church to express that the Holy Spirit descended from the Father and the Son, rather than *from* the Father and *through* the Son, as the Byzantine Church expressed. *(page 86)*

Franks A Germanic tribe that inhabited the Roman provinces of Gaul (roughly coinciding with modern-day France) starting in the sixth century. *(page 76)*

friars Members of religious orders of men who serve the Church through teaching or preaching. *(page 101)*

G

grace The free and undeserved gift of God's loving and active presence in our lives, empowering us to respond to his call and to live as his adopted sons and daughters. Grace restores our loving communion with the Holy Trinity, lost through sin. *(page 24)*

Great Western Schism A split within the Church that lasted from 1378 to 1417, when there were two or three claimants to the papacy at once. Also called the Papal Schism. *(page 95)*

Gregorian chant A monophonic, unaccompanied style of liturgical singing that takes its name from Pope Gregory the Great (540–604). *(page 206)*

H

hermit A person who lives a solitary life in order to commit himself or herself more fully to prayer and in some cases to be completely free for service to others. *(page 69)*

humanism A cultural and intellectual movement that emphasized classical learning, such as Latin and Greek literary and historical texts, and that focused on human achievements rather than on the divine. *(page 121)*

hypostatic union The union of Jesus Christ's divine and human natures in one Divine Person. *(page 61)*

I

iconoclasm The deliberate destruction of religious icons and symbols. *(page 85)*

illuminated manuscript A manuscript in which the text is supplemented with artwork such as decorated initials, borders, and illustrations, often using gold and silver. During the Middle Ages, manuscripts were copied and illuminated by hand, work often done by monks. *(page 70)*

indulgence The means by which the Church takes away the punishment that a person would receive in Purgatory. *(page 89)*

J

justification Justification is an invitation toward conversion, which happens as a response to God through the active life of faith. It involves the removal of sin and the gift of God's sanctifying grace to renew holiness. Justification was accomplished by Christ's Paschal Mystery, in his sacrificial death for all humanity. *(page 136)*

L

Logos A Greek word meaning "Word." *Logos* is a title of Jesus Christ found in the Gospel of John that illuminates the relationship between the three Divine Persons of the Holy Trinity. (See John 1:1,14.) *(page 60)*

M

Magisterium The Church's living teaching office, which consists of all bishops, in communion with the Pope, the bishop of Rome. *(page 32)*

Marks of the Church The four essential features or characteristics of the Church: One, Holy, Catholic (universal), and Apostolic. *(page 237)*

martyrdom Witness to the saving message of Christ through the sacrifice of one's life. *(page 36)*

Marxism An economic, social, and political philosophy or system based on the theories of social scientist and philosopher Karl Marx (1818–1883). The system eschews the notion of private property and seeks to control wealth by taking the means of production away from the upper class for the benefit of the rest of society. *(page 199)*

Medieval Inquisition An inquisition established by the Church in the thirteenth century aimed at rooting out heresies. Sometimes called the Papal Inquisition. *(page 114)*

mendicants Members of religious orders that rely on charity for support. *(page 100)*

merit God's reward to those who love him and by his grace do good works. We cannot "merit" justification or eternal life, which are a free gift of God. The source of any merit we have before God is due to the grace of Christ in us. *(page 136)*

Messiah Hebrew word for "anointed one." The equivalent Greek term is *christos*. Jesus is the Christ and the Messiah because he is the Anointed One. *(page 17)*

mystic A person who regularly has an intense experience of the presence and power of God, resulting in a deep sense of union with him. *(page 93)*

N

nave The main body of a church or cathedral, where the assembly gathers. *(page 106)*

New Covenant The covenant or law established by God in Jesus Christ to fulfill and perfect the Old Covenant, or Mosaic Law. It is a perfection here on earth of the Divine Law. The law of the New Covenant is called a law of love, grace, and freedom. The New Covenant will never end or diminish, and nothing new will be revealed until Christ comes again in glory. *(page 11)*

new evangelization A renewed effort, called forth by Pope Saint John Paul II, to bring the Gospel of Christ to individual believers, especially to those who, though baptized, have never fully heard or accepted the Christian message. *(page 266)*

P

pantheism The belief that everything is God; in particular, the belief that God is identical to nature and everything in it, and that God therefore changes just as nature changes. *(page 174)*

papal bull An official letter or charter issued by the Pope, named for the *bulla*, or wax seal, that was used to authenticate it. *(page 79)*

Papal States An independent country ruled by the Pope until 1870, covering a wide strip of land in the middle of the Italian Peninsula. The Papal States were awarded to the papacy in 756 in a formal deed called the Donation of Pepin. *(page 76)*

pastoral From the Latin *pastor*, meaning "shepherd" or "herdsman"; refers to the spiritual care or guidance of others. *(page 227)*

patriarch (Eastern) In the Old Testament, a patriarch is the father of a group or tribe. In the Eastern (or Greek) Church, a patriarch is a spiritual father. The title is given to the highest ranking bishops in the Church. *(page 85)*

predestination The belief that each person's fate after death is predetermined by God and that no one can do anything to change it. *(page 129)*

presbyter A synonym for "elder" in the Acts of the Apostles and an alternative word for "priest" today. *(page 48)*

providence of God God's loving care throughout salvation history and in each individual life, bringing what is needed into every situation and even bringing good out of evil. *(page 11)*

R

rationalism A term that refers to a broad range of philosophical positions that maintain that human reason is the final determinant of truth. *(page 162)*

redemption From the Latin *redemptio*, meaning "a buying back," referring, in the Old Testament, to Yahweh's deliverance of Israel and, in the New Testament, to Christ's deliverance of all Christians from the forces of sin. *(page 11)*

Reign of Terror A period of violence that occurred after the start of the French Revolution, marked by mass executions of "enemies of the revolution." *(page 165)*

S

Sacred Tradition From the Latin *tradere*, meaning "to hand on." Refers to the process of passing on the Gospel message. It began with the oral communication of the Gospel by the Apostles, was written down in Sacred Scripture, and is interpreted by the Magisterium under the guidance of the Holy Spirit. *(page 32)*

scholasticism The method of thinking, teaching, and writing devised in, and characteristic of, the medieval universities of Europe from about 1100 to 1500. Although concerned with all of scientific learning, scholasticism is most closely identified with knowledge about God. *(page 108)*

secularism A focus or emphasis on matters of this world, and a separation from, or rejection of, religion and religious values and beliefs. *(page 280)*

simony Buying or selling something spiritual, such as a grace, a Sacrament, or a relic. *(page 79)*

social doctrine The Church's body of teaching on economic and social matters that includes moral judgments and demands for action in favor of those being harmed by unjust social and economic policies and conditions. *(page 197)*

social encyclical A teaching letter from the Pope to the members of the Church on topics of social justice, human rights, and peace. *(page 198)*

socialism An economic system in which there is no private ownership of goods and the creation and distribution of goods and services is determined by the whole community or by the government. *(page 199)*

Spanish Inquisition An inquisition process established in the late fifteenth century by the Spanish monarchs Ferdinand and Isabella intended to maintain Catholic orthodoxy in Spain. *(page 114)*

subsidiarity The moral principle that large organizations and governments should not take over responsibilities and decisions that can be carried out by individuals and local organizations, and that large corporations and governments have the responsibility to support the good of human beings, families, and local communities, which are the center and purpose of social life. *(page 200)*

T

theocracy A form of government in which God is understood to be head of the state, ruling by divine guidance granted to its clergy or other ruling officials. *(page 129)*

Theotokos A Greek title for Mary meaning "God bearer." *(page 60)*

V

Vikings The Scandinavian explorers, merchants, and warriors who invaded and settled in Europe from the late eighth to the eleventh centuries. *(page 78)*

Vulgate The version of the Bible translated from Hebrew and Greek into Latin by Saint Jerome and which became the definitive version and officially promulgated by the Church. *(page 58)*

Index

Page numbers in italics refer to illustrations.

Acknowledgments

Scripture texts used in this work are taken from the *New American Bible, revised edition* © 2010, 1991, 1986, 1970 Confraternity of Christian Doctrine, Inc., Washington, D.C. All Rights Reserved. No part of this work may be reproduced or transmitted in any form or by any means, electronic or mechanical, including photocopying, recording, or by any information storage and retrieval system, without permission in writing from the copyright owners.

The excerpts labeled *Catechism* and *CCC* are from the English translation of the *Catechism of the Catholic Church* for use in the United States of America, second edition. Copyright © 1994 by the United States Catholic Conference, Inc.—Libreria EditriceVaticana (LEV). English translation of the *Catechism of the Catholic Church: Modifications from the Editio Typica* copyright © 1997 by the United States Catholic Conference, Inc.—LEV.

The quotations on pages 13, 49, 235, 236–237, and 239 from *Dogmatic Constitution on the Church* (*Lumen Gentium*, 1964), numbers 48, 23, 13, 4, and 8, respectively; the quotation on page 32 from *Dogmatic Constitution on Divine Revelation* (*Dei Verbum*, 1965), number 10; the quotations on pages 232 and 233 from *Pastoral Constitution on the Church in the Modern World* (*Gaudium et Spes*, 1965), number 1; the quotation on pages 233–234 from *Declaration on the Relation of the Church to Non-Christian Religions* (*Nostra Aetate*, 1965), number 2; and the quotation on page 245 from *Decree on the Catholic Churches of the Eastern Rite* (*Orientalium Ecclesiarum*, 1965), number 24; are taken from *Vatican Council II: Constitutions, Decrees, Declarations*, Austin Flannery, general editor (Northport, NY: Costello Publishing Company, 1996). Copyright © 1996 by Reverend Austin Flannery. Used with permission of Costello Publishing Company.

The prayers from the Mass on pages 15, 29, 60, and 84 are from the English translation of *The Roman Missal* © 2010, International Commission on English in the Liturgy Corporation (ICEL). All rights reserved. Used with permission of the ICEL.

The quotations on page 42 are from *The Didache*, translation by Alexander Roberts and James Donaldson, at *www.earlychristianwritings.com/text/didache-roberts.html*.

The excerpt on page 44 is from the English translation of the Letter to the Romans by Saint Ignatius, from *The Liturgy of the Hours* © 1970, 1973, 1975, ICEL (New York: Catholic Book Publishing Company, 1975), volume IV, page 1491. Illustrations and arrangement copyright © 1975 by the Catholic Book Publishing Company, NY. Used with permission of the ICEL.

The basic characteristics of the Fathers of the Church on page 55 are adapted from *The Catholic Church Through the Ages,* by John Vidmar (New York / Mahwah, NJ: Paulist Press, 2005), pages 46 and 48. Copyright © 2005 by John Vidmar.

The quotation on page 73 is from "Meeting with Muslim Religious Leaders, Members of the Diplomatic Corps, and Rectors of Universities in Jordan," at *www.vatican.va/holy_father/benedict_xvi/speeches/2009/may/ documents/hf_ben-xvi_spe_20090509_capi-musulmani_en.html*. Copyright © 2009 LEV. Used with permission of LEV.

The excerpt on page 90 is adapted from a Pope Innocent III letter translated in *The Crusades: A Documentary History*, by James Brundage (Milwaukee: Marquette University Press, 1962), found at *www.fordham.edu/ halsall/source/1204innocent.asp*.

The quotations on page 91 are from "Message for the End of Ramadan, 2011," numbers 3 and 6, by the Pontifical Council for Interreligious Dialogue, at *www.vatican.va/roman_curia/pontifical_councils/interelg/*. Copyright © LEV. Used with permission of LEV.

The excerpt on pages 94–95 is quoted from *How to Read Church History, Volume 1: From the Beginnings to the Fifteenth Century*, by Jean Comby (New York: Crossroad Publishing, 1985), page 176. Translation © 1985 John Bowden and Margaret Lydamore.

The quotations on page 95 are from *The Imitation of Christ*, by Thomas à Kempis, translated by William C. Creasy (New York: Book-of-the-Month Club, 1995), pages 50 and 57. Copyright © 1989 by Ave Maria Press.

The excerpt on page 110 is from *Inquisitor's Manual of Bernard Gui*, translated in *Readings in European History: A Collection of Extracts from the Sources Chosen with the Purpose of Illustrating the Progress of Culture in Western Europe Since the German Invasions*, by James Harvey Robinson (New York: Ginn and Company, 1904–1906), found at *www.fordham.edu/ halsall/source/gui-cathars.asp*.

The quotation and excerpt in the sidebar on page 111 are from *On the Eucharist in Its Relationship to the Church* (*Ecclesia de Eucharistia*), number 1, at *www.vatican.va/holy_father/special_features/encyclicals/documents/ hf_jp-ii_enc_20030417_ecclesia_eucharistia_en.html*. Copyright © LEV. Used with permission of LEV.

The excerpt on page 113 is from *The Life of Saint Clare: Ascribed to Fr. Thomas of Celano of the Order of Friars Minor (A.D. 1255–1261),* translated and edited from the earliest mss. by Fr. Paschal Robinson (Philadelphia: Dolphin Press, 1910), pages 36–37.

The quotation on page 125 is from "Joint Declaration on the Doctrine of Justification," number 15, by the Lutheran World Federation and the Catholic Church, at *www.vatican.va/roman_curia/pontifical_councils/ chrstuni/documents/rc_pc_chrstuni_doc_31101999_cath-luth-joint- declaration_en.html*. Copyright © LEV. Used with permission of LEV.

The quotations on page 131 are from *The Life of Sir Thomas More*, by William Roper (New York: Collier, 1910), found at *www.fordham.edu/ halsall/mod/16Croper-more.asp*.

The excerpts on pages 136–138 are from *The Canons and Decrees of the Sacred and Ecumenical Council of Trent*, edited and translated by J. Waterworth (London: Dolman, 1848), pages 54, 78, 153, 187, and 197, respectively.

The quotation on page 146 is from a United States Conference of Catholic Bishops' (USCCB) news release, April 28, 2010, at *usccb.org/news/archived.cfm?releaseNumber=10-081*. Copyright © USCCB, Washington, D.C. Used with permission of the USCCB.

The excerpts on pages 147, 167, and 177 are quoted in *How to Read Church History, Volume 2: From the Reformation to the Present Day*, by Jean Comby with Diarmaid MacCulloch (New York: Crossroad Publishing, 1985), pages 68, 136, and 113, respectively. English edition copyright © 1989 SCM Press Ltd.

The quotation on page 150 is from *Story of a Soul: The Autobiography of St. Thérèse of Lisieux*, third edition, translated by John Clarke (Washington, DC: ICS Publications, 1996), page 193. Copyright © 1975, 1976, 1996, by the Washington Province of Discalced Carmelites, Inc.

The carol on page 157 was translated from the Huron language by John Steckley, and reprinted here from *cockburnproject.net/songs&music/ia.html*. Used with permission of John Steckley.

The quotation on page 168 is from *Progress and Religion: An Historical Enquiry*, by Christopher Dawson (New York: Longmans, Green and Company, 1929), page 192.

The excerpt on page 168 and the quotation on page 283 are from *Memory and Identity: Conversations at the Dawn of a Millennium*, by Pope John Paul II (New York: Rizzoli International Publications, 2005), pages 107 and 149. Originally published in Italian in 2005 by RCS LibriS.p.A. Copyright © 2005 LEV; copyright © 2005 RCS LibriS.p.A.

The quotations on page 174 are quoted in *The A to Z of Catholicism*, by William J. Collinge (Lanham, MD: Scarecrow Press, 2001), pages 499 and 500. Copyright © 2001 by William J. Collinge.

The quotation on page 175 is quoted from *www.lourdes-pilgrimage.com/Youth2009.html*.

The excerpt on page 178 is quoted from *Documents of the Christian Church*, fourth edition, edited by Henry Bettenson and Chris Maunder (Oxford, England: Oxford University Press, 2011), page 277. Selection © 1963, 1999, 2011 by Oxford University Press.

The prayers on pages 178 and 196 are adapted from the English translation of *The Roman Missal* © 1973, ICEL (New York: Catholic Book Publishing Company, 1985), pages 873 and 907. Illustrations and arrangement copyright © 1985–1974 by the Catholic Book Publishing Company. Used with permission of the ICEL.

The excerpt on page 184 is quoted in *John Carroll of Baltimore: Founder of the American Catholic Hierarchy*, by Annabelle M. Melville (New York: Charles Scribner's Sons, 1955), page 287. Copyright © 1955 by Annabelle M. Melville.

The excerpt on page 198 and the quotation on page 199 are from *On the Condition of Labor (Rerum Novarum)*, numbers 3 and 11, at *www.vatican.va/holy_father/leo_xiii/encyclicals/documents/hf_l-xiii_enc_15051891_rerum-novarum_en.html*. Copyright © LEV. Used with permission of LEV.

find an error in, or have a question or concern about, any of the information or sources listed within, please contact Saint Mary's Press.

Endnotes Cited in Quotations from the *Catechism of the Catholic Church, Second Edition*

Introduction
1. *Roman Catechism* I, 10, 20.

Section 1
1. Tertullian, *Apol.* 50, 13: J. P. Migne, ed., Patrologia Latina (Paris: 1841–1855) 1, 603.
2. Tertullian, *Apol.* 50, 13: J. P. Migne, ed., Patrologia Latina (Paris: 1841–1855) 1, 603.
3. St. Justin, *Apol.* 1, 65–67: J. P. Migne, ed., Patrologia Graeca (Paris, 1857–1866) 6, 428–429.
4. St. Justin, *Apol.* 1, 65–67: J. P. Migne, ed., Patrologia Graeca (Paris, 1857–1866) 6, 428–429.
5. St. Justin, *Apol.* 1, 67: J. P. Migne, ed., Patrologia Graeca (Paris, 1857–1866) 6, 429.
6. Tertullian, *Apol.* 50, 13: J. P. Migne, ed., Patrologia Latina (Paris: 1841–1855) 1, 603.

Section 2
1. St. John Chrysostom, *prod. Jud.* 1:6: J. P. Migne, ed., Patrologia Graeca (Paris, 1857–1866) 49, 380.

Section 4
1. Pius IX, *Ineffabilis Deus*, 1854: Denzinger-Schönmetzer, *Enchiridion Symbolorum, definitionum et declarationum de rebus fidei et morum* (1965) 2803.
2. *Lumen Gentium* 25; cf. Vatican Council I: Denzinger-Schönmetzer, *Enchiridion Symbolorum, definitionum et declarationum de rebus fidei et morum* (1965) 3074.